Praise for *Quirky*:

"A fascinating journey through the minds, experiences, and ideas of breakthrough innovators, Melissa Schilling's *Quirky* is an exceptionally rewarding marriage of biography and social science that will change the way you think about winners and winning."

—Ron Adner, Tuck School of Business, Dartmouth College, author of *The Wide Lens*

"We all benefit from the work of few giants who massively changed the world. What sets them apart? Melissa Schilling has written by far the best book on this topic I've ever read, weaving together spellbinding stories about seven amazing mega-innovators with serious, grounded science. Read it and then and give a copy to a friend, and you just might unleash two more world-changers."

—Erik Brynjolfsson, MIT, coauthor of *The Second Machine Age* and *Machine | Platform | Crowd*

"*Quirky* is an interesting and well-crafted journey through the lives of those 'quirky' women and men who transformed the world through innovation. Melissa A. Schilling compares the lives of Edison, Musk, Einstein, Curie, and many others through themes of creativity and originality, effort and persistence, and situational advantage."

—David Brin, NASA advisor, astrophysicist, and award-winning author of *The Postman*, *The Transparent Society*, and *Existence*

"Melissa A. Schilling masterfully derives powerful and fresh insights for invention and innovation based on her careful analysis of some of the top inventors in our economic history. Anyone interested in the history of science, innovation, and increasing the flow of useful knowledge around the world will find this an invaluable resource."

—Henry Chesbrough, University of California, Berkeley, author of *Open Innovation*

"I love this book because it makes me think about thinking. Schilling very strongly makes the point that in a society where broad statistical approaches in education and science seem to point us toward some mediocre median, that the big innovations—the industry and civilization-changing innovations—still generally come from cranky individuals who are determined that their way is the better way. How do you make another Tesla, Curie, Jobs, or Musk? Schilling tells us how."

—Robert Cringely, author of *Accidental Empires, Triumph of the Nerds,* and *Nerds 2.0.1.*

"*Quirky* is . . . well, quirky! A compelling multi-case study of amazing innovators. Yet while these people are breathtaking in their ingenuity, Schilling also wisely blends in sharp insights for the rest of us to step up our own innovation 'game.' Bravo!"

—Kathleen M. Eisenhardt, S.W. Ascherman Professor of Strategy at Stanford University and coauthor of *Simple Rules: How to Thrive in a Complex World*

"The clarion call to be innovative sounds loud and clear, but how to respond to this call is far less clear. Schilling provides us with not a recipe, but the fundamental ingredients as illustrated by the lives of an extraordinary set of diverse innovators. The key to her secret sauce is a 'distance' that provides the perspective to think differently, the passion to bring an insight to fruition, and the good fortune of context to facilitate these elements. A captivating read with inspirational biographies and valuable lessons to help light that innovative flame."

—Daniel Levinthal, The Wharton School, University of Pennsylvania

"*Quirky* is a great reminder that when it comes to understanding the extraordinary, outliers and exceptions are invaluable teachers. To be able to break with social expectations, to have the confidence to tackle seemingly intractable problems, and to have the social skills to inspire others are unusual, indeed. Schilling's book takes us on an inspiring journey of discovery—leading us to see clearly what was always there but hidden in plain view. You'll finish the book understanding something of true genius."

—Rita McGrath, Columbia University

"It is not often that a business school professor writes a real page-turner, but *Quirky* definitely is. Melissa Schilling offers a fascinating mixture of the life stories of radical innovators, such as Elon Musk and Marie Curie, but also expertly deconstructs them to reveal their underlying commonalities. What transpires is both wonderfully insightful and inspiring. Having finished the book, I felt strangely elated."

—Freek Vermeulen, London Business School

Quirky

The Remarkable Story of the Traits, Foibles, and Genius of Breakthrough Innovators Who Changed the World

Melissa A. Schilling

PUBLICAFFAIRS
New York

PublicAffairs
Hachette Book Group
1290 Avenue of the Americas, New York, NY 10104
www.publicaffairsbooks.com
@Public_Affairs

Printed in the United States of America
First Edition: February 2018

Published by PublicAffairs, an imprint of Perseus Books, LLC, a subsidiary of Hachette Book Group, Inc. The PublicAffairs name and logo is a trademark of the Hachette Book Group.

The Hachette Speakers Bureau provides a wide range of authors for speaking events. To find out more, go to www.hachettespeakersbureau.com or call (866) 376-6591.

The publisher is not responsible for websites (or their content) that are not owned by the publisher.

The Library of Congress has cataloged the hardcover edition as follows:
Names: Schilling, Melissa A., author.
Title: Quirky : the remarkable story of the traits, foibles, and genius of breakthrough innovators who changed the world / Melissa A. Schilling.
Description: First edition. | New York, NY : PublicAffairs, [2018] | Includes bibliographical references and index.
Identifiers: LCCN 2017043370 (print) | LCCN 2017050137 (ebook) | ISBN 9781610397933 (ebook) | ISBN 9781610397926 (hardcover)
Subjects: LCSH: Inventors—Psychology. | Personality and creative ability. | Genius. | Inventions. | Technological innovations.
Classification: LCC T39 (ebook) | LCC T39 .S3185 2018 (print) | DDC 609.2/2—dc23
LC record available at https://lccn.loc.gov/2017043370
ISBNs: 978-1-61039-792-6 (hardcover), 978-1-61039-793-3 (ebook), 978-1-5417-6239-8 (international)

LSC-C

10 9 8 7 6 5 4 3 2

Contents

Introduction
"Don't tell me it's impossible. Tell me you can't do it." 1
What Makes Some People Spectacularly Innovative?

1 **"I gang my own gait. . . . "** 21
A Sense of "Separateness"

2 **"He's like a walking moonshot."** 63
Extreme Confidence

3 **"Ideas came in an uninterrupted stream. . . . "** 87
The Creative Mind

4 **"Once she had recognized a certain way as a right one, she pursued it without compromise. . . . "** 123
A Higher Purpose

5 **"Work made the Earth a paradise for me."** 157
Driven to Work

6 **"The sixties produced an anarchic mind-set. . . . "** 187
Opportunities and Challenges of an Era

7 **"It's not about the money. It's about the people you have, how you're led, and how much you get it. . . . "** 211
Access to Resources

8 **"You get creative people, you bet big on them, you give them enormous leeway and support. . . . "** 245
Nurturing the Potential That Lies Within

Acknowledgments 263
Notes 265
Selected References 289
Index 299
Photo section between pages 156–157

> Everyone who's ever taken a shower has had an idea. It's the person who gets out of the shower, dries off and does something about it who makes a difference.
>
> —Nolan Bushnell

Introduction

"Don't tell me it's impossible. Tell me you can't do it."

What Makes Some People Spectacularly Innovative?

Why are some people so remarkably innovative? Not the one-hit wonders with a single great idea or the people who seize a unique opportunity offered by a moment in time, but the people who create one game-changing innovation after another: people who spend most of their lives generating and pursuing startling ideas, challenging assumptions, and accomplishing the seemingly impossible. Is there something special about them that makes them so willing and able to change the world? Consider, for example, Elon Musk.

Musk created and sold his first video game when he was twelve and became a millionaire by the time he turned twenty-eight. Over the next ten years he developed an electronic payment system that would be merged into a company we now know as PayPal; founded SpaceX, a company with no less of an objective than to colonize Mars; and helped to create Tesla Motors, the first new-car company to go public in the United States in more than fifty years. In 2010 SpaceX successfully launched a spacecraft into orbit and then brought it safely back to Earth, a remarkable achievement that hitherto had been accomplished only by the national governments of three countries: the United States, Russia, and China. Furthermore, he demonstrated the viability of reusable rockets, something the space industry had long said was impossible.

Musk did not come from a family with strong connections to any of these industries, nor did he come from exceptional wealth or political advantage. Musk did not grow up with any special access to computing, automotive, or space technology prior to founding these companies, nor did he spend years accumulating unusually deep experience in these fields prior to his innovations. Thus, he had no special experience or resources that enabled him to accomplish these feats—his successes seem to have been attained through sheer force of will. What made Musk both able to and driven to create such a remarkable series of profoundly important innovations?

Nikola Tesla (the man for whom Musk's car company is named) was equally prolific, or perhaps even more so. During his lifetime he achieved more than two hundred stunningly advanced innovations, including the first long-distance wireless communication systems, alternating-current electrical systems, and remote-control robots. His fervor in pursuit of innovation was hard for most people to understand, especially given the skepticism and lack of financing he encountered throughout his life. Like Musk, Tesla had no family background or other advantage in the fields he would come to revolutionize. Although he studied physics in college, it is not clear that he ever completed a degree. Also like Musk, he left his home country as a young man and arrived in the United States nearly penniless. Tesla was an unusual man, to put it mildly. He was riddled with phobias and odd habits, and he lacked the kind of social intelligence and charisma that could have made it easier to get financial support for his projects. Yet also like Musk, he would accomplish a series of technological achievements that most observers had deemed impossible.

Albert Einstein achieved equally remarkable accomplishments in physics: during a four-month period, when he was all of twenty-six years old, he wrote four papers that completely altered the scientific world's understanding of space, time, mass, and energy. Each was a significant breakthrough, including work on particle physics that would set the stage for quantum mechanics to overthrow classical physics. What is all the more remarkable is that he accomplished these feats while working as a patent examiner because every physics department he applied to turned him down for an academic post. His disrespect for authority had earned him the ire of his college professors, and they refused to support him in his quest for a university position. Even after writing his four remarkable papers, he faced considerable resistance: having the impudence to challenge well-established theories and being Jewish in a time of rampant anti-Semitism combined to make him the subject of frequent attacks. These attacks made his life harder, but they did not induce him to show more reverence for the work of his peers. For Einstein, bowing to authority—including the authority of social norms—was a corruption of the human spirit. He had no intention of marching to anyone else's drum. This stance would make it harder for him to gain support and legitimacy for his ideas, yet it also freed him to think beyond the existing theories of his time. He would go on to win the Nobel Prize and become, arguably, the most famous scientist of all time.

What is it, then, that makes these people so spectacularly innovative? Is it genetics, parenting, education, or luck? Although innovation has long been a popular research topic in both psychology and business, we don't have good answers to the question. In part this is because serial breakthrough innovators—people who are extreme outliers of innovative productivity—don't make great research subjects. Because they are rare, it's next to impossible to gather data on a large sample of them and run statistical analyses. And because they are busy, you would have an equally hard time getting them into a laboratory to run experiments. Thus, in business schools we tend to focus our research on problems such as how to organize innovation teams, how to choose alliance partners, and how to structure ideation exercises. Those are, after all, things we can measure and manage. The innovation research has not told us where serial breakthrough innovators come from, nor has it told us how we can foster breakthrough innovation in ourselves, in people with whom we work, or in our children.

The research in psychology on individual creativity gets us a bit closer, but most of that research has focused on the general process of creativity—how ordinary people use creativity to solve problems, for example—rather than telling us why some people become outliers. The smattering of research on creative geniuses is sparse, disconnected, and short on conclusions and implications. For example, it has suggested that there may be a genetic component of genius, which is true, though not particularly helpful if you are seeking to increase your innovativeness. Other writers have argued that true genius requires a very large number of hours of practice or very large numbers of chunks of information—a claim that is diminished by a vast number of highly visible exceptions. As noted, Elon Musk did not revolutionize space travel because he had extensive information and experience in that field—quite the opposite. When both US and Russian rocket manufacturers told Musk that his idea for economical reusable rockets was simply not feasible, he started teaching himself by studying rocket science textbooks on his own, and within months he created a spreadsheet that detailed the costs, materials, and performance specifications of the rocket he intended to build. Musk is an outsider who has done the impossible, in part because he didn't know (or believe) that it was impossible.

Musk crosses boundaries because some of the quirks of his personality are that he enjoys tackling new, difficult problems and he doesn't care very much about whether you think he has the ability or right to do that. This is an extremely important point—most research shows that we tend to penalize people for crossing boundaries. We discount generalists and are suspicious of people who engage in activities that seem inconsistent with their identity. However, outsiders such as Musk bring an advantage that insiders and industry veterans often lack. Outsiders aren't trapped by the paradigms and assumptions that become calcified in industry veterans, nor do they have the existing investments in tools, expertise, or supplier and customer relationships that make change difficult and unappealing. For example, Gavriel Iddan, a guided-missile designer for the Israeli military, invented a revolutionary way to allow doctors to see inside a patient's gastrointestinal system. The traditional approach for obtaining images inside the gut is a camera on the end of a long flexible rod. This method is quite uncomfortable, and it cannot reach large portions of the small intestine, but it was the industry standard for many decades. Most gastroenterologists have invested in significant training to use endoscopic tools, and many have also purchased endoscopic equipment for their clinics. Not surprisingly, most innovation in this domain has focused on incremental improvements in the rod, the camera, and the imaging software. However, Iddan approached the problem of viewing the inside of the gut like a guided-missile designer, not like a gastroenterologist. He did not have the same assumptions about the need either to control the camera with a rod or to transmit images with a wire. Instead, he invented a capsule (called the PillCam) with a power source, a light source, and two tiny cameras that the patient can swallow. The patient then goes about her day while the camera pill broadcasts images to a video pack worn by the patient. Roughly eight hours later, the patient returns to the doctor's office to have the images read by a software algorithm that can identify any locations of bleeding (the camera pill exits naturally). The PillCam has proven to be safer and less expensive than traditional endoscopy (the PillCam costs less than $500), and it is dramatically more comfortable. For patients, the camera pill was a no-brainer; getting doctors to adopt it has been slower because of their existing investment and familiarity with endoscopy. The PillCam is currently sold in more than sixty countries, and several companies now offer competing products. The camera pill is a remarkable solution to a difficult problem, and it is easy to see why it came from an outsider rather than from an endoscope producer.

Similarly, it is easy to see why Uber, Lyft, Didi Chuxing, and Grab are disrupting the taxi business and why Airbnb, Homestay, and Couchsurfing are disrupting the hotel business. Although taxi companies and hotel chains undoubtedly have knowledge and assets that would be useful in these new business models, they also have assets and strategic commitments that are tied to (or designed for) their original way of doing business and making money. Change would be painful, and it is not obvious that they could outcompete the newcomers in the new business models even if they tried. These are the reasons that disruptive innovation often comes from new entrants rather than industry stalwarts, despite the fact that existing businesses with decades of experience in an industry would seem to have some advantages in resources such as cash, equipment, and clout.

However, most outsiders do not become serial breakthrough innovators. Neither do most extremely experienced people. An individual's degree of experience may play a role in her emergence as a breakthrough innovator, but it is not clear that it is particularly important or reliable. What, then, is important or reliable? Is there some combination of traits or resources that increases the likelihood of an individual becoming a serial breakthrough innovator?

Can we help people tap their own potential to be a breakthrough innovator (and would we want to)?

I first tried to address this question through standard research methods: conducting large-sample studies on innovators and gathering as much data as I could about hundreds of innovators identified by aggregating lists made by others.[1] Invariably these studies proved unsatisfying. Most inventors and entrepreneurs are one-hit wonders, leaving us with doubt about how much they could teach us about being innovative. Furthermore, when you try to study a large sample of innovators, you typically find that there is very little information available about their lives, leaving you to draw only a few conclusions about their education or work experience. These studies do not give us the kind of insight into breakthrough innovation that we really want. It is easy to conclude that this is a problem that cannot really be studied or that no insights can be gleaned from trying. Perhaps the problem is too complex, or innovators are too idiosyncratic, for us to learn much of use from studying them.

The question really started coming to a head in early 2011 as people saw the visible deterioration of Steve Jobs's health. Many, including students in my course on innovation strategy, began asking me about the fate of Apple if it lost its famous leader. I wondered too. Did Apple's innovativeness arise from something in the organization's DNA, or was it specific to Steve Jobs? Could his "magic" be handed down to a successor? Was it embedded in the routines at Apple? Or was it in the man himself? It was a question so intriguing that it was worth pursuing even if it didn't lead to anything useful. I thus began to study Steve Jobs, comparing every detail I could find on him with the existing research on innovation and creativity. I had already been following Apple for years in the course of my research and teaching, but now I began to study Jobs as a person. I read biographies, watched recorded interviews, and scavenged his statements from wherever I could find them. I wanted to understand what he was really like: his talents, his weaknesses, his beliefs and biases. I wanted to understand what drove him and enabled him. I was lucky that a great deal had been written about Steve Jobs and that he had done numerous recorded interviews: it was possible to get a rich, multifaceted perspective on him.

I soon noticed some striking commonalities between Jobs and other breakthrough innovators. For example, I had written a teaching case on Dean Kamen (inventor of the Segway, the first portable kidney dialysis machine, the first wearable drug infusion pump, and much more), and the similarities between Jobs and Kamen were strange and intriguing. Both men had dropped out of college and started companies in their early twenties, and neither had extensive training in the fields to which they would contribute. Both were quirky, with eccentric traits such as wearing the same clothes every day. Jobs didn't put a license plate on his car and routinely parked in the spots reserved for people with disabilities—those rules just didn't apply to him. Kamen bought an island (North Dumpling), built his own power grid, and declared his intention to secede from the United States so that its rules would not apply to him. Both men also had unusual homes. Jobs didn't put furniture in his house—nothing quite fit his stark aesthetic tastes. Kamen's home was a four-story hexagon with at least one secret passage. Its hallways were designed to look like mine shafts, and a huge cast-iron steam engine that had once belonged to Henry Ford was built into the house's four-story central atrium. More importantly, both men had such great faith in their own capacity for reasoning and insight that they disregarded the "rules" that constrained the problem-solving efforts of others. For example, when people told Kamen that his idea for a wheelchair that would balance on two feet was impossible, he retorted, "Don't tell me it's impossible. Tell me you can't do it," and pointed out that many of the scientific principles we take as given are just "man's laws" that we don't know to be actually true.[2] Steve Jobs said something remarkably similar in a video-recorded interview: "Life gets a lot broader once you realize one simple fact: Everything around you that you call life was made up by people that were no smarter than you, and you can change it."[3] Both men were also driven much more by idealistic goals than materialistic gain: Jobs saw the computer as a means to revolutionize human cognition the way that bicycles had revolutionized human mobility; Kamen wanted to liberate people from the constraints of disease or injury.

As I pondered my notes on these two men—both so profoundly innovative and both sharing some peculiar personal traits that broke with social norms—I suddenly understood that we could gain insight into what makes some people serial breakthrough innovators by studying a smaller sample of exceptional innovators *very deeply,* using what is known as a multiple case study approach. A multiple case study process begins with writing a description or story of the case (like a biographer writes about her subject) but extends well beyond that as the researcher compares the cases, working iteratively through every possible pair, attempting to recognize commonalities and differences, and capturing the categories and patterns that emerge. Because this is a study of people who are rare outliers of innovative productivity and impact, the control group (what the cases are compared to) is the rest of us.[4] That is, we are looking for characteristics that the innovators have in common that stand out for being unusual, such as traits they exhibit to a much greater degree than we would expect for a person drawn at random. Any dimension that figures prominently in one or a few cases is scrutinized closely in the other cases. Humans are prone to overgeneralizing from small samples, so one of the most important tasks is to try to strip away spurious commonalities. For example, Thomas Edison and Marie Curie were the youngest children of their families, and Benjamin

Franklin was the youngest son (though not the youngest child) in a family of sixteen children. People have speculated about the effect of birth order on personality and behavior since at least the early 1900s. At that time, Austrian psychiatrist Alfred Adler proposed that firstborns would be more prone to neuroticism and substance abuse because of the excessive responsibility of looking after the younger children, and youngest children would be prone to having poor social empathy as a consequence of being overindulged. It would be easy to speculate that breakthrough innovators might be more likely to be youngest children because, as we shall see, not fitting in socially is a recurring theme among such innovators. But birth order does not survive closer scrutiny: Steve Jobs, Albert Einstein, and Elon Musk were the oldest children in their families, and Nikola Tesla and Dean Kamen were middle children. Furthermore, of the innovators studied here, the one that *least* exhibits poor social empathy is Benjamin Franklin. It turns out that most empirical work on birth order has found zero effect on personality or behavior, despite the persistence of the myth!

It quickly became clear that it would be important to focus on people who had innovated repeatedly so that we could go beyond "right time, right place" explanations. They also had to be world renowned as innovators so that there would be no doubt about their accomplishments. And their innovations had to be important—they had to leave an indelible imprint on the world because that is the capability that we really want to understand. For practical purposes, they also had to be people who had been extensively written about because only then would we know something about their childhoods, their educations, their hobbies, their personalities, their talents, their motives, their experiences, and more. Once we understood them deeply as people, we could compare and contrast their characteristics and backgrounds, and integrate this with what we know from the science of creativity and innovation. I hoped such an integration would help illuminate what really matters. In the end, it did that and more. It exposed both the exhilaration that the innovators experienced and the great personal costs that they bore while pursuing something that they believed was incredibly important. It revealed the opportunities and constraints that have ensured that the lists of famous innovators have historically been dominated by men from developed economies. And, perhaps most importantly, it revealed that even though some factors have made these innovators unique and inimitable, there are also ways in which we can increase the breakthrough innovation potential in us all.

How the Innovators Were Chosen and Studied

To CHOOSE A LIST of people that I could confidently identify as profoundly important serial breakthrough innovators, I first scoured dozens of lists of the most famous innovators, looking for people who topped multiple lists and whose contributions would be indisputable. It quickly became clear that there was much more consensus about contributions to technology and science than, for example, contributions to art and music. The appreciation of art and music is a subjective experience, and people vary enormously in how they will rank an innovation in these fields. Furthermore, once artists or musicians have earned acclaim, their subsequent work receives more attention. This can lead to a self-reinforcing advantage in being considered "important." Technology and science innovations can also have subjective components and self-reinforcing advantages, but they usually have performance dimensions that are objectively measurable, leading to greater agreement about what is important. For example, when Marie Curie discovered the most powerful radioactive substance known at that time (radium), its importance was indisputable. When

Albert Einstein first proposed his General Theory of Relativity, its value was at first subject to the interpretation of his peers. However, in 1919, when Sir Arthur Addington verified that Einstein's predictions were correct during a complete solar eclipse, the theory's merit was no longer subjective. When Elon Musk demonstrated that a rocket could, in fact, be landed and reused—and at a much lower price than the space industry had dreamed—the value of this innovation could not be denied, even by the space industry stalwarts whose competitive positions it threatened. A small group of technology and science innovators show up near the top of every famous innovators list; the same is not true for innovation in the arts. Thus, to sidestep the sometimes contentious issue of the definition of an important innovation, I decided to limit my focus to technological or scientific innovators and let public lists identify the candidates.

Second, I limited the set to individuals who were widely associated with *multiple* innovations. The vast majority of people on famous innovator lists are associated with only a single important invention—for example, Percy LeBaron Spencer's microwave oven, Leopold Godowsky Jr.'s Kodachrome color film, or Hedy Lamarr's frequency-hopping spread spectrum technology for torpedoes. When an individual is associated with only a single major invention, it is much harder to know whether the invention was caused by the inventor's personal characteristics or by simply being at the right place at the right time. To really know that we are gaining insight into what makes someone an exceptional innovator, it is important to identify *serial* breakthrough innovators who innovate for most of their lives. These are the rare people whose life's purpose is based on making one breakthrough after another.

And, third, developing case studies of the innovators that are as complete and unbiased as possible requires both multiple published biographies of the individual and extensive first-person narratives such as autobiographies, interviews, and videos. In practice, this criteria tended to eliminate many innovators that I would have liked to study who either emerged too recently (for example, Larry Page) or lived too long ago (for example, Leonardo da Vinci). Finally, from the individuals prominent on the remaining list, I attempted to choose people from different areas of industry or science (e.g., medicine, aerospace, electricity, information technology) and from different time periods in order to avoid oversampling from particular "blooms" of innovation associated with a technological shock. Choosing individuals from different periods and fields helps to separate individual factors from contextual factors and improves the opportunity to triangulate about breakthrough innovation more generally. The final set of innovators that I chose to study and focus on in this book includes Marie Curie, Thomas Edison, Albert Einstein, Benjamin Franklin, Steve Jobs, Dean Kamen, Elon Musk, and Nikola Tesla, although I occasionally include examples about other innovators (such as Grace Hopper and Sergey Brin) to illustrate particular concepts.

Closely studying these breakthrough innovators reveals some important commonalities that help give us insight into what made them able—and made them driven—to change the world in such dramatic ways. Although they were extremely intelligent, that is not enough to make someone a serial breakthrough innovator. Other factors played key roles. The innovators displayed some unusual characteristics—quirks—that had important implications for both the ideas they generated and the intensity with which they pursued them. For example, nearly every innovator I studied exhibited very high levels of social detachment. Marie Curie's unconventionality and chronic depression led her to seek what she referred to as an "anti-natural" life,[5] largely isolated from the social world and often isolated even from her children. Marie Curie was aware of her self-imposed isolation and knew that the way she had lived her life was not for everyone. Albert Einstein was similarly aware of his own detachment and isolation, recognizing both its benefits to his independence and originality and its costs to his psychic comfort. Thomas Edison's deafness made him extremely uncomfortable in social settings, and his near-maniacal work habits meant that he spent most of his life in his laboratory, even sleeping on a table many nights. And Elon Musk, though sometimes referred to as a "playboy" in his adulthood, describes himself as bookish, nerdy, and devoid of friends as a child. In fact, he was so introspective that his family at one point considered the possibility that he was deaf. Separateness helped these innovators become original thinkers. Their isolation meant that they were less exposed to dominant ideas and norms, and their sense of not belonging meant that even when exposed to dominant ideas and norms, they were often less inclined to adopt them.

All of the innovators also exhibited extreme faith in their ability to overcome obstacles (what psychologists would call "self-efficacy") from an early age. Consider Elon Musk's decision (at the age of six) to walk ten miles across the city of Pretoria, South Africa, to get to a cousin's birthday party or his later decision to personally resurrect the space program when he discovered that NASA had no plans to go to Mars. Musk is sometimes referred to as a "walking moonshot"[6] because of his willingness to take on seemingly impossible goals. Many of the breakthrough innovators took on such goals because they had such high faith in their own ability to overcome obstacles that they did not buy in to the rules that other people accept as given. This is why some people referred to Steve Jobs as having a "reality distortion field" and why Dean Kamen could dismiss the four laws of thermodynamics as "man's laws" rather than universal principles. Nikola Tesla similarly challenged what was possible and made statements about what he would achieve in the world that were so grand that people often dismissed him as having delusions of grandeur—until, of course, he proved he was right!

All of the innovators also pursued their projects with remarkable zeal, often working extremely long hours and at great personal cost. Most were driven by idealism, a superordinate goal that was more important than their own comfort, reputation, or families. Nikola Tesla wanted to free mankind from labor through unlimited free energy and to achieve international peace through global communication. Elon Musk wants to solve the world's energy problems and colonize Mars. Benjamin Franklin was seeking greater social harmony and productivity through the ideals of egalitarianism, tolerance, industriousness, temperance, and charity. Marie Curie had been inspired by Polish positivism's argument that Poland, which was under Tsarist Russian rule, could be preserved only through the pursuit of education and technological advance by all Poles—*including women*. Idealism is a very powerful intrinsic motivator that can induce individuals to exert exceptional effort toward a problem. In fact, it may occupy their energy and time to such a level that it causes them to disregard motives that other individuals might find more important, such as the desire for social interaction or leisure. This might partially explain why so many breakthrough innovators have been criticized for abandoning or neglecting their families (e.g., Benjamin Franklin, Thomas Edison, Steve Jobs, Marie Curie). Idealism helps focus innovators by making their long-term purpose very clear, helping them to make choices among the competing demands of their attention. Having lofty superordinate goals, such as Tesla's desire to achieve global wireless transmission of energy and to free mankind from physical toil, or Musk's ambition to colonize Mars, gave these innovators a drive and single-mindedness that helped them avoid getting caught up in other interesting problems. They often led their lives as if they had blinders on to keep their attention locked on target. It also made them resilient to failure or criticism because they believed that their goals were important and intrinsically honorable and valuable. For example, Franklin once had to endure a brutal attack by prosecutor Alexander Wedderburn in England's Privy Council while facing a jeering crowd of England's elite. However, Franklin remained stoic and silent during the proceedings and never shrank from public life because his belief that he was pursuing his duty to serve God and mankind gave him a moral high ground that helped make him resilient to such attacks.

Idealism was not the only force that drove the innovators. Most of them also worked so hard and so tirelessly because they found work extremely rewarding. Some had an extremely high need for achievement (a personality trait associated with a strong and consistent concern with setting and meeting high standards, and accomplishing difficult tasks), so they took great pleasure in amassing accomplishments. Many also appeared to experience the pleasure of "flow" from working incredibly hard (i.e., work was *autotelic*—rewarding for its own sake). For example, Edison was competitive by nature and enormously energetic. He enjoyed the process of achieving things, and the physical and mental activity of work gave him pleasure. Many of Edison's projects turned out to be unprofitable, and he was known to berate the patent system's inability to defend inventors from "pirates." However, in general he expressed little remorse or discouragement about disappointing outcomes. The work itself was his primary joy. "I never intend to retire," he stated. "Work made the earth a paradise for me."[7]

In sum, there are very strong commonalities among exceptional breakthrough innovators that make these people similar to one another and also make them atypical, or quirky. Studying these people and integrating what we learn about them with existing research on creativity and innovation helps us understand the mechanisms by which the characteristics led these innovators to create one profound innovation after another. This distinction between the *characteristics* and the *mechanisms* by which the characteristics led to innovation is important because even though serial breakthrough innovators are rare and in many ways inimitable, we can still harness some of these mechanisms to discover and unleash innovative potential in ourselves and others. For example, understanding the innovator's sense of separateness points out the importance of giving people time alone to pursue their own interests and form their own ideas. It highlights how dangerous norms of consensus are to innovation and reveals the advantages of helping people to embrace their weird sides. People also find it illuminating—and often a relief—to see just how many innovators did not do well in school precisely because of their creativity or their tendency to challenge rules. A surprisingly large portion of the breakthrough innovators have been autodidacts—self-taught people—and excelled much more outside the classroom than inside. Although many people will have heard anecdotally that some innovators did not do well in school, this book shows exactly *why* innovators might not flourish in school and *how* they were successful anyway.

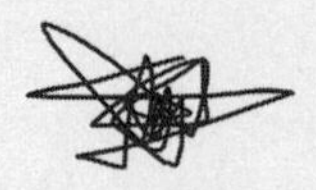

I HAVE ORGANIZED *QUIRKY* around the three main themes of creativity and originality, effort and persistence, and situational advantage. Almost all breakthrough innovation starts with an unusual idea or with beliefs that break with conventional wisdom. Thus, my focus in the first few chapters is on the factors that helped to inspire the innovators to be unconventional, to be creative, and to generate original ideas. We will see here how the breakthrough innovators' quirky natures make them less likely to buy into established theories and paradigms, and more likely to come up with pathbreaking solutions.

However, creative ideas alone are almost never enough. Many people have creative ideas, even brilliant ones. But usually we lack the time, knowledge, money, or motivation to act on those ideas. For example, we may not know whether our idea will work or how it could be implemented. It may seem too difficult or too risky. Thus, most insightful, creative ideas are brief wisps of thought that are swept away by other, more immediate concerns. It is rare that someone with a breakthrough idea has the motivation, resources, and persistence to pursue it, and although a person could give such an idea to someone else with better motivation and resources—an established inventor or firm, perhaps—it is probably rarer still that this "someone else" will pursue the breakthrough idea. This is because by their very nature, original ideas are often initially hard for others to understand and value. The odds of one person's breakthrough idea fitting well with another person's resources, motivation, and worldview are slim. This is why when breakthrough innovations have been brought to the world, it is usually because the innovator has invested remarkable effort and persistence in executing the idea—often in the face of failure and opposition. Every breakthrough innovator studied here demonstrated *extraordinary* effort and persistence. Most worked extremely long hours, forfeiting leisure, sleep, and time with their families in single-minded pursuit of their mission. Many stuck doggedly to a solution that others had deemed irrational or doomed. Where does such fierce commitment and energy come from? Chapters 4 and 5 show that idealism, need for achievement, unusual energy levels, and "flow" provide some answers to this question.

Next, although we will see that most breakthrough innovators share some personal traits that make them more likely to generate and execute breakthrough ideas, being at the right place at the right time still matters. Chapters 6 and 7 look at the situational advantages—opportunities (and challenges) of an era and access to resources—that aided the rise of these innovators. Finally, as noted above, although this book will show that breakthrough innovators often have some unique and some difficult-to-imitate characteristics or experiences, we can still learn a great deal from them about enhancing innovation. Chapter 8 will summarize the implications for how we can nurture and shape the breakthrough innovation potential in ourselves, in the people we work with, and in our children.

Be a loner. That gives you time to wonder, to search for the truth.

—Albert Einstein[1]

1

"I gang my own gait. . . ."

A Sense of "Separateness"

Many of the most prolific breakthrough innovators exhibit a marked sense of "separateness," perceiving themselves as different or disconnected from the crowd. This separateness can reveal itself in a lack of interest in social interaction, a rejection of rules and norms, and often isolation even from family members. It is not always easy to tell whether an innovator made a voluntary choice to be separate, was born with innate personality traits that led to separateness, or acquired a sense of separateness involuntarily because of circumstances beyond the innovator's control. However, that sense of separateness is usually sharply discernible by both the innovator and those around her, and it typically emerges quite early in life. Albert Einstein provides an excellent example—he not only exhibited a sense of separateness; he also wrote about it and reflected extensively on how it influenced his ability to be an original thinker.

Albert Einstein was known for great warmth and love for mankind, but in his direct interpersonal relationships he was often cold or detached. Einstein loved humanity and was an avid champion of human rights, pacifism, and nondiscrimination. He could be funny and make and appreciate close friendships. Yet he never lost his sense of disconnect from others and was notoriously aloof and rebellious. He articulated it poignantly in a book titled *The World as I See It:*

> My passionate sense of social justice and social responsibility has always contrasted oddly with my pronounced freedom from the need for direct contact with other human beings and human communities. I gang my own gait and have never belonged to my country, my home, my friends, or even my immediate family, with my whole heart; in the face of all these ties I have never lost an obstinate sense of detachment, of the need for solitude—a feeling which increases with the years. One is sharply conscious, yet without regret, of the limits to the possibility of mutual understanding and sympathy with one's fellow-creatures. Such a person no doubt loses something in the way of geniality and light-heartedness; on the other hand, he is largely independent of the opinions, habits, and judgments of his fellow and avoids the temptation to take his stand on such insecure foundations.[2]

Born in Germany on March 14, 1879, Einstein was slow to learn to talk, not uttering his first words until after the age of two, and for most of his life exhibited a form of echolalia—the repetition of phrases, often under the breath. Echolalia is extremely common in autistic children (roughly 75 percent of children on the autism spectrum are estimated to exhibit echolalia), but it can also appear in the absence of any disorder and is sometimes exhibited by children learning to speak. Einstein himself attributed his echolalia to his delay in speaking and noted that he liked to quietly repeat sentences over and over in hopes of perfecting them before voicing them out loud.

Although Einstein's childhood home and garden were often bustling with children, he tended to keep to himself, pursuing quieter activities. As his longtime colleague Phillipp Frank noted, "From the very beginning he was inclined to separate himself from children his own age and to engage in daydreaming and meditative musing."[3] Some psychologists have speculated that Einstein might have had a mild form of autism that caused him to have far greater ability to analyze the dynamics of the universe than to sense and care about the humans around him. Similar speculations about autism have also at times been made about Bill Gates, in part because he constantly rocks his body while working. He lowers his upper body to a forty-five-degree angle and raises it again, repetitively, with the intensity of the rocking varying with his mood. Many autistic people exhibit repetitive or automatic movements such as rocking, but Gates believes that "it is just excess energy. . . . I should stop, but I haven't yet. They claim I started at an extremely young age."[4] Gates is also described as an introvert, not having strong social skills, and sometimes exhibiting a disregard for personal hygiene. However, none of these characteristics suggest that he is actually autistic. Gates is extremely intelligent, highly functional, and, according to his former girlfriend Ann Winblad, a very open and emotional person. He is quite capable of expressing his feelings and understanding those of others. It is just that, as Winblad mentions, Gates is often in a "pure mind state" where hygiene and social graces are a low priority. This aspect of Gates's nature is exhibited by many serial breakthrough innovators, serial entrepreneurs, and other exceptionally driven people: the prioritization of intellectual pursuits or extreme goals can cause some people to disregard personal appearance or social graces, as we shall see with not only Einstein but also Steve Jobs, Marie Curie, and Dean Kamen.

When Einstein began attending school, at age six, he was withdrawn and quiet, and he did not make many friends. He did not like sports, and his classmates often teased him. He spoke slowly, and his teachers perceived him as inattentive. On one occasion a teacher remarked to him that he would never amount to anything because of his inability to exhibit the necessary discipline for the type of education provided in the school.[5] On another occasion, when Einstein's father inquired with a teacher about what profession the boy should pursue, the teacher responded that it did not really matter as he was unlikely to excel in anything. Einstein would later criticize his childhood school by noting, "The worst thing seems to be for a school principally to work with methods of fear, force and artificial authority. Such treatment destroys healthy feelings, the integrity of and self-confidence of pupils."[6] Yet despite the mutual enmity with which Einstein and his teachers appeared to feel for each other, Einstein often earned the highest grades in the class. Although the regimented rules and rote memorization of school inspired only resentment by the young Einstein, at home he reveled in practicing algebra and showed a strong interest in science. Max Talmud, a medical student who had meals with the Einstein family once a week, noted the boy's intense interest and began bringing him science and math books. As Talmud would later note, "In all those years, I never saw him reading any light literature. Nor did I see him in the company of schoolmates or other boys of his own age." Also, "He showed a particular inclination toward physics and took pleasure in conversing on physical phenomena. I gave him therefor for reading matter A. Bernstein's *Popular Books on Physical Science* and L. Buchner's *Force and Matter,* two works that were then quite popular in Germany." Talmud noted that Einstein read the books with "breathless suspense."[7] By the time he was twelve, Einstein was teaching himself higher mathematics from books—well ahead of his school curriculum—and, as Talmud noted, "Soon the flight of his mathematical genius was so high that I could no longer follow."[8]

Up to the age of twelve, Einstein had (in his own words) a "deep religiosity," despite having nonreligious parents.[9] However, at the age of twelve he became convinced that the stories in the Bible could not be true and that the state was deliberately deceiving young people through religion. This planted the seeds of distrust for authority that would come to define his personality. As he recounted, "Suspicion against every kind of authority grew out of this experience, a skeptical attitude towards the convictions which were alive in any specific social environment—an attitude which has never again left me even though later on, because of better insight into the causal connections, it lost some of its original poignancy."[10] Einstein would later return to believing in a greater spiritual being, but he would never lose his distaste for authority. This had direct consequences on his success in school; although Einstein was a natural and gifted student, his disrespect created friction with his teachers. Little evidence exists that Einstein was overtly rebellious in class, but his disdain for his professors was readily apparent. As his Greek professor said to him, "You sit there in the back row smiling. And that undermines the respect a teacher needs from his class."[11] When Einstein was sixteen, the family business collapsed, so the family moved to Milan, intending for Einstein to stay behind to finish his studies in Munich. Instead, the sixteen-year-old decided to drop out of high school, determined to study on his own and seek admission into a technical college in Zurich. He left Germany and soon renounced his German citizenship (likely in order to avoid joining the army, which would have been required when he turned seventeen). To continue his pursuit of self-education, he bought all three volumes of Jules Violle's advanced physics text and set to work studying them intensely.

In the fall of 1895 he received permission to take the entrance exam at Zurich Polytechnic two years ahead of time. Although he easily passed the math and science sections, he failed to pass the general section (which included literature, zoology, botany, French, and politics), and he ended up going to a cantonal school in Aarau based on the teaching philosophy of Swiss education reformer Johann Heinrich Pestalozzi. This proved to be a wonderful move for Einstein. Pestalozzi's philosophy was that students should be able to reach their own conclusions. They should have the opportunity to observe, experiment, and exercise their own intuition. Instead of an authoritarian environment that emphasized rote memorization, as Einstein had experienced in his German gymnasium, the school in Aarau nurtured each student's individuality and emphasized each student's free will and responsibility. Perhaps because he was now more comfortable in the Aarau culture, Einstein began to be more social, making friends and cultivating a sense of wit and charm. His classmate Hans Byland described him as "sure of himself. . . . Nothing escaped his sharp eyes. . . . Unhampered by convention, his attitude toward the world was that of the laughing philosopher."[12]

Pestalozzi also emphasized the value of a visual understanding of concepts (rather than numbers and language)—a fundamental principle that would influence Einstein his entire life. It was at Aarau that Einstein began using "thought experiments," whereby he would explore physics concepts by picturing them visually in his mind, such as lightning strikes and moving trains, blind beetles crawling on curved branches, and devices designed to identify the location and velocity of speeding electrons.[13] One of his most famous visual thought experiments pertained to light: to understand how light moves, he imagined what it would be like to travel alongside a light beam.[14] What would it look like? If light were indeed a wave, then the light beam itself would be stationary. It was a puzzle that motivated a large part of his future work.

Einstein was accepted into Zurich Polytechnic the following year at the age of seventeen. He was frequently quoted much later in life that the years in Zurich were some of the happiest of his life. It was here he met Michele Besso and Marcel Grossmann, who would become lifelong friends and would sometimes help him work out the mathematics of his theories. At Zurich his intelligence was frequently acknowledged, but he was also known as irreverent. He had a distracted and disorganized air about him, and he paid scant attention to his clothes or grooming. He was also very prone to skipping class, preferring instead to study subjects on his own. This was perceived as arrogance and disrespect, which earned him uneven grades and animosity from some of the faculty. His physics professor, Heinrich Weber, was quoted as saying, "You're a clever fellow, but you have one fault: You won't let anyone tell you a thing!"[15] In 1900 Einstein graduated from Zurich Polytechnic near the bottom of his class.

The next couple of years were difficult. Einstein did not want to join his father's company as an engineer, and his former professors at Zurich Polytechnic were not interested in offering him a job as an assistant professor or in writing him the glowing recommendations he would need to get one elsewhere. He was twenty-one years old, was in love with Mileva Marić (a classmate from Zurich Polytechnic whom his parents found to be unsuitable as a wife because, in part, she suffered from chronic ill health and a limp), and was subsisting on sporadic jobs as a math tutor. In despair, he wrote to nearly every physics professor in Europe, pleading for a job so that he could continue his studies. Most did not respond, and those that did rejected him. During this period Marić and Einstein also produced a daughter, whom he appears to have never publicly acknowledged (in fact, scholars of Einstein were surprised to make the discovery of her existence in 1986, when a stash of letters were found in a California safe-deposit box). Without a job he could not marry Marić, and without a marriage he could not be seen with their child.

Finally, with the help of his friend Marcel Grossman, he got a job as an examiner at the Swiss Patent Office in 1902. Although this job was considered well beneath his qualifications, the move turned out surprisingly well. Einstein found he was able to complete his work in a few hours each day, leaving him time to do his own study and thought experiments. Gainful employment also meant that he could finally marry Marić, which he did on January 6, 1903, although their child had apparently already been given up for adoption. Einstein later expressed gratitude that he ended up as a patent examiner rather than an assistant professor, for academia might have induced him to publish "safe" papers that embraced accepted theories. In the academic world, papers must go through a process of peer review prior to publication; a paper is accepted for publication only if reviewers deem it worthy. If a paper challenges popular ideas or does not show reverence for those who have previously published in the area (who may also be reviewing the paper), it is far less likely to be accepted for publication. Furthermore, after being published, an article gains legitimacy and becomes well-known only if others cite it, build upon it, and teach with it. If an article is ignored, the ideas in the paper may quietly die on the vine without ever having reached a wide audience. Needless to say, it was thus risky for Einstein to write papers that boldly challenged consecrated ideas by well-respected physicists. However, because Einstein did not yet really "belong" to academia, he had less to lose by flouting its norms. It was not in his nature to be deferential to others in order to curry favor. Furthermore, in his role as a patent examiner he was encouraged to be a skeptical and independent thinker.

The year 1905 turned out to be pivotal. In a four-month period from March to June, he wrote papers at a frenzied pace and developed multiple significant breakthroughs in physics, alluded to in a letter he wrote to his friend Conrad Habicht in May 1905:

> Why have you still not sent me your dissertation? Don't you know that I am one of the 1½ fellows who would read it with interest and pleasure, you wretched man? I promise you four papers in return. The first deals with radiation and the energy properties of light and is very revolutionary, as you will see if you send me your work first. The second paper is a determination of the true sizes of atoms. . . . The third proves that bodies on the order of magnitude 1/1000 mm, suspended in liquids, must already perform an observable random motion that is produced by thermal motion. Such movement of suspended bodies has actually been observed by physiologists who call it Brownian molecular motion. The fourth paper is

> only a rough draft at this point, and is an electrodynamics of moving bodies which employs a modification of the theory of space and time.[16]

The first paper that Einstein describes made a theoretical case for light being in the form of discrete particles of energy then called "quanta" (later known as photons) and arguing that the wave effect of light was actually the observation of averages of where those particles were at any point in time. He performed some basic empirical tests that yielded results consistent with his hypothesis. The implications of quantum mechanics would eventually overthrow much of classical physics, but in 1905 it was only a hesitantly considered idea. His second paper on the size of molecules underwent a few rounds of corrections before being submitted as a doctoral dissertation to Dr. Kleiner at the Zurich Polytechnic. This paper earned Einstein his doctorate in April 1905. In May his third paper created quite a stir by providing a theoretical reasoning for the empirical observation of Brownian motion, while at the same time providing a compelling argument that Avogadro's number could be determined from observations with an ordinary microscope. His paper was widely considered by the physics community to be astonishing and impressive.

Around this time Einstein started to experience a "state of psychic tension" about the conflict between Newton's laws and Maxwell's equations: "At the very beginning, when the special theory of relativity began to germinate in me, I was visited by all sorts of nervous conflicts. . . . When young, I used to go away for weeks in a state of confusion."[17] Although Einstein was interested in the work of both Newton and Maxwell, he knew that their ideas were incompatible. As he would later note, "[T]he constancy of the velocity of light is not consistent with the law of the addition of velocities."[18] This problem gnawed at him, and he spent almost a year trying to resolve it. He had almost given up on it when his "aha!" moment came. He suddenly realized that there was no such thing as absolute time and thus no such thing as absolute simultaneity; there was no ether (the substance that nineteenth-century physicists believed filled all of space and enabled propagation of electromagnetic and gravitational forces), no absolute rest: time is relative based on an observer's motion, and so is space. He made his arguments by means of thought experiments involving moving trains and clocks (it is probably not inconsequential that he lived next to the Bern train station and was at the time receiving a flood of patent applications at the patent office directed at finding a way to synchronize clocks with an electrical signal).

He came to his insight by casting off Newtonian misconceptions that had held back his contemporaries such as Lorentz or Poincaré, who had come close to the realization made by Einstein but never made the full leap.[19] In other words, his insight was made possible precisely because he was able to disregard accepted wisdom. Einstein believed in the existence of simple, harmonious, universal principles. He thus preferred a theory that could sweep away the clutter of fuzzy and thus-far-unverified assumptions such as the existence of ether. Einstein also worked in isolation, away from other scholars and university libraries, so there is some speculation that he may not have even been aware of all of the work of Lorentz and Poincaré. Perhaps more importantly, his rebellious nature and his fundamental belief that deference to authority was a corruption of the human spirit meant that for Einstein, pursuing the discovery of truth was far more important than showing deference to other physicists by adhering to old principles. Theoretical physicist Freeman Dyson described the situation as follows:

> The essential difference between Poincaré and Einstein was that Poincaré was by temperament conservative and Einstein was by temperament revolutionary. When Poincaré looked for a new theory of electromagnetism, he tried to preserve as much as he could of the old. . . . Einstein, on the other hand,

> saw the old framework as cumbersome and unnecessary and was delighted to be rid of it. His version of the theory was simpler and more elegant. There was no absolute space and time and there was no ether. All the complicated explanations of electric and magnetic forces and elastic stressed in the ether could be swept into the dustbin of history, together with the famous old professors who believed in them.[20]

As one of his biographers put it, "His early suspicion of authority, which never wholly left him, was to prove of decisive importance, for without it he would not have been able to develop the powerful independence of mind that gave him the courage to challenge established scientific beliefs, and thereby revolutionize physics."[21]

Einstein published his special theory of relativity in June 1905. Then, in a state of exhaustion, he took to his bed for two weeks. (In September he would write a three-page paper with one more consequence that occurred to him from his special theory of relativity—namely, that mass m was a measure of the energy E contained within it, and the relationship between speed and mass was $E=mc^2$, with c referring to the speed of light.)

Throughout his life, Einstein possessed a child's gift of awe at the wonders of the universe, and he had the ability to "hold two thoughts in his mind simultaneously, to be puzzled when they conflicted, and to marvel when he could smell an underlying unity."[22] Einstein was driven to find unifying theories—he believed that a harmonious reality was the basis of the laws of the universe and that science's goal was to discover it.[23] He could often sense when there was a simpler, unified answer to problems that were assumed to be separate. For example, he intuitively understood that gravitational force and inertial force must be definable by a single explanation. It should not be surprising that after completing his special theory of relativity, he immediately began to work on generalizing it so that it could handle changes in velocity or direction.

Despite his astonishing productivity (he published sixteen papers during 1906 and 1907) and the irrefutable impact he was having on physics, he still had difficulty attaining an academic post. He had not made many friends while at Zurich Polytechnic, and his teaching—demonstrated when he lectured as a *privatdozent* at the University of Bern—left much room for improvement. These personal deficiencies, combined with the anti-Semitism pervasive in European society at the time, created an uphill battle for Einstein. Finally, in 1909, with the support of his former professor Alfred Kleiner, the faculty of Zurich Polytechnic voted to award Einstein a professorship. He would go on to become one of the most famous scientists of all time. He would also leverage his fame to promote pacifism, disarmament, and the abolition of compulsory military service. He was a worldwide celebrity, revered both for his profound intellectual contributions to science and his effort in working toward a kinder, gentler world, even though in many ways he was a detached observer of it. As described by his friend Thomas Bucky, "He had a shy attitude toward everybody. He was gentle, considerate of others, and the opposite of pompous. But I never heard even a close friend call him by his first name. When someone did treat him with undue familiarity, he would shrink back."[24] As we shall see later in the chapter, this detachment is likely to have played multiple roles in helping Einstein to develop his breakthrough ideas.

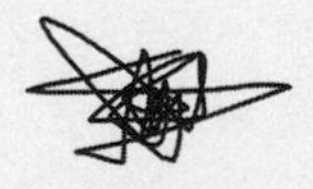

Marie Curie, whose story is told in Chapter 6, is also a poignant example of separateness and isolation. She discovered radium and polonium, and she identified radioactivity as an atomic property. She was the first woman to earn a Nobel Prize, she was the first person ever to win Nobel Prizes in two different fields, and she is likely the most famous female scientist of all time.

To say that Curie was an exceptional student is to understate it—she learned to read so early that it stunned family and friends, and she was the top student of her class all through school despite also usually being the youngest. However, women could not attend university in Poland. Thus, after graduating from the gymnasium she began to focus on self-education, reading science, politics, literature, poetry, and more, while developing a plan to further her educational career. She took a job as a governess in Szczuki, a rural town roughly fifty miles north of Warsaw, hoping to raise enough money to eventually help both her and her sister go to France to attend the Sorbonne. In the meantime she diligently pursued an educational curriculum of her own design, as she described in a letter to her cousin Henrietta:

> At nine in the evening I take my books and go to work, if something unexpected does not prevent it. . . . I have even acquired the habit of getting up at six so that I work more. . . . At the moment I am reading:
>
> 1. Daniel's *Physics,* of which I have finished the first volume,
> 2. Spencer's *Sociology,* in French;
> 3. Paul Bers' *Lessons on Anatomy and Physiology,* in Russian.
>
> I read several things at a time: the consecutive study of a single subject would wear out my poor little head which is already much overworked. When I feel myself quite unable to read with profit, I work problems of algebra or trigonometry, which allow no lapses of attention and get me back into the right road.[25]

She also wrote that she had "acquired the habit of independent work,"[26] a habit that would enable her to challenge accepted practices and paradigms and would help develop her ability to make her profound discoveries later in life.

During this period Curie also began to gain more awareness of her own sense of disconnect from the social expectations of young women. She was shy and uncomfortable when meeting new people. She disdained small talk and refused to go to the dances that other young women her age were attending. Separateness would become a defining characteristic of her nature, even after she managed to get to the Sorbonne, where she lived (according to her daughter Eve) "a Spartan existence, strange and inhuman."[27] She avoided friendly meetings and other human contact, and similarly rejected material wealth, thinking it of no importance. For fifteen or twenty francs per month, she rented a small attic without heat, lighting, or water. She would subsist for weeks at a time on only buttered bread and tea. Her entire life was organized around her work at the Sorbonne, and on more than one occasion she fainted at her lab table and had to be reminded to rest and eat.

Even after falling in love and marrying Pierre Curie, she lived a socially isolated life. She had found her match: he was not only brilliant, but he also shared her lack of interest in the social world. As Pierre once wrote, "We dreamed of living in the world quite removed from human beings." Their daughter Eve wrote about her parents, "United by their tenderness, united by their intellectual passions, they had, in a wooden shack, the 'anti-natural' existence for which they had both been made, she as well as he."[28] In her obsession with her work, Marie chose to relinquish much of her child-care duties to Pierre's father, a cheerful and loving man without whom the daughters would have led bleak lives.[29] Although her daughters expressed great adoration and respect for their mother, they also suffered from her insensitivity and neglect. Marie carefully monitored their education and development but gave them scant time and even less overt affection. In a biography that Eve would later write about her mother, she describes her as a person who was fragile yet determined, generous yet austere, lonely yet always painfully distant: "Marie had no time to give to friendship or to love. She loved mathematics and physics." However, Eve appears to justify her mother's behavior when she notes that "In all ages women who burn to become great painters or great musicians have disdained the norm, love and motherhood."[30]

Like Einstein, Curie was aware of her unconventionality and self-imposed isolation. She also knew that the way she had lived her life was not for everyone, telling Eve, "It isn't necessary to lead such an anti-natural existence as mine. . . . I have given a great deal of my time to science because I wanted to, because I loved research."[31]

As later chapters will indicate, all the breakthrough innovators I studied (with the notable exception of Benjamin Franklin) exhibited this marked sense of separateness as an integral part of their nature. This is not to be confused with the personality trait that psychologists call "introversion." Introverts are said to be reflective, reserved, and predominantly interested in ideas and their own mental self than action. Extroverts, on the other hand, are said to be sociable, energetic, and often assertive and outspoken.[32] None of the innovators studied here fit neatly into these categories, and certainly many of them would be characterized as assertive or outspoken—sometimes even domineering. The sense of separateness exhibited by the innovators is not reserve; rather, it reflects the degree to which they felt they did not belong to, or were not a part of, the social world around them.

Steve Jobs perceived himself as different from his peers and family, in part because of the angst he suffered from the knowledge that his birth parents gave him up, in part because he realized at a young age that he was more intelligent than his parents, and probably in part because his strong-willed and somewhat abrasive personality made it difficult for him to sustain intimate friendships. Chrisann Brennan, his first girlfriend and the mother of his first child, notes how even in high school Jobs was "disconnected and awkward" and that he had "a mix of genius, authenticity, and emotional woodenness."[33] Thomas Edison was born with an "abnormally large though well-shaped head," and doctors feared he might have some type of problem with his brain. Because of his presumed delicacy, he was sent to school for only three months of his life. While other boys were playing sports, Edison spent nearly every free moment in a laboratory he had set up in the cellar of his parents' home. Later in life he would be described by more than one biographer as "jocular," and he was a known lover of pranks. He also spent most of his life in his laboratory, where he was surrounded by his large team of employees. However, he also became mostly deaf, and this condition made him uncomfortable in social situations (although he saw it as a great boon to his ability to focus). He later married and had children but was chronically preoccupied with work and spent most nights in its laboratory, neglecting his family.[34] As his second wife, Mina, wrote of him, "Mr. Edison has few friends. Because of his work he has had to live a great deal by himself and in himself—shut out from the social contacts open to most men."[35]

Nikola Tesla, whose life is discussed at length in Chapter 3, similarly worked alone and obsessively, mostly at night, with little social interaction and few friends. In a statement that is remarkably similar to remarks made by Einstein, he told his father, "It is not humans that I love, but humanity." Although he had the ability to be a charismatic storyteller, he was also noted for having poor social skills and being extremely unconventional. For example, he wrote at length about his love for a pigeon that he believed to be his soul mate. In 1895 a *New York Times* article described him: "He seems to be a man who dwells apart. He has no kith or kin in this country, and only a few friends who share his confidences. Even in moments of closest social intercourse he will become abstracted, and there is never a time when he would not prefer his laboratory to any other spot on earth."[36]

Even Elon Musk, the boy wonder behind SpaceX and Tesla Motors, exhibits this sense of separateness. According to his mother, as a child Musk was the smallest in his class, was a "super nerd," and was often bullied. He is repeatedly described as "bookish." His family had also moved frequently (Musk went to seven different schools growing up), making it even more difficult for him to build strong social connections. Musk notes that he "never truly had a chance to make friends."[37] He responded to this sense of separation by escaping into books (Jules Verne and J. R. Tolkien were favorites) and computer programming, ultimately writing and selling his first video game at the age of twelve.

It is difficult to know to what degree these individuals experienced a sense of suffering or regret from their separateness—what people feel may not be what they convey publicly. For example, Eve Curie's description of her mother paints a picture of a terribly sad and lonely woman, but Marie Curie's own writings indicated that she experienced a sense of bliss in her self-imposed isolation and immersion in work—at least until Pierre's death. Of the innovators studied here, only Einstein extensively reflects on his separateness in a written form to which we have access, and although his expressions include a discernible twinge of melancholy, for the most part he confidently extols the importance of such independence. Einstein is famously quoted as having said "It is strange to be known so universally and yet to be so lonely." Yet in writing about his detachment he noted that it was extremely important for his ability to think independently: "The really valuable thing in the pageant of human life seems to me not the State but the creative, sentient individual, the personality; it alone creates the noble and sublime, while the herd as such remains dull in thought and dull in feeling."[38]

By nurturing the independent thinking of the breakthrough innovators, separateness helped them to generate and pursue big and unusual ideas. By not belonging, they were buffered from the norms that help to bring groups of people to consensus and foster cooperation. When separateness is a result of, or results in, social isolation, individuals are less exposed to conventional wisdom; their ideas can develop less contaminated by those shared by the crowd. Furthermore, perceiving oneself as separate can also make an individual more prone to resisting conventional wisdom even if amply exposed to it. When an individual is not well integrated into the social fabric, there is less to lose by being unconventional. In fact, being unconventional or iconoclastic can become an important part of an individual's identity. These dynamics are vividly illustrated by the lives of serial breakthrough innovators: Einstein was initially shunned by academia and was subsequently able to reject established ideas about ether and absolute time that held back Lorentz and Poincaré; Edison was kept out of grammar school and learned to trust only those things he could prove himself; Curie intensely pursued self-education because women were not allowed in universities in Poland, and she consequently acquired the independent thinking and resolve that were the wellsprings of her success; Jobs felt "abandoned, but special"[39] because he knew that he'd been put up for adoption and that he was smarter than his adoptive parents, and he consequently decided that the rules other people lived by did not apply to him. Rejecting the constraints of what other people deemed impossible was fundamental to his inspiration to build computers in a garage and to his commitment to put "1,000 songs in your pocket."[40]

Many things can give rise to a sense of separateness. An individual might be physically or socially isolated because of circumstances in childhood. Tesla was emotionally abandoned by his parents for a while after his brother's death, and he was later confined to bed for nine months with cholera. Separateness can also have a physical origin, such as physical disabilities or mental disorders. Edison's hearing impairment made him not only uncomfortable in social gatherings but also extremely reluctant to speak in public.[41] Charles Darwin appears to have suffered from extreme anthrophobia (fear of social contact) that made him avoid contact even with his close family members.[42] Economic, cultural, and language barriers can also create a sense of separateness, offering a partial explanation for why immigrant communities are so often identified as a source of innovation and entrepreneurship: if the "typical" route to prosperity is not available to an individual or a group, they may be more likely to pursue "atypical" routes. Many studies show that immigrants start up new companies at twice the rate of natives, in part because traditional employment opportunities are often not available to them and in part because of different attitudes about risk that are both cause and consequence of leaving the home country and starting over in a new one. Sergey Brin, cofounder of Google, emigrated to the United States with his family at the age of six—Russian Jews were among the few who were allowed to leave the Soviet Union. As he describes it, "The US was very good to us. It was a great place, but we started with nothing. We were poor. . . . When we first moved to the States we rented a little house, and my parents didn't have a proper room to sleep in. They had to wall off the kitchen. It was a very humble beginning. . . . We learned to get by. I think being scrappy and getting by is important. . . . The most important thing in the background [of being Jewish]—of just having gone through hardship and being able to survive and thrive. I think that's at the core of the Jewish experience."[43]

A sense of separateness can also be self-reinforcing: individuals who perceive themselves as not fitting in may socially isolate themselves because of shyness or fear of rejection. They may not develop social skills that make it easy for them be comfortable in social settings and may also experience failed social encounters that cause them to retreat still further. Others may have excellent social skills but use them only in selective occasions (both Jobs and Einstein were noted as being capable of exceptional charisma yet were also famous for their detachment and for their rejection of social norms). Such people may become so accustomed to doing things their own way that conforming to the structure or routines of others is difficult or irritating for them. On a more positive note, they may also learn to relish and make productive use of their time alone.

These latter two points may explain why so many of the most famous innovators struggled with (or skipped) formal schooling but keenly pursued self-education. Albert Einstein, as described previously, was a difficult and irregular student who graduated at the bottom of his class but studied intensively on his own. Steve Jobs and Dean Kamen both dropped out of undergraduate programs. Jobs famously said that "looking back it was one of the best decisions I ever made. The minute I dropped out I could stop taking the required classes that didn't interest me, and begin dropping in on the ones that looked far more interesting."[44]

Kamen, who is probably best known for inventing the Segway personal transporter (his most famous though not most successful invention), also developed the first portable drug infusion pump, the first portable kidney dialysis machine, several prosthetic limbs, and the iBot, a wheelchair that can climb stairs. He is widely regarded as one of the most accomplished electromechanical engineers in the world and is often compared to Thomas Edison and Henry Ford.[45] He has won many awards (including the US National Medal of Technology and the United Nations Global Humanitarian Action Award) and has received roughly a dozen honorary doctoral degrees despite having never finished an undergraduate program. Kamen had earned mediocre grades in middle school and high school, and had frequent conflicts with his teachers. He resented being told what to do and would argue with them over the way they taught math and physics. He also frequently refused to answer test questions, explaining, "I decided taking a test is a fool's errand. Because the ones you know the answer to, don't waste your time writing down. And the ones you don't know the answer to, why shine a bright light on how stupid you are?"[46] Later, when he was enrolled at the Worcester Polytechnic Institute, he refused to go to classes: "I said, 'I'm paying my tuition to have the entire faculty as business consultants. I recognize that is not consistent with your model, which is, You know better than I and I have to take this much math and these electives, and all that stuff is valuable, but *right now* I'm focused, I'm allowed to make a rational decision, I can pay you this tuition and avail myself of this extraordinary faculty, but I'm not going to waste my time in class because the opportunity costs would be too high.'"[47] He ended up dropping out before graduating but remained an avid reader of science texts.

Elon Musk and Sergey Brin both dropped out of doctoral programs. Musk's approach to his early schooling was utilitarian: he excelled in classes that appealed to him and ignored the others. As he puts it, "I just look at it as 'What grades do I need to get where I want to go?' There were compulsory subjects like Afrikaans, and I just didn't see the point of learning that. It seemed ridiculous. I'd get a passing grade and that was fine. Things like physics and computers—I got the highest grade you can get in those."[48] He also noted, "When I went to college I rarely went to class. I'd just read the textbook and show up for the exams."[49] Although he earned excellent grades and was admitted to Stanford's doctoral program in physics, he dropped out on the second day after deciding he would rather spend his time revolutionizing methods of payment and banking. Brin has a similar story. Bored in high school, he dropped out a year early and was accepted by the University of Maryland. Like Einstein, he had a tendency to correct his professors; unlike Einstein, his quieter and more studious demeanor did not inspire the rancor that Einstein's careless wit had provoked. He graduated with a dual degree in math and computer science in 1993 and went straight into the Stanford doctoral program, where he passed all of his qualifying exams within the first couple of months (most students do not take the exams until their third year). Brin thus didn't need to take any classes—he just needed to write a thesis to graduate. Instead, Brin worked on various projects that interested him (one of which was with Larry Page and evolved into the Google search engine) and never bothered to complete the thesis.

Some breakthrough innovators had almost no formal education. For example, Benjamin Franklin went to school from the age of eight to ten and was almost wholly self-educated. Thomas Edison, despite his mere three months of grammar school, was a voracious reader and by the age of twelve had read Gibbon's *Decline and Fall of the Roman Empire,* Hume's *History of England,* Sears's *History of the World,* Burton's *Anatomy of Melancholy,* and the *Dictionary of Sciences.*[50]

When people see that brilliantly successful people drop out of school, many infer that education had nothing to do with their success or was even an impediment. However, that is far from the case. All of the breakthrough innovators I studied invested heavily in self-education. They were avid consumers of knowledge, but they followed their own rhythms rather than an instructor's pace. They went deeply into a topic or broadly across topics they chose rather than following the path of a syllabus. They were fueled by intrinsic motivation—a true love of learning—even if they had no love for school.

TIME ALONE CAN BE both cause and consequence of a sense of separateness. Most of the innovators had childhoods and young-adult periods characterized by significant time spent in solitude, pursuing their own interests. Solitude is valuable for creativity; it affords people the time to think about and pursue those things they find intrinsically interesting.[51] It can help them to develop their own beliefs about how the world works and to develop a self-concept that is less structured by the interpretations or opinions of others.

Solitude also enables people to pursue cognitive paths of association without the contaminating effect or interference of the associations made by others, a point we will return to when we discuss brainstorming groups.

Henry David Thoreau, Emily Dickinson, Rudyard Kipling, and Franz Kafka are among the many famous writers noted for the role that solitude played in their creative processes.[52] Thoreau's journals and works are filled with statements about how he valued time alone:

> By my intimacy with nature I find myself withdrawn from man. My interest in the sun and the moon, in the morning and the evening, compels me to solitude. (journal, July 26, 1851)
>
> I thrive best on solitude. If I have had a companion only one day in a week, unless it were one or two I could name, I find that the value of the week to me has been seriously affected. It dissipates my days, and often it takes me another week to get over it. (journal, December 28, 1856)
>
> You think that I am impoverishing myself withdrawing from men, but in my solitude I have woven for myself a silken web or chrysalis, and, nymph-like, shall ere long burst forth a more perfect creature, fitted for a higher society. (journal, February 8, 1857)
>
> I have an immense appetite for solitude, like an infant for sleep, and if I don't get enough for this year, I shall cry all the next. (letter to Daniel Ricketson, September 9, 1857)[53]

Solitude is not, of course, the ideal that most people seek. Many find it very uncomfortable because, as noted in more detail later, humans are social animals. If time alone is valuable for creativity, then perhaps the degree to which people are comfortable being alone influences their likelihood of tapping their latent creative capability. If this is the case, it explains why so many studies have concluded that creative geniuses are more likely to be introverts—introversion could be an *enabling* trait for creative people. Consistent with this idea, noted creativity researcher Mihaly Csikszentmihalyi observed in 1996 that adolescents who could not tolerate solitude often failed to develop their creative talents because that development typically requires solitary engagement in such activities.

Separateness does not mean that the entire creative process is conducted alone—even for serial breakthrough innovators. Many creative ideas arise through the recombination of ideas or the knowledge of others, and still more require the cooperation or collaboration of others in order to refine and implement them. Steve Jobs could not have built computers without the help of Steve Wozniak or developed the iPhone, iPod, or iPad without the help of Jonathan Ive and others; Einstein sought help from Michele Besso and Marcel Grossmann for some aspects of his work; Elon Musk and Thomas Edison built laboratories full of technical experts to help them execute their ideas; and even Marie Curie, as we shall see in Chapter 6, required considerable assistance from her husband to discover radium. However, it is also true that all of the innovators exhibited extraordinary independence and developed many of their most important ideas or inventions on their own. As noted above, many of Einstein's breakthrough discoveries were developed in almost complete isolation. Tesla, as described in Chapter 3, worked almost entirely alone, bringing others into his projects only when the designs were complete. Musk astonished space industry veterans when he designed his own reusable rocket by studying aerospace in borrowed rocket science textbooks. And although Edison is famous for having built research and development (R&D) laboratories, he was a consummate tinkerer from a very early age, and his earliest inventions, such as his first improved telegraph transmitter, a stock-price printer, and an electric vote recorder, were solo creations. As shown in Chapter 5, Edison was virtually immune to the influence of others and, as described by one biographer, "Edison's need for autonomy was primal and unvarying; it would determine the course of his career from beginning to end."[54]

STUDIES BY PSYCHOLOGISTS OF groups engaged in brainstorming reinforce the benefits of solitude for creativity. Brainstorming groups have been a tenet of faith in business schools for close to a half-century, ever since Alex Osborne, in his highly influential book *Applied Imagination,* opined that "the average person can think up twice as many ideas when working with a group than when working alone." Brainstorming groups have been extremely popular in both businesses and business schools, and doubts about brainstorming's efficacy border on heresy. However, dozens of subsequent laboratory studies found results opposite to Osborne's claim: brainstorming groups produced fewer ideas, and ideas of less novelty, than the sum of the ideas created by the same number of individuals working alone.

Three theories have emerged to explain why brainstorming groups are less productive than people working alone. First is the free-rider issue: the possibility that some people may shirk when others in the group start generating ideas. Second is evaluation apprehension. People may self-censor many of their ideas in group brainstorming sessions for fear of being judged negatively by others. The third explanation is production blocking. As people take turns voicing their ideas, those bringing up the rear may forget their ideas before having a chance to voice them. Furthermore, the process of attending to another person's ideas redirects a listener's train of thought, essentially hijacking her own idea-generation process.

Professors Michael Diehl and Wolfgang Stroebe set out to test these theories with a series of experiments that compared brainstorming groups with people working alone whose ideas are combined, using high school and college students.[55] First, to test the free-rider explanation, they told some groups that ideas would be evaluated for each person individually and some groups that ideas would be evaluated collectively. Groups that were told ideas would be evaluated collectively generated slightly fewer ideas, explaining a significant, though minor, amount of the productivity losses in brainstorming groups. Next, to test the evaluation-apprehension explanation they told some groups that their ideas would be evaluated by anonymous judges and told other groups that their ideas would be evaluated by their peers, under the assumption that judgment by peers would induce the greatest evaluation apprehension. They found stronger results for the evaluation-apprehension explanation: groups that were told their ideas would be judged by their peers generated significantly fewer and less novel ideas than groups that were told they would be evaluated by anonymous judges. Finally, to evaluate the possibility of production blocking, the researchers created several different conditions. In some conditions, individuals worked alone in rooms and spoke their ideas into a microphone, but lights indicated when they were allowed to contribute their ideas and when they needed to wait while others contributed. In some of the rooms the individuals could hear the contributions of others, and in some they could not. This study resulted in the largest production losses by far: being required to wait to give ideas caused people to submit far fewer ideas, an outcome that many of us have experienced. Now imagine what happens when people do not have to take turns but instead volunteer ideas at will: the most outgoing people in the group may dominate all of the idea submission while the quieter people, or those more worried about social pressure, do not submit many (or any) of their ideas. Furthermore, if they do submit their ideas, they may submit only those ideas that build upon the ideas that were already contributed—a sure way to drive out novelty.

Professor Brian Mullen and his coauthors Craig Johnson and Eduardo Salas decided to assess how reliable these findings were by conducting a meta-analysis (where the results of multiple studies are combined) of twenty studies of brainstorming groups. They found that productivity losses in both quantity and quality of ideas were highly significant and were large in magnitude. Losses increased with larger groups and with supervision by an experimenter or other authority. Like Diehl and Stroebe, these analysts found that only negligible losses were caused by free riding, but unlike Diehl and Stroebe, they found that production losses were greatest for evaluation apprehension, followed by production blocking.[56]

Together, then, these studies show that brainstorming groups diminish creative outcomes because we lose our ideas when others are talking, and we do not express our most novel ideas because we worry about what others will think. Isaac Asimov, one of the most famous science fiction writers of all time and also a biochemistry professor at Boston University, presaged these findings in an unpublished essay written in 1959: "My feeling is that as far as creativity is concerned, isolation is required. The creative person is, in any case, continually working at it. His mind is shuffling his information at all times, even when he is not conscious of it. (The famous example of Kekule working out the structure of benzene in his sleep is well-known.) The presence of others can only inhibit this process, since creation is embarrassing. For every new good idea you have, there are a hundred, ten thousand foolish ones, which you naturally do not care to display."[57]

Later, a series of studies by Professor Eric Rietzschel and coauthors showed that group *selection* (rather than *generation*) of ideas also reduces novelty as groups of people tend to prefer and select ideas that are feasible over those that are original.[58] For example, both interactive groups (people brainstorming together) and nominal groups (people brainstorming separately and then combining their ideas) were asked to generate ideas for improving course instruction in a psychology department. Then all of the groups were instructed to interactively select the "best" ideas. The ideas were then assessed by independent raters for their originality and feasibility. For example, the idea "Use hypnosis to increase students' concentration" was considered highly original, whereas "Teach courses in smaller groups" was considered unoriginal. "Maintain a stricter policy against cell phones during exams" was considered highly feasible, but "Make all course books available in digital form" was considered infeasible. Overall, these studies found that when groups interactively ranked their "best" ideas, they chose ideas that were less original than the average of the ideas produced and more feasible than the average of the ideas produced. In other words, people tended to value feasibility more than originality. If a brainstorming group is intended to elicit novel ideas, asking groups to select and submit their best ideas is not the way to achieve that outcome. This also highlights the importance of both the breakthrough innovator's tendency to have different beliefs about what is possible and the breakthrough innovator's willingness to pursue projects even if they have a high likelihood of failure—points that are further discussed in the chapters on self-efficacy and idealism.

Nonconformity and Rebelliousness

THE INNOVATOR'S SENSE OF separateness can also give rise to a sharp tendency to disregard or rebel against rules. For example, nonconformity was a central element of Einstein's moral philosophy. His study of the philosophies of Hume and Mach taught him to be skeptical of things that he could not observe and to question conventional theories. Further, his job at the patent office did not subject him to the homogenizing norms of academia, and his job required him to ferret out false claims or flawed logic in patent applications. Each of these factors played a part in helping Einstein become a profoundly independent thinker. As Walter Isaacson described him, "His success came from questioning conventional wisdom, challenging authority, and marveling at mysteries that struck others as mundane. This led him to embrace a morality and politics based on respect for free minds, free spirits, and free individuals. Tyranny repulsed him, and he saw tolerance not simply as a sweet virtue but as a necessary condition for a creative society. Einstein argued, 'It is important to foster individuality, . . . for only the individual can produce the new ideas.'"[59]

Edison had a very similar nature. As he noted about himself in a 1908 interview, when he was a child he "involuntarily challenged" everything he read and desired to demonstrate whether it was right or wrong. His individualistic style of acquiring knowledge and his reflexive challenging of received wisdom eventually led him to question many of the prevailing theories of electricity.[60] One of his biographers, Gerald Beals, noted that even as a boy, Edison became irritated and impatient with the way Newton's theories were written. He felt that the classical aristocratic terms were unnecessarily confusing, and he developed a strong dislike for "hightone" language and mathematics. In response, he developed his own theories through objective examination and experimentation. As he frequently declared, "I accept almost nothing dealing with electricity without thoroughly testing it first." His keen memory, intelligence, and extraordinary perseverance served him well in this objective. As is discussed in Chapter 5, it was this perseverance that led him to test thousands of different potential filaments until he found one that would yield a long-lasting light bulb and to run nine thousand experiments to develop a storage battery.

Sometimes the nonconformity of breakthrough innovators is displayed in a distinct sense that the rules do not apply to them. Steve Jobs's nonconformity was particularly notorious in this respect. Rules, as he demonstrated throughout his life, applied to other people. Jobs was comfortable being different from other people and engaged in unconventional behaviors such as extreme diets, not wearing shoes, and staring intensely without blinking at people. Although Jobs was frequently abrasive, he could also be intensely charismatic, and he used this ability to be charismatic to alter other people's perception of the rules—a phenomenon people commonly referred to as a "reality distortion field." As Bud Tribble, a software designer on the original Macintosh team, described it, "In his presence, reality is malleable. He can convince anyone of anything. It wears off when he's not around, but it makes it hard to have realistic schedules. . . . It was dangerous to get caught in Steve's distortion field, but it was what led him to actually be able to change reality." Andy Hertzfeld, another software designer on the team, added that "The reality distortion field was a confounding mélange of a charismatic rhetorical style, indomitable will, and eagerness to bend any fact to fit the purpose at hand. . . . Amazingly, the reality distortion field seemed to be effective even if you were acutely aware of it. We would often discuss potential techniques for grounding it, but after a while most of us gave up, accepting it as a force of nature."[61] Debi Coleman, a member of the original Macintosh team who later became head of Macintosh manufacturing at Apple, likened Jobs's charisma to a form of hypnosis: "He laser-beamed in on you and didn't blink. It didn't matter if he was serving purple Kool-Aid. You drank it. . . . It was a self-fulfilling distortion. . . . You did the impossible because you didn't realize it was impossible."[62]

Dean Kamen is another archetypal example of an innovator who does not let himself be constrained by the rules and laws that govern others. An iconoclastic and quirky genius who has taken on one grand challenge after the other, Kamen is also described as "spectacularly stubborn." As his brother Mitch notes, "He was always focused on what he wanted to do, and nobody could ever talk him into doing something he didn't want to do."[63] In the early 2000s he began developing a water purification machine called the Slingshot that can turn anything wet into drinkable water. In fact, in a demonstration at a 2004 conference, Kamen ran his own urine through the purifier and drank the clean water it produced.

When Kamen set out to develop the iBot, he realized that if it had wheels that could turn back and forth quickly and precisely enough, it would be able to stay upright on just two wheels, balancing much the same way a person does through rapidly shifting weight back and forth. The ability to balance upright would enable it to climb stairs, go over curbs, handle rough terrain, and more. When people said it was impossible to develop such a balancing device, he replied, "Don't tell me it's impossible . . . tell me you can't do it. . . . Tell me it's never been done. Because the only real laws in this world—the only things we really know—are the two postulates of relativity, the three laws of Newton, the four laws of thermodynamics, and Maxwell's equation—no, scratch that, the only things we really know are Maxwell's equations, the three laws of Newton, the two postulates of relativity, and the periodic table. That's all we know that's true. All the rest are man's laws. . . . "[64]

The rejection of rules by Jobs and Kamen also hints at another key trait of the most fecund innovators: a profound faith in their ability to achieve their objectives known as "self-efficacy," which will be further explored in the next chapter.

There are multiple self-reinforcing pathways connecting a sense of separateness, time alone, nonconformity, and heterodox thinking. First, having the time and liberty to pursue one's own interests enables individuals to develop opinions and expertise, and directly reduces exposure to homogenizing norms. This is captured eloquently in a biographer's description of Marie Curie, which notes that instead of socializing, Curie relentlessly pursued self-education and by the age of eighteen had "acquired the habit of independent work," which gave her the ability to draw her own conclusions unconstrained by others' perceptions and accepted paradigms. Time alone may also directly increase or reinforce one's sense of "separateness," or lack of belonging, because of reduced bonding time with others and, indirectly, because a person who spends less time with others may suffer in her social skill development, which can lead to poor social experiences. For some people, a reduced sense of belonging will result in greater effort to fit in; for others, it releases them from the pressure of social norms, increasing their ability to be nonconforming. As noted previously, the fact that Einstein was initially rejected by academia made it easier for him to disregard its norms and widely accepted ideas. This, in turn, helped him to throw out conventions like absolute time and ether and to develop his breakthrough theories. Curie was considered highly unconventional because she was a woman of science; perhaps this made her more likely to stand up to those who discriminated against her. Time alone and separateness can thus increase both the *opportunity* to develop divergent ideas and the *willingness* to be nonconforming.

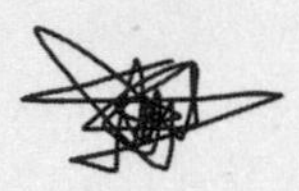

SEPARATENESS HAS BOTH BENEFITS and costs. On the positive side, a sense of separateness can liberate people from the constraints of conventions and paradigms, freeing them to pursue more original ideas and activities. Paradigms are like well-trodden paths in science: they can accelerate your pace of travel along a known trajectory, but they discourage you from finding more novel directions for exploring the environment. As a result, hidden opportunities go undiscovered.

On the other hand, separateness can lead to psychic distress. Homo sapiens is a highly interdependent creature; evolution has ensured that most individuals instinctively know and feel their interconnectedness with others. It is thus not surprising that most people will feel some distress about separateness. The fact that the people discussed here did not express such distress might mean that other traits (such as high self-efficacy or introversion) possessed by breakthrough innovators moderate the anxiety normally produced by separateness, or it may reflect bias in how the sense of separateness is remembered or presented to the outside world.

Second, separateness can impair influence and access to resources, especially when it is caused by (or results in) actual social or physical isolation. Information, capital, and other resources are often attained through personal social networks. The size and structure of an individual's personal network can influence access to resources as diverse as restaurant recommendations, jobs, and potential marriage partners. Individuals with larger networks, who are connected directly or indirectly to many people or whose networks have considerable range (that is, the people with whom they are connected are diverse, causing the network to span multiple occupational, social, or other spheres), reap significant advantages in their access to resources. Although isolation from information could help prevent an individual from converging on the same ideas possessed by others, it could also impair her ability to access information and other resources that would help her develop or execute her ideas.

Similarly, the size and structure of a person's network also directly influence the degree to which she can influence the world around her. Having strong ties to others (connections that involve frequent and intense exchange) and a dense personal network (one in which many of a person's contacts are also connected to one another) enhances the speed and accuracy with which information can be transferred. Dense networks usually have high levels of mutual understanding, trust, and willingness to exchange information. Ideas are more easily comprehended and assimilated in a dense network. If an innovator's network is both dense and of great range, it greatly increases her potential influence; a poorly connected innovator may find it harder to get people to accept or use her ideas.

Thus there is a tradeoff: separateness enables inventors to create heterodox ideas, but strong cohesive networks are likely to be better for getting them implemented. The benefits and costs of a cohesive interpersonal network were explored by Professors Lee

Fleming, Santiago Mingo, and David Chen. They studied every patent granted by the US Patent and Trademark Office between 1975 and 2002. Patents list their inventors, and many patents have more than one inventor, indicating that the work on the patent was a collaborative effort. Fleming, Mingo, and Chen then looked at each inventor's network of collaborators: Did they coinvent with many others? Did many of their collaborators also coinvent with one another? If the latter is true, the inventor is said to have a "cohesive" network. In social network terms this corresponds to the situation where many of a person's friends are also friends of one another, forming a tightly woven-together clique. On the other hand, an inventor might not collaborate very much at all (and thus have a small network) or might collaborate with inventors who do not coinvent with one another. In the latter case the inventor is said to have a "brokerage" position because the inventor can broker knowledge (or other resources) between other inventors who would otherwise be unconnected. In social terms, this is similar to the situation that occurs when an individual has friends who would otherwise be unconnected. For example, a person might have a friend on her soccer team, a friend in a church group, and some friends at work. If most of those friends are not friends of one another, that individual occupies a brokerage position. Brokers are important because they provide access to information (or other resources) that their connections would not otherwise have. For example, the broker who has a friend on the soccer team might know someone in the church group whom the soccer teammate might like to date, or she might be able to introduce her friend from the church group to someone at the broker's workplace who can help him get a job.

On the other hand, being in a brokerage position could have its downsides. When many of your friends are friends of your friends, information flows quickly among the members of the group. People who are densely connected may understand and trust one another more, leading to better exchange and cooperation. The broker, unfortunately, may not benefit from the trust and deep knowledge of being centrally embedded in a densely connected group. She may have access to a broader variety of information, but it may not flow as rapidly to her or be assimilated as rapidly by the connections she transmits it to. Not surprisingly, Fleming, Mingo, and Chen found that inventors who had more-cohesive collaboration networks were less likely to generate creative ideas but that when they did generate creative ideas, those ideas were more likely to be adopted and built upon by other inventors. Inventors who were in "brokerage" positions generated many creative ideas but were less likely to have those ideas adopted.[65] This was aptly illustrated in the case of Einstein: after he published his flurry of revolutionary papers in 1905, he expected to be warmly embraced by the academic community to which he did not yet really belong. Instead, he was greeted by a chilly silence that surprised and disappointed him. It was not until the revered physicist Max Planck published a paper in 1906 building on Einstein's theory of relatively that he began to gain widespread recognition and legitimacy.

The lack of a strong and dense network can especially handicap ideas whose benefits are harder to observe in advance of their use or that require the cooperation of other stakeholders to implement. This contrast is well illustrated by comparing Benjamin Franklin to Marie Curie. Many of Franklin's innovations were social institutions, such as the creation of the Philadelphia Public Library, the implementation of a system for sweeping and lighting the city's streets, and the country's first volunteer firefighting cooperative. These institutions required the considerable cooperation of others, and their outcomes were difficult to estimate in advance. To gain the support and cooperation necessary to implement them, Franklin wielded an extensive network of personal contacts, his masterfully crafted persona, and his exceptional oratorical and writing skills. Franklin invested considerable time and effort in developing and practicing a form of speech that was designed to not arouse opposition. He refrained from using words such as "certainly" and "undoubtedly" and instead would say "I conceive or apprehend a thing to be so and so," "It appears to me," or "I imagine it to be so." As he noted in his autobiography,

> This habit, I believe, has been of great advantage to me when I have had occasion to inculcate my opinions, and persuade men into measures that I have been from time to time engag'd in promoting; and as the chief ends of conversation are to inform or to be informed, to please or to persuade, I wish well-meaning, sensible men would not lessen their power of doing good by a positive, assuming manner, that seldom fails to disgust, tends to create opposition, and to defeat every one of those purposes for which speech was given to us, to wit, giving or receiving information or pleasure. For, if you would inform, a positive and dogmatical manner in advancing your sentiments may provoke contradiction and prevent a candid attention.[66]

Now compare Franklin to Curie, who was altogether different. Curie's innovations were based on chemistry and physics, and could not be ignored—after all, they *glowed*. Whereas Franklin was a skilled and enthusiastic social networker who demonstrated extreme interest in managing his image and influence, Curie was a very private person who worked long hours, often only in the company of her laboratory equipment, and showed little interest in managing her image or influence. Consider the sequence of events that occurred just after her husband's untimely death, in 1905. Marie was devastated by the loss of Pierre and characteristically turned to her work for solace. When a former pupil and close friend wrote to her complaining of her neglect, she wrote, "I no longer am able to devote any time to social life. All our friends in common will tell you that I never see them anymore except for business, for questions concerning work or education of the children. No one visits me, and I don't see anyone and I haven't been able to avoid offending some people in my circle and my laboratory who don't find me sufficiently friendly. . . . I have completely lost the habit of conversation without a set goal."[67]

In 1910, however, a longtime friend and colleague, Paul Langevin, somehow managed to convince Marie to open her heart. He was tall, handsome, and a brilliant physicist and mathematician. Unfortunately, he was also married, with four children. The two began a passionate—and secret—affair. Rumors began to swirl by the summer of 1911, and the press whipped the scandal into a frenzy. Marie did little to defend herself and instead retreated still further into her private life. Langevin's wife found out about the affair and released to the press Langevin and Curie's intimate letters, with details of both Curie's passion for Langevin and her urgings that he leave his wife. For a man in France at the time, an affair was a nonissue—perhaps even to be expected. For a woman, however, it was a despicable act, inspiring vicious attacks. As Bertram Boltwood publicly declared, "She is exactly what I always thought she was, a detestable idiot!"[68] People surrounded Curie's home and threw stones at her windows. Many of her friends turned on her, and a group of professors at the Sorbonne demanded that she leave France.

On the same day that news of the affair broke, Curie received a telegram notifying her that she had won a second Nobel Prize—this time in chemistry. Shortly after, however, a member of the Nobel Committee wrote her requesting that she not come to Sweden to collect the prize because of the scandal. The wounded yet resolute Curie wrote back:

> You suggest to me . . . that the Academy of Stockholm, if it had been forewarned, would probably have decided not to give me the Prize, unless I could publicly explain the attacks of which I have been the object. . . . I must therefore act according to my convictions. . . . The action that you advise me would appear

> a grave error on my part. In fact the Prize has been awarded for discovery of Radium and Polonium. I believe there is no connection between my scientific work and the facts of private life. . . . I cannot accept the idea in principle that the appreciation of the value of scientific work should be influenced by libel and slander concerning private life. I am convinced that this opinion is shared by many people.[69]

Curie went to Stockholm and collected her prize. She was the only woman to have ever won two Nobel Prizes and, at the time, the only person to have ever won two Nobel Prizes in different fields. At the ceremony she paid homage to the contribution of other scientists in the field, but as she also firmly stated, "[I]solating radium as a pure salt was undertaken by me alone."[70] Though appearing somewhat hardened and proud at the ceremony, afterward she experienced a complete nervous breakdown. Her weight dropped to 103 pounds. She told her daughter Eve that she wanted to kill herself, and she spent weeks in a darkened room under medical care. She gradually recovered, in part because her daughters needed her and in part because of the tender nursing she received from her close friend Hertha Ayrton. She did little to manage people's impressions of her, nor did she seek the support of those who might have defended her. She was a woman who stood largely alone in the face of opposition, criticism, and discrimination. Fortunately, her scientific contributions were so indisputable that they were readily assimilated and used by others because of their enormous benefits. Curie's separateness had enabled her to conceive and pursue scientific paths of which most other women at the time would not have dreamed; her separateness gave her the strength and resolve to continue on her path even when many people were against her. However, she also paid a significant emotional toll for her separateness, in part because she did not live in a time or place that embraced unconventional women.

Nurturing Independence and Creativity

THERE ARE A NUMBER of implications for nurturing creativity in individuals, families, and organizations that come from understanding the benefits and costs of separateness. The first and most straightforward pertains to spending time alone: if we are seeking creative ideas, it is very beneficial to give individuals time to work alone before engaging in collaboration. Individuals should be encouraged to not fear being unorthodox, and they should be asked to write down their ideas before any sharing or comparison takes place. Evaluation or judgment should be downplayed. Some companies, such as Google and 3M, take this idea several steps further and give employees in creative roles time (20 percent of work hours for Google and 15 percent of work hours for 3M) in which they are supposed to pursue projects of their own creation and choosing. Children are also likely to benefit from time to think, read, and write alone—overscheduling them and turning all activities into collaborative engagements could prevent them from fully developing their own ideas and discovering those things in which they are intrinsically interested.

Second, norms of meritocracy and a tolerance for unconventionality have a surprising synergy, as we have often seen in the information technology industry. For example, consider what happened when Steve Jobs applied for a job at Atari in 1974. Jobs had seen a help-wanted ad in the *San Jose Mercury* that said "Have fun, make money." He showed up in the lobby of the video game manufacturer wearing sandals and disheveled hair, and he told the personnel director that he wouldn't leave until he was given a job. Al Alcorn, then chief engineer at Atari, was called and told, "We've got a hippie kid in the lobby. He says he's not going to leave until we hire him. Should we call the cops or let him in?" Alcorn said to send him in. Despite Jobs's startling appearance, Alcorn hired him. As Alcorn described it, "He just walked in the door and here was an eighteen year old kind-of a hippy kid, and he wanted a job, and I said 'Oh, where did you go to school?' and he says 'Reed.' 'Reed, is that an engineering school?' 'No, it's a literary school,' and he'd dropped out. But then he started in with this enthusiasm for technology, and he had a spark. He was eighteen years old so he had to be cheap. And so I hired him!"[71] Atari cofounder Nolan Bushnell noted that Jobs was "brilliant, curious, and aggressive,"[72] but soon it was apparent that Jobs could also be very difficult to work with, openly mocking other employees and making several enemies in the process. To make matters worse, he had significant body odor. Jobs adhered to a fruitarian diet and believed (incorrectly) that it prevented body odor, so he did not shower regularly or use deodorant. Unfazed by the complaints, Alcorn resolved the problem by having Jobs work only at night.[73] As Bushnell later recalled, "I always felt to run a good company you had to have room for everybody—you could always figure out a way to make room for smart people, so we decided to have a night shift in engineering—he was the only one in it."[74] Many organizations would have sent Steve Jobs—one of the most profoundly successful innovators of our time—away without even giving him an interview. However, Alcorn could see the creativity and passion of Jobs, and he was not about to let unconventionality be an obstacle to employing him.

The third implication is in the way we teach or emphasize social skills. Social skills such as persuasiveness and the ability to build trust and rapport are, of course, valuable for acquiring the cooperation of others or accessing resources. They undoubtedly make many aspects of life easier and more pleasant. But we have to be careful that in our emphasis on social skills we do not extinguish either individualism or a person's willingness to challenge norms. Rigid adherence to convention and agreeability is the surest way to prevent innovation. Furthermore, not all innovations will require extensive cooperation or accessing large amounts of resources. Marie Curie's ambitious pursuit of science made her a very unconventional woman for her time, and she was subject to intense criticism and discrimination. If she had bowed to social norms, she would have neither achieved her remarkable accomplishments nor lived the life that fulfilled her. Furthermore, ultimately her discoveries of radium and radioactivity were so fundamental, so valuable, and so irrefutable that in the end it did not matter very much whether people accepted her. They had to accept her innovations.

None of this means that we should actively turn our employees or family members into social pariahs, nor should we assume that all individuals are unconventional by nature or want to be breakthrough innovators. However, it does suggest that there are valuable reasons to signal that being unconventional is acceptable. By embracing weirdness, we might better allow the natural creativity of people to flourish. In fact, if we learn to embrace unconventionality, creative people will have better access to cooperation and resources—thereby giving us the best of both worlds.

The people who are crazy enough to think they can change the world are the ones who do.

—Apple's "Think Different" commercial, 1997

2

"He's like a walking moonshot."

Extreme Confidence

Dean Kamen and Steve Jobs, as we have seen, had such great faith in their own capacity for reasoning and insight that they felt free to disregard the "rules" that constrained others. That faith in themselves enabled them to think big, fearlessly tackling projects that seemed impossible to others. Psychologists call a person's confidence in her ability to solve problems and achieve her objectives "self-efficacy." Exceptionally high self-efficacy can lead people to pursue problems that are bigger or more complex than most people would typically take on. Elon Musk and his quest to bring humanity to Mars and solve the problem of sustainable energy production illustrate the power of self-efficacy in its extreme.

Elon Musk was born on June 28, 1971, in Pretoria, South Africa. His father, Errol Musk, a successful electrical and mechanical engineer, had family roots in South Africa that stretched back two hundred years. Elon's brother, Kimbal, described their father as "ultra-present and very intense."[1] Elon's mother, Maye, grew up in the same neighborhood as Errol, but the story of how her family arrived in South Africa is interesting, and it perhaps suggests that a rejection of norms and a deep need for adventure were in Elon's genes. His maternal grandfather, Joshua Haldeman, was born in the United States but lived most of the first half of his life in Canada. A deeply independent man, Haldeman had a distaste for the mainstream political parties of Canada and instead aligned himself with a political philosophy called Technocracy. The Technocracy movement argued for replacing politicians and businesspeople with scientists and engineers, who, the movement believed, had the technical expertise to run society and make it more rational and productive.[2] The movement even had a plan for a new calendar that would divide the population up into seven groups, each working a workweek that began and ended on a different day so that industries could have uninterrupted production and there would be no "weekend effect." At one point the Canadian government outlawed the movement, fearing its members would attempt to overthrow the government by force.[3] Haldeman, who by 1940 was Canada's leader of the Technocracy Party, defied the ban and on June 26, 1940, placed this notice in the *Regina Leader-Post:*

> STATEMENT OF PATRIOTISM BY THOSE WHO WERE TECHNOCRATS
>
> The political Government of Canada by Order-in-Council has declared Technocracy Inc. to be an illegal organization. This action was unjustified and unwarranted and can be classified as a tactical, political blunder. Technocracy Inc. from its inception has been unequivocally opposed to Nazism, Fascism, and Communism. On Sept. 5 1939, Technocrats all over Canada wired Prime Minister Mackenzie King that they stood ready to defend Canada from any alien attack. Following the issue of Technocracy's General Regulations on Home Defence on June 1, which was published in most newspapers, Technocrats all over Canada contacted the R.C.M.P., the city police, and the military authorities offering their services in any capacity required for the Defence of Canada. Those who were members of Technocracy Inc. as loyal Canadian citizens will continue to render full support to the defence program of the

> Dominion of Canada. Technocracy Inc. was the outstanding patriotic organization in Canada, therefore those who were its members must view the present action of the political government as an attempt at subversive sabotage of a national patriotic organization, unless this action is immediately rescinded.[4]

Haldeman faced three legal charges for the notice but was undeterred. However, in 1941 the Technocracy movement changed its official policy from "unequivocally opposed to Communism, Fascism, Nazism and Socialism" to "complete economic and military collaboration with Soviet Russia" in response to Hitler's invasion of Russia. Although the decision now appears to have been a practical choosing of sides, Haldeman could not accept any justification for allying with Stalin's dictatorship and resigned from the Technocracy movement. For a few years he attempted (unsuccessfully) to establish his own political party and then in 1943 joined the Social Credit Party, a conservative-populist political party. In 1950, believing that Canadian bureaucracy interfered too much in the lives of individuals and also that the moral character of Canada had begun to decline, the iconoclastic Haldeman made the startling decision to move his wife, Winnifred, and four children (including Elon's mother, Maye) to South Africa, a place he had never even visited. Haldeman was also a pilot and owned his own private plane, a single-engine Bellanca Cruisair. Upon arriving in South Africa he reassembled the plane, which he had shipped in crates to his new country, and used it to survey the area and pick a place to live. They decided on Pretoria.

The Haldeman children grew up in a household where adventure was the norm. On one occasion in 1954, Joshua and Winnifred Haldeman flew their plane to Australia and back, a round trip of 33,000 miles. They may still be the only private pilots to have accomplished this feat. On another occasion they tied for first place in the 8,000-mile Cape Town to Algiers Motor Rally. Joshua Haldeman also became famous in South Africa for taking his family on rugged and daring expeditions through the bush of Botswana on an enthusiastic mission to find the Lost City of Kalahari. It is fitting, then, that he would have a grandson who would take on the even more daring mission of bringing humanity to Mars. Elon's mother and her siblings grew up in a home where goals were to be big and boundaries to be challenged. Maye's brother Scott noted that they were raised to believe "there's nothing a Haldeman can't do."[5]

In school, Maye was a nerdy child who loved math and science, but her stunning good looks led her into a career of modeling. After marrying Errol Musk, the couple had three children, Elon (the oldest), Kimbal, and Tosca. Elon was smaller than the other children his age and was often bullied in school. He also had such a curiously introspective streak that his family worried that he might be deaf. After tests revealed that his hearing was normal, his family realized he was just an avid thinker and gave him the nickname of "genius boy." Although he was quiet, his independent and confident nature was evident at a very early age. Once, for example, when Elon was six, his parents told him he could not go to a cousin's birthday party. The defiant young Elon walked there on his own, making a four-hour, ten-mile journey across Pretoria.

Musk was a zealous reader, with a particular taste for science fiction and fantasy. He devoured books by Jules Verne, J. R. Tolkien, and Robert Heinlein, and he was particularly influenced by Douglas Adams's *The Hitchhiker's Guide to the Galaxy*. As Kimbal notes, "It was not unusual for him to read ten hours a day," and adds, "if it was the weekend he could go through two books in a day."[6] Elon himself notes, "At one point, I ran out of books to read at the school library and the neighborhood library. This is maybe the third or fourth grade. I tried to convince the librarian to order books for me. So then I started to read the Encyclopedia Britannica. That was so helpful. You don't know what you don't know. You realize there are all these things out there."[7] As Musk's mother pointed out, "He would just find everything interesting. He wanted to explore everything."[8] He also had an exceptional memory (discussed in more detail in Chapter 3) and was able to recite facts from the encyclopedia at will. If, for example, his sister happened to wonder aloud what the distance was to the moon, he would immediately provide the exact measurement at both perigee and apogee, much to the shock and awe of those around him.[9]

At the age of ten, Musk bought a computer and taught himself to program. By the age of twelve he had created and sold his first piece of software—a video game called Blastar that he sold to a computer magazine for $500.[10] This kind of very early success undoubtedly taught Musk some important lessons about what he was capable of achieving.

Musk began to dream of America as a refuge for smart and innovative people. As he noted in an interview, "I remember thinking and seeing that America is where great things are possible, more than any other country in the world."[11] And, if he stayed in South Africa, he would also soon be subject to that country's compulsory military service, which he desperately wanted to avoid. According to Musk, he was not against the military per se, but he did not think it would be a good use of his time. He began to badger his parents about moving to America, but his father, who had business interests that kept him entrenched in South Africa, had no intention of moving. Furthermore, he did not want Elon to leave on his own and said he would pay for college only in South Africa. Not to be thwarted, the fearless sixteen-year-old Musk took a bus to the Canadian Embassy and obtained a passport (his mother is a Canadian national), and at seventeen, against his father's wishes, moved to Canada. He supported himself with odd jobs such as shoveling grain, cutting wood, and cleaning the boiler room of a lumber mill, and he began attending Queen's University. Musk's parents had divorced when he was nine, and his departure inspired Maye, Kimbal, and Tosca to move as well; soon all four were living in Canada.

Musk was similar to Albert Einstein, Dean Kamen, and Steve Jobs in not being a diligent student in the traditional sense. He found it difficult to apply himself to topics that he did not see as directly useful. However, his remarkable intelligence and memory made up for his poor attendance and uneven attention, enabling him to get grades good enough to secure a scholarship to the University of Pennsylvania. He transferred there after one year at Queens and ended up completing two degrees, one in physics and the other in economics. He was then accepted into Stanford's doctoral program in physics.

Musk moved to Palo Alto after graduation, planning to start the doctoral program in the fall of 1995. That summer, however, as he watched Marc Andreessen, a man even younger than himself, take the start-up Netscape Communications public for an astonishing market value of $2.9 billion, he suddenly began to question his plans. It was clear to him that the Internet was going to change the world in a fundamental way, and this struck a deep chord within him. It was extremely important to Musk that he work on "stuff that really mattered."[12] After only two days on the Stanford campus and with only $2,000, a car, and a computer, he withdrew from school and began creating an Internet company.

In 1994 Elon teamed up with Kimbal, and the pair borrowed $28,000 from their father to start Global Link Information Network, later renamed as Zip2. The company sold a software platform that enabled newspapers to create and host their own online "city guides," websites that would help users find events, restaurants, and other services. The timing was perfect: the penetration of the Internet was growing exponentially, but most businesses did not yet fully understand how to harness it. As Musk noted, "When we tried to get funding in November 1995, more than half the venture capitalists we met with didn't know what the internet was and had not used it."[13] However, soon Musk's company was hosting the websites of nearly two hundred media companies, including the *New York Times* local directory site called "New York Today." It also hosted newspapers owned by Hearst, Times Mirror, and Pulitzer.[14] In February 1999, Compaq bought Zip2 for $307 million in hopes that it could use the platform to help one of its other products, AltaVista, become a top portal for search, media, and shopping.[15] Elon and Kimbal received, respectively, $22 million and $15 million from the sale.

Now a millionaire at the age of twenty-eight, Musk was faced with the prospect of what to do next. Spending a life in leisure was absolutely not an option for the fiercely driven Musk. As he notes, "The idea of lying on a beach as my main thing sounds horrible to me. . . . I would go bonkers. I'd have to be on serious drugs. . . . I like high intensity."[16] In trying to assess what he would do with his life, he asked himself, "What would most influence the future? What are the problems that we have to solve?"

It seemed obvious to Musk that financial institutions were ripe for technological revolution, so he founded X.com to operate as an online financial services and e-mail payment company. The company's premier product was a person-to-person e-mail payment system. Later, X.com would merge with Confinity, which had also developed a person-to-person payment system, called PayPal. Preferring the PayPal brand name, Musk agreed to drop the X.com brand from the merged product. In 2002 Ebay bought PayPal for $1.5 billion in stock; Musk got $165 million from the sale.

Musk now had a serious nest egg he could use in his pursuit of changing the world. One unusual possibility had begun to take shape in his mind. Musk had been very disturbed to discover that NASA had no intentions of going to Mars, and he began to ponder what it would take. The major problem was not one of technological feasibility, he concluded, but rather expense. Rockets could get into orbit, but they were expensive and typically not reusable. In a comparison he would often make, this was like throwing away your Boeing 747 after every flight across the Atlantic. It made space travel ludicrously impractical. In a move that evinces a man with a spectacular sense of self-efficacy, Musk decided to pick up where NASA had left off. He began to study rocket science texts such as *Rocket Propulsion Elements*, *Fundamentals of Astrodynamics*, and *Aerothermodynamics of Gas Turbine and Rocket Propulsion*.

He then traveled to Russia to see if he could obtain an affordable rocket upon which to base his plans, but the Russians sent him away, telling him his plan was impossible. Undaunted, he came up with his own preliminary design for an affordable rocket.[17] Investing $100 million of his own funds, he founded a company in June 2002 called Space Exploration (SpaceX) and began developing a method that would streamline the production of rockets that could be used more than once. If NASA was not going to bring humanity to Mars, Musk would do it himself.

The interest in colonizing Mars was part of an even grander mission to save the world. Musk was worried about the limits of finite resources on Earth. It was clear to him that humanity was at risk of extinction if we didn't come up with better ways to produce, use, and conserve energy. Mars was the backup plan—by creating colonies on other planets, it would increase the likelihood of survival of the human species if we ended up destroying our home planet. Only a person with an astonishing sense of self-efficacy and a keenly idealistic nature would decide to personally take on the job of saving humanity from its own destruction. Musk began to contemplate ways to improve both energy production and consumption. To address energy production, he sketched out a business plan for a company that would accelerate the installation of solar panels on homes. He proposed this plan to his cousins, Peter and Lyndon Rive, and agreed to fund the start-up personally. This company launched in 2006 as Solar City.

To reduce energy consumption, Musk decided to develop an electric car. He planned to base his car on one that had been created by Al Cocconi, founder of AC Propulsion and one of the original engineers of GM's ill-fated EV1. GM had launched the EV1 in 1996 as an experiment in the feasibility of producing and marketing an electric car. GM did not actually sell any EV1s, only making them available through leases. After three years, GM concluded that the cars would not be profitable and ended their production, and by 2002 GM had recalled almost all of the cars and had them crushed (about forty were sent to museums). After the EV1 program was discontinued, Cocconi developed an electric sports car by incorporating an electric drivetrain into a Piontech Sportech fiberglass kit car.[18] The result was the tzero—a two-hundred-horsepower electric vehicle with the styling of a race car that could accelerate from zero to sixty miles per hour in a heart-pounding 3.7 seconds. The moment Musk drove it, he knew it had potential to reinvent people's perception of the electric car.

Another engineer and entrepreneur, Martin Eberhard, had already approached Cocconi with the idea to substitute the tzero's heavy lead acid batteries with much lighter lithium ion batteries. A tall, slim man with a mop of gray hair, Eberhard was a serial entrepreneur who had launched a number of start-ups. Now, with concerns about global warming and the US dependence on the Middle East for oil, he was looking to build a sports car that would be environmentally friendly. Tom Gage, then AC Propulsion's CEO, suggested that Eberhard and Musk collaborate. Both Eberhard and Musk believed that for an electric car to be successful, it had to be sexy and fast. Soon they had agreed upon a plan, and in February 2004 Musk committed $6.3 million to fund a project to build a new kind of electric vehicle, the sleek and powerful Tesla Roadster. Musk would be the company's chairman and Eberhard its CEO.

The two men worked well together at first, but soon personality clashes began to emerge. Both men were technically savvy and opinionated about the design of the car and the running of the company. Eberhard could be abrasive and critical. Musk, in turn, was not content to just financially back the company. He began to get intimately involved in decisions about the car's design and the operation of the company. The conflicts began to multiply. For example, Eberhard preferred to stick with the fiberglass body panels used in the original Lotus Elise car body upon which the Roadster was based; Musk wanted to use the lighter, stronger—and more expensive—carbon fiber. Eberhard hired public relations agents to hype the car before its launch; Musk fired them, believing his own involvement and the car itself would generate enough publicity. Eberhard wanted to save money by using the Elise's original crash-tested, off-the-rack chassis; Musk wanted to lower the doorsills by two inches to make the car easier to enter and exit. Musk also wanted to redesign the headlights and door latches, and replace the Elise's seats with more comfortable—and again, more expensive—custom seats.[19] In each case, Musk prevailed. His views were hard to ignore given that, by 2007, he had put $55 million of his own money into the company and had also raised money from wealthy friends, including eBay's second employee, Jeff Skoll, and Google cofounders Sergey Brin and Larry Page. In 2007 tensions reached a head, and Eberhard was ousted from the company.

Numerous production delays and cost overruns plagued the project, but in July 2008, when the first seven Roadsters—the "Founder's Series"—hit the road, the production problems were forgotten. The car had four hundred volts of electric potential, liquid-cooled lithium ion batteries, and a series of silicon transistors that gave the car acceleration so powerful the driver was pressed back against the seat.[20] It was about as fast as a Porsche 911 Turbo, did not create a single emission, and got about 220 miles on a single charge.[21]

Nearly all of the early reviews were effusive. As the online auto review site Autoguide.com reported, "The Tesla Roadster 2.5 S is a massively impressive vehicle, more spacecraft than sports car. Theories like global warming, peak oil and rising oil prices should no longer bring heart palpitations to car fans. The Tesla shows just how good zero-emissions 'green' technology can be. Quite frankly, getting into a normal car at the end of the test drive was a major letdown."[22] *Motortrend* called the acceleration "breathtaking"; *Automobile Magazine* editor Jason Cammisa said the Roadster "explodes off the line, pulling like a small jet plane. . . . It's like driving a Lamborghini with a big V-12 revved over 6000 rpm at all times, waiting to pounce—without the noise, vibration, or misdemeanor arrest for disturbing the peace."[23]

Although the car was a huge technological success and attracted considerable attention from the public, it was incredibly expensive to produce, and the company posted an $82 million loss for the year. Furthermore, to really have an impact on energy consumption, Tesla Motors would need to produce a car for the mass market—not just the luxury niche—and that meant it would also have to find a way to overcome the huge challenge of ensuring that enough charging stations were available. Without a robust network of charging stations, the mass market could not be induced to buy.

To make matters worse, SpaceX's first three rocket launches had failed, putting yet another company of the Musk business empire in crisis. In 2008, at the age of thirty-seven, Musk was in debt and on the verge of a nervous breakdown. He was also embroiled in a divorce from his first wife, Justine Wilson. Antonio Gracias, chief executive officer of Valor Equity Partners, a friend of Musk and an investor in both Tesla and SpaceX, became deeply impressed by Musk's strength and resolve during this time: "He has this ability to work harder and endure more stress than anyone I've ever met. What he went through in 2008 would have broken anyone else. He didn't just survive. He kept working and stayed focused." He adds, "Most people who are under that sort of pressure fray. Their decisions go bad. Elon gets hyperrational. He's still able to make very clear, long-term decisions. The harder it gets, the better he gets. Anyone who saw what he went through firsthand came away with more respect for the guy. I've just never seen anything like his ability to take pain."[24]

Fortunately, in September 2008 SpaceX's fourth launch of its Falcon 1 rocket went flawlessly and landed SpaceX a $1.5 billion contract from NASA to service the space station. Musk and his team were elated; many (including Musk) fought back tears. SpaceX had become the first purely commercial from-the-ground-up development to have a space vehicle reach orbit. As Scott Pelley, anchor of *CBS Evening News,* said in 2014, "Only four entities have launched a space capsule into orbit and successfully brought it back: the United States, Russia, China, and Elon Musk."[25]

Musk was now the CEO of two companies (SpaceX and Tesla) and chairman of a third (Solar City). Musk must have understood how unusual both his intellectual abilities and strength of will were, because when pressed about whether he could find someone else to act as CEO at SpaceX, he replied, "This may be presumptuous, but I have not met anyone who could do this. . . . Well wait, that's not true. Jeff Bezos could do this. Larry Page could do this. Bill Gates could do this. But there's just a really small list of people with the sufficient technical and business ability to do this job."[26]

The years to follow brought more success. Tesla's next car, the Model S, was rated by *Consumer Reports* as the best car it had ever reviewed. The Model X—a luxury sports utility vehicle—also received high marks, and by the end of 2017 the market was eagerly awaiting the Model 3, which promised to be the first truly affordable Tesla automobile. Musk also expanded the company's product scope by building a massive factory that would produce batteries for automobiles (the Gigafactory, built in Nevada) and by launching a line of "Powerwall" batteries that people could use to store electricity generated by solar power in their homes. Tesla Motors still had not turned a profit, but it had survived its infancy, appeared to be solvent, and was meeting its sales objectives. It was also competing against companies with far greater scale. As noted by John O'Dell, senior editor at auto information site Edmunds .com, "A lot of people have been very, very skeptical . . . when you want to be an automaker, you are competing with multibillion-dollar conglomerates. . . . It's entrepreneurism on steroids. . . . They had a huge learning curve but they've powered through it." Theo O'Neill, an analyst at Wunderlich Securities, added that "It's going to prove everybody in Detroit wrong. . . . They all say what Tesla is doing isn't possible."[27] SpaceX was also making history: in March 2017 it successfully launched a *reused* Falcon 9 rocket into orbit, and minutes later the first stage of the rocket made a controlled landing back on a drone ship in the Atlantic while an ecstatic audience cheered.[28] Musk had achieved what the space industry had repeatedly said was impossible.

Musk's aspirations and victories were larger than life. J. B. Straubel, one of the men who helped design the Tesla, characterized it this way: "Elon drives this think-bigger mentality. . . . As engineers we tend to want to keep things small, but Elon is always imagining something so large it's terrifying, and he's incredibly demanding and hard-driving."[29] While giving a speech at the famous annual film, media, and music conference South by Southwest, Google's Astro Teller called Elon Musk a "national treasure" and then stated, "It's not just that he's built some exciting and really meaningful, positive things . . . that's great. But he's like a walking moonshot. He's so audacious. It seems limitless." Teller then added, "It's his bravery and creativity that make him exceptional."[30] John Seely Brown, a scholar of innovation and former chief scientist at Xerox, added, "When I first heard about the space stuff, I said, 'By God, this guy is crazy. . . . ' But that's the point."[31]

As Kimbal Musk observed, his brother is "a guy with unlimited ambition. His mind needs to be constantly fulfilled. The problems that he takes on therefore need to be more and more complex over time to keep him interested."[32] Friends and colleagues describe him as "Steve Jobs, John D. Rockefeller, and Howard Hughes, rolled into one,"[33] and the director Jon Favreau has openly declared that he modeled his version of the playboy-rocket-scientist-action-hero Tony Stark in his *Iron Man* movies on Musk. While observers are likely to describe Musk's achievements with amazement and hyperbole, for his own part Musk tends to be coolly confident and focused on the problems he still wants to solve: to create truly sustainable energy production and to make humans an interplanetary species. Max Levchin, who cofounded PayPal with Musk, says, "He is very much the person who, when someone says it's impossible, shrugs and says, 'I think I can do it.'"[34] That "I think I can do it" is key—Musk's gut-level faith in his ability to achieve any goal and overcome any obstacle is one of the most important aspects of his character that has made him a larger-than-life innovator. He takes on enormous challenges and sticks with them no matter how hard they become because he knows he will usually succeed. In Musk we can see very clearly that exceptional self-efficacy gives rise to bigger ideas and fuels greater tenacity in pursuing them.

How High Self-Efficacy Works

Self-efficacy is a form of task-specific self-confidence, such as a person's faith in her ability to solve particular kinds of problems and achieve particular kinds of objectives. A person with high self-efficacy with respect to her reasoning and judgment will have great faith in her ability to assess the nature of a problem and the utility or feasibility of a solution. This, in turn, can empower her to believe in an idea even if others do not—she trusts her own judgment and doesn't expect others to always be able to follow her reasoning. After all, one of the ways that she may have acquired this self-efficacy is by having early experiences where she discovered that she was smarter, or more creative, than those around her. When Elon Musk witnessed people's surprise at his comprehension and recall of facts from the encyclopedia, for example, he was learning both about his own capabilities and the fact that others might not always be able to keep up. Steve Jobs learned a similar lesson when he realized as a teenager that he was smarter than his parents. Marie Curie discovered at the tender age of five that she was reading well ahead of her older siblings, and the shock of her parents at this discovery made her burst into tears, fearing she had done something wrong. Albert Einstein must have realized he had a gift for math when his skills as a young boy quickly passed those of his college-age tutor. Nikola Tesla also had many such moments, although the most definitive would arrive when he realized that he had proven his college professors wrong about producing electricity without a commutator (this is discussed in more detail in Chapter 3).

Exceptionally high self-efficacy does not guarantee a person will engage in nonconforming thinking and behavior, but it does increase the likelihood: a person who believes she knows better than the crowd is less likely to bow to the crowd's will. Many people who come up with an unusual idea will doubt themselves and may abandon their idea at the first sign of criticism. They will assume that if their idea were good, it would face less opposition or would already be implemented. The very unusualness of their idea is a signal that it is not likely to be a good idea. But a person with high self-efficacy doesn't interpret unusualness as a negative signal because she has faith in her own ability to assess the merit of the idea, and she doesn't always expect others to "get it."

Self-efficacy also mediates the relationship between idea and action: a person is much more likely to take on a task that she believes she will be successful in achieving. Because she believes she can achieve what she takes on, she may exert more effort toward a task and persist in the face of obstacles or failure.[35] Initial difficulties or setbacks are not signals to her that she will not succeed; they are just prompts for her to dig in harder until she has mastered her objective. For example, although Marie Curie tended to be self-deprecating, Barbara Goldsmith notes that "At twenty-three Manya's [Marie's] character had been formed. She had learned that if she had enough patience and tenacity, the seemingly impossible could be accomplished."[36] Eve Curie described her mother's tenacity with the following: "Her brain was so precise, her intelligence so marvelously clear. . . . She was supported by a will of iron, by a maniacal taste for perfection, and by an incredible stubbornness. Systematically, patiently, she attained each of the ends she had set for herself: she passed first in the master's examination in physics in 1893, and second in the master's in mathematics in 1894."[37] We can see Marie Curie's belief in the ability of the individual to overcome all obstacles, and the importance of persevering, expressed in her own words in a letter to her brother: "I want you to pass your doctor's thesis. . . . It seems that life is not easy for any of us. But what of that? We must have perseverance and above all confidence in ourselves. We must believe that we are gifted for something, and that this thing, at whatever cost, must be attained."[38] Curie's perseverance, as discussed further in Chapters 4 and 6, was so extreme that she would often work to the point of exhaustion, and on more than one occasion she fainted in her laboratory for lack of food and rest.

Thomas Edison's self-efficacy is also exhibited in his dogged perseverance. Edison is renowned for trying thousands of different filaments in his objective of creating a long-lived light bulb—beginning with platinum but then turning to cotton threads, different kinds of paper and cardboard, various woods, and even horsehair. As he described it in his own words, "I speak without exaggeration when I say that I have constructed three thousand different theories in connection with the electric light, each one of them reasonable and apparently to be true. Yet only in two cases did my experiments prove the truth of my theory. My chief difficulty, as perhaps you know, was in constructing the carbon filament, the incandescence of which is the source of the light. Every quarter of the globe was ransacked by my agents, and all sorts of the queerest materials were used, until finally the shred of bamboo now utilized was settled upon."[39] Edison's friend Walter S. Mallory recounts a similar story about Edison's development of a storage battery.

Albert Bandura, a psychologist who wrote most of the earliest seminal works on self-efficacy and who has dedicated a substantial part of his career to studying how self-efficacy emerges and shapes the behavior of those who have it, notes that those with high self-efficacy are more likely to view difficult tasks as something to be mastered rather than avoided.[40] Consider Elon Musk, in February 2002, flying back from Moscow having just been told by Russian rocket manufacturers, patronizingly and in no uncertain terms, that he could not obtain rockets for the price that he wanted ($8 million for two rockets). While the rest of "Team Musk" (which included two aerospace engineers, Jim Cantrell and Mike Griffin, and one of Musk's buddies from college, Adeo Ressi) sat having drinks and nursing the wounds of defeat, Musk was furiously typing away on his computer. Before they could ask him what he was doing, he spun around and showed them a spreadsheet with detailed cost calculations and performance characteristics for a modest-sized rocket that would significantly undercut the prices charged by existing launch companies. As the men looked at him, dumbfounded, he stated, "Hey guys, I think we can build this rocket ourselves."[41] A moment that would have humbled and disheartened just about anyone else spurred Musk to take on more of the problem himself.

Note that perseverance and self-efficacy can be self-reinforcing: those who persevere at tasks are more likely to accomplish them, reinforcing their confidence in their ability to achieve what they set out to do. It should not be surprising, then, that numerous studies have shown that self-efficacy can lead to greater risk taking and entrepreneurship.[42] Things that other people think are impossible may not seem impossible to a person who believes that she can overcome any obstacle. Ideas or methods that most people would find risky might not seem risky to someone who has greater faith in both her ability to assess the idea or method and her ability to execute it. Many researchers have argued that innovators and entrepreneurs are often more "risk seeking" or "risk tolerant" than most people; however, if the innovators or entrepreneurs have high self-efficacy, it might not really be risk seeking or risk tolerance that we are observing. What appears to be risk tolerance may simply be a different assessment of risk based on the individual's differential belief in her ability to overcome difficult obstacles.

Where Does Self-Efficacy Originate?

The three main factors that give rise to high self-efficacy are personal experience (one's own prior experience of succeeding at a problem or task), vicarious experience (seeing how others succeed at a problem or task), and verbal persuasion (being told that one will succeed at a problem or task). Of these, not surprisingly, personal experience is the most powerful. As noted previously, it is likely that all of the breakthrough innovators had moments early in their lives that revealed they were smarter or more capable than many of the people around them. Many also had notable "early wins" that provided strong evidence of their innovative or entrepreneurial abilities. Musk's creation and sale of a video game at the age of twelve is one example. Although kids of today can gain ready access to tools that enable them to design their own games, this was not the case in 1984, when the first personal computers had been on the market for only a few years.

Thomas Edison's early success as an entrepreneur provides another example of powerful early wins: between the ages of twelve and fifteen, Edison opened a newsstand and a produce stand, and even hired two boys to work for him. By the age of fifteen, he was also publishing his own newspaper, the *Weekly Herald*. Edison was also an avid experimenter and tinkerer from a very young age and received his first patent—for an electronic vote recorder—by the age of twenty-two.

Benjamin Franklin, whose story is told in more detail in Chapter 4, provides yet another excellent example of an early win. As a sixteen-year-old, Franklin yearned to write articles for the *New England Courant,* the newspaper published by his elder brother, James, to whom Benjamin was apprenticed. Franklin knew that his brother would not knowingly publish the works of a teenage boy even—or perhaps especially—if they were written by his own brother. Franklin thus invented a fictitious character, a middle-aged woman by the name of Silence Dogood. Between April 1722 and October 1722, he wrote fourteen letters under her name, using disguised handwriting and sliding the letters under the print shop's door after dark. The letters were a mix of storytelling and homespun philosophy, and they gained an enthusiastic following. This delighted Franklin, who noted in his autobiography, "They read it, commented on it in my Hearing, and I had the exquisite Pleasure, of finding it met with their Approbation, and that in their different Guesses at the Author none were named but Men of some Character among us for Learning and Ingenuity."[43] The success emboldened Franklin, who would go on to write increasingly provocative moral and political opinion pieces for his brother's paper, and later for his own.

Steve Jobs explicitly described how an early win in developing the "blue box" played a crucial role in giving him and Steve Wozniak the confidence to create a computer. In 1971, when Jobs was still in high school and Wozniak was in college, Wozniak picked up a copy of *Esquire* that his mother had left on the kitchen table and ended up reading an article by Ron Rosenbaum titled "Secrets of the Little Blue Box." Rosenbaum described how hackers had replicated the tones that routed calls on the AT&T network, enabling them to make long-distance calls for free. Rosenbaum also noted that the tones could be found in an issue of the *Bell System Technical Journal.* AT&T had already started contacting libraries, demanding that the issue be pulled from the shelves. Wozniak sprang into action. He called Jobs, and the two raced to the library at the Stanford Linear Accelerator Center. Although the library was closed, Jobs and Wozniak gained entrance through a door they knew was rarely locked and began furiously searching the stacks. According to Jobs, "It was Woz who finally found the journal with all the frequencies. It was like, holy shit, and we opened it and there it was. We kept saying to ourselves, 'It's real. Holy shit, it's real.' It was all laid out—the tones, the frequencies."[44] Together, using parts from Sunnyvale Electronics and diodes and transistors from Radio Shack, they built a digital version of a blue box.

After using the blue box to perform several pranks (including calling the Vatican and waking a bishop at 5:30 A.M.), Jobs suggested that they build and sell the boxes for a profit. They bought parts for about $40 and sold the boxes for $150. As Jobs recalled, "We made a hundred or so Blue Boxes and sold almost all of them."[45] The blue box business came to an end when a would-be customer drew a gun on the two young men and stole one of their devices. However, as Jobs noted, "If it hadn't been for the Blue Boxes, there wouldn't have been an Apple. I'm 100% sure of that. Woz and I learned how to work together, and we gained the confidence that we could solve technical problems and actually put something into production. . . . You cannot believe how much confidence that gave us."[46]

In 1994 Jobs would articulate the sense of empowerment with which he lived his life in a videotaped interview for the Santa Clara Historical Association:

> When you grow up you tend to get told that the world is the way it is and your life is just to live your life inside the world, try not to bash into the walls too much, try to have a nice family life, have fun, save a little money. But life. . . . That's a very limited life. Life can be much broader once you discover one simple fact. And that is everything around you that you call life was made up by people no smarter than you. And you can change it, you can influence it, you can build your own things that other people can use. And the minute that you understand that you can poke life and actually something will, if you push in something will pop out the other side, you can change it, you can mold it.
>
> That's maybe the most important thing, is to shake off this erroneous notion is that life is there and you are just going to live in it versus embrace it, change it, improve it, make your mark upon it. I think that's very important and however you learn that once you learn it, you'll want to change life and make it better cause it's kind of messed up in a lot of ways. Once you learn that you'll never be the same again.

Although studies of self-efficacy unanimously conclude that the most reliable source of self-efficacy is personal experience, other evidence suggests that vicarious experience can increase self-efficacy. That is, people learn about what they are capable in part by observing the achievements of others.[47] Seeing others accomplish their objectives even in the face of great obstacles can inspire an individual, giving her the sense of "If they can do it, I can too." As a complex, learning, social creature, much of what a human learns about how to interact with the world comes from watching others, viewing their behaviors and the consequences of those behaviors. Like most social animals, we learn what is safe to eat not by randomly tasting things but by watching what others eat; we form beliefs about what we can physically or mentally accomplish in part by experimentation and in part by observing what others can physically or mentally accomplish. Musk's decision to drop out of the doctoral program and start an Internet company after witnessing Marc Andreessen's successful IPO of Netscape is an apt example.

Experimental studies have shown that giving people an opportunity to witness someone else's success can create large and enduring effects on self-efficacy.[48] Although most people do not follow the experimental research on vicarious learning, many intuitively understand its powerful effect. Managers and teachers have long taken advantage of this principle by using hero stories as a form of role modeling that shapes how we perceive and respond to problems. Hero stories are particularly effective if the hero is someone we can identify with and do not feel is innately smarter or stronger than us. When organizations celebrate the story of a person who took initiative to overcome significant obstacles or who showed persistence when others had given up, they are using a hero story to signal to others what is valued in the organization and what employees are capable of. For example, Nike uses the story of track coach Bill Bowerman's efforts to make a better running shoe. Bowerman wanted to create a running shoe that would provide excellent traction without the metal spikes that were the standard of the day. His inspiration came one morning while he contemplated his waffles: what if you reversed the pattern and formed a material with raised waffle-grid nubs? Several experiments (and several ruined waffle irons) later, Bowerman had created waffle-soled shoes that debuted at the 1972 Olympics. Bowerman's Waffle Trainers put Nike on the global athletic footwear map and initiated a period of unparalleled growth.[49] Nike employs this story frequently, ensuring that all employees are familiar with it, and notes, "Bowerman's legacy as an original thinker and innovator will forever be linked with the waffle sole, which like many brilliant inventions is so simple and intuitive it resonates immediately and broadly."[50] The Bowerman story is effective because it shows that powerful innovation can come from anyone. Bowerman was a track coach—not an engineer or from another technical background—and because Bowerman's inspiration came from waffles, the story shows that inspiration for innovation can come from literally anywhere.

The effects of personal experience and vicarious experience on self-efficacy raise an interesting question about failure: Does experiencing failure or witnessing failure lower self-efficacy? The short answer is "yes, but probably not to the degree that success can increase it, on average." There is an interesting asymmetry in how humans process failure. We tend to attribute successes to our personal abilities, and we tend to attribute failure to external factors beyond our control. This is known as the "self-attribution bias" or the "self-serving bias." It is an instinctive process that helps to preserve self-esteem, and at the species level it probably helps to ensure that we generally learn through errors of commission rather than errors of omission. We are, on average, overconfident, and from the perspective of fueling innovation, that is a great thing. Some important factors temper this, of course. For example, depressed people tend to have less of a self-serving bias and also have lower self-efficacy. People in collectivist cultures such as Korea or Japan, where the self is perceived as highly interdependent with others, might have lower self-attribution bias than people in individualistic cultures such as those in North America or Western Europe, where the self is perceived to be autonomous and independent (although the evidence on this is mixed and is complicated by the challenges of adapting a study across different cultures).[51]

Last, we should consider the role of verbal persuasion in self-efficacy. That is, can you convince people they are capable by simply telling them? Studies show that verbal persuasion can be effective in increasing the self-efficacy of children but that it is not particularly effective in adults. Telling adults that they will achieve their objectives will often fail to convince them if they have not experienced such success themselves or seen it among people with whom they identify.[52] Furthermore, verbal persuasion will not be effective even in children if it is not perceived as substantive and genuine.[53] Interestingly, although Bandura argued that negative feedback was more effective at diminishing self-efficacy than positive feedback was at increasing self-efficacy, the subsequent empirical research on this question is scant and mixed.[54]

The overwhelming conclusion of the research on self-efficacy is that if we want to increase it, we want people to witness and experience success at overcoming difficult problems. We want to set people up for early wins by giving them problems that are hard enough to be challenging yet are likely to be solved. This will help to build both their repertoire of approaches to problem solving and their confidence. We also want to avoid the destructive effect of "rescuing" individuals when they face obstacles that they might ultimately overcome on their own. Although providing generous assistance to others can be valuable for social bonding, it can also create or reinforce the belief that they could not solve the problem themselves. In some instances it may be better to instead just offer encouragement and show our faith in their ability to overcome the obstacle. We can also increase the likelihood of people finding their own "early wins" by lowering the price of failure or even by celebrating bold-but-intelligent failures, a topic that we will return to in Chapter 8.

The creative genius may be at once naïve and knowledgeable, being at home equally to primitive symbolism and rigorous logic. He is both more primitive and more cultured, more destructive and more constructive, occasionally crazier yet adamantly saner than the average person.

—Frank Baron

3

"Ideas came in an uninterrupted stream. . . ."

The Creative Mind

How much of a serial breakthrough innovator's capacity or drive is nature versus nurture? Do these individuals have "gifts" hardwired into their biology that we could never hope to imitate? Or are they primarily empowered by their context—their families, their resources, their moment in time? When people discuss the possible roles of nature in breakthrough innovators, two questions loom particularly large: Are they smarter than most people? Are they crazier? My research indicates that the answers to these questions, at least with respect to *exceptional* serial breakthrough innovators, are "yes" and "probably."

A long history of research in psychology and a recent surge of research in neuroscience have explored the ways in which particularly creative people might differ in their intellectual capabilities, patterns of association, and neurochemical balances. This body of research is diverse and rapidly changing—for example, new techniques in imaging brain activity have given rise to rapidly advancing trajectories of research in this area, and it is impossible to summarize everything here. However, there are a few main threads that stand out: primary process thinking and remote association, working memory and executive control, the personality trait "openness to experience," and rapidly emerging evidence on neurotransmitters such as dopamine and their effects on things such as latent inhibition and psychopathologies often associated with creative genius.

Nikola Tesla's story provides ample evidence of the separateness and self-efficacy discussed in the previous two chapters; he was a loner who fearlessly asserted his ambitions and theories, taking on tasks that others would have deemed impossible. However, Tesla's story also highlights something else quite distinct: the potential for atypical mental faculties and psychopathologies to influence creativity. Tesla had an interesting combination of exceptional intellectual ability, extraordinary working memory, and probable neurotransmitter irregularities that gave rise to symptoms of mania, obsessive-compulsive disorder, and oversensitivity to sensory stimuli. Tesla thus aptly illustrates what research in neuroscience has only recently begun to elucidate: the biological bases of creativity. Many of the innovators are extremely intelligent, and as will be noted later in the chapter, several exhibit some symptoms of mania, but none exhibit both traits at such extreme levels as Nikola Tesla. His case turns out to be exceptionally valuable in helping us to understand the creative mind. Tesla's unusual traits and capabilities are so extreme, and the mechanisms by which they aided his innovation so clear, that it is like having a giant searchlight that points out dimensions we need to examine in the other innovators. For example, a person might not notice that most of the serial breakthrough innovators sleep significantly less than the average for the population. It isn't usually highlighted in articles or biographies about them, and it's not something that is generally brought up in the creativity literature. But after you note Tesla's extreme in this regard, you start to pay more attention. You hunt down references that indicate the actual hours they sleep, and you do the math. The difference is big enough that you wonder how you missed it before, but you could have never missed it with Tesla—he slept two hours a night when he slept at all. Before studying Tesla you might not notice references to other innovators' memories, but after being exposed to Tesla's eidetic (photographic) memory and how he used it, you pay attention, and you begin to notice that the stories of innovators are littered with statements about their exceptional memories. Just as you might not notice moles on your skin until a particularly large one catches your attention, or you might not realize you have mice in your house until a brazen one pauses to stare you down, you could have easily overlooked some of the interesting traits of serial breakthrough innovators until you discovered Tesla, who had those traits turned up to a volume that you could not ignore.

Tesla was an astonishingly brilliant and unusual man who, in his life, would invent AC electricity, many systems of fluorescent lighting, the first remote-control devices, wireless communication, and much more. His accomplishments are all the more remarkable because he primarily worked alone, often with little money or other support. He was passionate and driven by ideals, and many other more strategic and materialistic people would try to lay claim to his discoveries and exploit his trusting nature. His name was literally erased from textbooks so that others could take credit for his work.

Tesla was born during a lightning storm on July 10, 1856, in Smiljan, a tiny village of just over a thousand people in the mountains of Croatia (then part of Austria-Hungary). About half of the population of Smiljan were Serbian Orthodox families that had settled there during the Great Turkish War of the seventeenth century. Tesla's father, Milutin, was a Serbian Orthodox minister who was sent to Smiljan to serve as a pastor. Milutin spoke many languages, was a talented mathematician, and was an avid reader with a large library. Tesla described him as "a very erudite man, a veritable natural philosopher, poet and writer. . . . He has a prodigious memory and frequently recited at length from works in several languages. He often remarked playfully that if some of the classics were lost he could restore them."[1] Both Tesla's mother, Djouka, and brother, Dane, were also endowed with extraordinary memories. According to Tesla, because his mother had never learned to read, she memorized the great epic Serbian poems and long passages from the Bible.[2] She also had exceptional mechanical talents and devised many kinds of household tools such as churns and looms. According to Tesla, his mother was "descended from a long line of inventors." She also had untiring work habits that would be shared by her son, rising before dawn each day and working until eleven o'clock at night.[3]

Smiljan was a farming community, and Nikola spent his childhood days frolicking in nature, playing with the barnyard animals and his beloved cat, and creating early boyish inventions such as a cornstalk popgun, a hook for catching frogs, and a propeller powered by May bugs glued onto tiny wooden blades. Exhibiting his tinkering nature from a very early age, he would disassemble and then reassemble his grandfather's clocks. He also played with his brother, who he described as being "gifted to an extraordinary degree; one of those rare phenomena of mentality which biological investigation has failed to explain."[4]

Tragedy struck in 1863. Dane was thrown from the family horse and died of his injuries. The family was devastated, and, as later noted by Nikola, Dane's "premature death left my parents disconsolate. . . . The recollection of his attainments made every effort of mine seem dull in comparison. Anything I did that was creditable merely caused my parents to feel their loss more keenly."[5] Feeling rejected by his parents and traumatized by the death of his brother, Nikola began to have nightmares and "lived in constant dread of the spirit of evil, of ghosts and ogres and other unholy monsters of the dark."[6]

Tesla was aware from an early age that he was uniquely intelligent. In his autobiography he recounts a story of a day when he was playing in the street with other boys and a wealthy alderman passed by. The alderman paused to give a silver piece to each of the boys, but when he reached Tesla, he suddenly stopped and commanded, "Look in my eyes." Tesla met his gaze, his hand outstretched to receive the valuable coin, when to his dismay, the alderman said, "No, not much; you can get nothing from me. You are too smart."[7] When he was ten years old, he solved math problems so quickly that his teachers contacted his parents, suspecting him of cheating. They asked him to repeat the feat in front of both his teachers and parents, which he did, convincing all who observed that they were in the presence of a child prodigy.

However, Tesla was also aware that his mind had some peculiar traits that were more discomfiting. He would frequently experience the appearance of images, accompanied by strong flashes of light, which interfered with his thoughts and actions. They were pictures of things or scenes that he had once seen, not just imagined. A word could invoke the image of an object in front of him, and he was incapable of distinguishing it from reality. In fact, he would sometimes need one of his sisters to tell him whether the vision was a hallucination or not.[8] The fact that the images were always something that Tesla had once seen suggests they were likely eidetic images—extremely clear mental images of an object that is no longer present—rather than hallucinations. Numerous studies of eidetic imagery suggest that it is an ability possessed by 2 percent to 10 percent of children and is almost nonexistent among adults. Not knowing or understanding the concept of an eidetic memory, however, Tesla and his family found the experiences worrying. Dane had experienced them too, provoking Tesla to speculate he was biologically predisposed to them.

Shortly after Dane's death, the family moved to the nearby city of Gospić, where Nikola's father served as the minister and also taught religion at the local gymnasium. Nikola missed his rural life and his animal playmates. He also began to have nightmares about Dane's death and to experience images of Dane's body in a casket:

> A vivid picture of the scene would thrust itself before my eyes and persist despite all efforts to banish it. . . . To free myself of these tormenting appearances, I tried to concentrate my mind on something else I had seen, and in this way I would often obtain temporary relief; but in order to get it I had to conjure continuously new images. . . . The remedy gradually lost all its force. Then I instinctively commenced to make excursions beyond the limits of the small world of which I had knowledge, and I saw new scenes. . . . I began to travel; of course, in my mind. . . . Every night, (and sometimes during the day), when alone, I would start on my journeys—see new places, cities and countries; live there, meet people and make friendships and acquaintances and, however unbelievable, it is a fact that they were just as dear to me as those in actual life, and not a bit less intense in their manifestations.[9]

By the age of twelve, he had begun exhibiting other peculiarities, perhaps stemming from the stress of his brother's death and his strained relationship with his parents.[10] He would practice acts of self-denial and self-mastery (for example, patterns of restricted eating would persist throughout his life). He acquired a strong aversion to many round things, noting "The sight of a pearl would almost give me a fit but I was fascinated with the glitter of . . . objects with sharp edges. . . . I would get a fever by looking at a peach." He also developed a germ phobia that caused him to feel repulsion at the idea of touching another person's hair and that would later lead him to worry considerably about the impurity of water and to frequently wear gloves. He counted the steps in his walks and calculated the cubical contents of soup plates, coffee cups, and pieces of food—otherwise, he could not enjoy his meal. All repeated acts had to be divisible by three, or he would feel compelled to do them over again, even if it took hours. Many of these habits suggest an obsessive-compulsive disorder, a point that I will return to later.

From ages ten to fourteen, Nikola attended the Real Gymnasium (equivalent to junior high school), which had a well-equipped physics department, and his interest in electricity began to quickly emerge: "I was interested in electricity almost from the beginning of my educational career. . . . I read all that I could find on the subject . . . [and] experimented with batteries and induction coils."[11] He also began experimenting with water turbines and motors, and began to develop the goal of creating a perpetual-motion machine. At fourteen, he proclaimed his intention to build a gigantic waterwheel under Niagara Falls (which he had seen in a drawing or photograph) and harness its energy—a remarkably accurate forecast of his future.

Although Tesla dreamed of studying engineering, his father intended him to enter the ministry. Then, in a twist of fate, shortly after graduating from the Higher Real Gymnasium (equivalent to high school), Tesla contracted cholera. He was bedridden for nine months, and his family feared that he would die. While his father sat at his bedside, Nikola told him, "Perhaps I may get well if you will let me study engineering." His father solemnly replied, "You will go to the best technical institution in the world."[12] Nikola recovered, and his father set about making good on his promise.

Tesla was known for being able to perform advanced calculus and physics equations in his head. At the age of seventeen, he began to turn his intelligence and capacity for imagery to invention:

> I observed to my delight that I could visualize with the greatest facility. I needed no models, drawings or experiments. I could picture them all as real in my mind. . . . It is absolutely immaterial to me whether I run my turbine in thought or test it in my shop. I even note if it is out of balance. There is no

> difference whatever; the results are the same. In this way I am able to rapidly develop and perfect a conception without touching anything. When I have gone so far as to embody in the invention every possible improvement I can think of and see no fault anywhere, I put into concrete form this final product of my brain. Invariably my device works as I conceived that it should, and the experiment comes out exactly as I planned it. In twenty years there has not been a single exception. Why should it be otherwise?[13]

While the reader may find this difficult to believe, there are numerous documented instances of Tesla's designs so constructed working perfectly upon execution. The process Tesla describes is closely analogous to what engineers now do with computer-aided design programs—but Tesla of course achieved it without the aid of a computer!

After spending a couple of years roaming in the mountains with "a hunter's outfit and a bundle of books" to recover his health and avoid being drafted into the Austro-Hungarian army, he began his studies in 1875 at the Polytechnic School in Graz, the most advanced school of the region. Tesla threw himself into his studies with near-frenzied intensity, studying upward of twenty hours per day.[14] As he noted, "I had made up my mind to give my parents a surprise, and during the whole first year I regularly started work at three o'clock in the morning and continued until eleven at night, no Sundays or holidays excepted. As most of my fellow-students took things easily, naturally I eclipsed all records."[15] Tesla studied so hard that his teachers worried that he might die from overwork. They wrote to his father suggesting that he persuade his son to leave school. His father tried to persuade Nikola to come back home to Gospić, but he was determined to continue his studies. He created his own extended curriculum that included not only those courses required for his major in engineering but also courses in languages (he could speak about nine) and self-directed study of the works of Descartes, Goethe, Spencer, and Shakespeare, many of which he committed to memory.[16] As he noted in his autobiography, "I had a veritable mania for finishing whatever I began, which often got me into difficulties. On one occasion I started to read the works of Voltaire, when I learned, to my dismay, that there were close to one hundred large volumes in small print which that monster had written while drinking seventy-two cups of black coffee per diem. It had to be done, but when I laid aside that last book I was very glad and said, 'Never more!'"[17] Tesla's use of the word *mania* is probably more prescient than he intended. As we shall see later, Tesla exhibited many of the diagnostic criteria for mania, such as oversensitivity to stimuli, periods of extremely intense goal-directed activity, and a sharply reduced need for sleep.

It was during his sophomore year at the Polytechnic that Tesla first saw a direct-current dynamo that was outfitted, as was customary, with a commutator that transferred the electric current (which is alternating in its natural state) to the motor. Tesla immediately intuited that the commutator was unnecessary: he knew there must be a way to harness alternating current unencumbered by the awkward commutator. When Tesla voiced this opinion spontaneously in class, his outraged professor spent the rest of the class detailing why this was impossible and remarked critically, "Mr. Tesla will accomplish great things, but he certainly will never do this. It would be equivalent to converting a steady pulling force like gravity into rotary effort. It is a perpetual motion scheme, an impossible idea."[18] Tesla would eventually prove the professor—and many other people—wrong.[19]

Unfortunately, during this time Tesla acquired a gambling addiction, and he sometimes wagered for twenty-four hours at a stretch. He failed his exams and was thrown out of school. Initially, he fled to Slovenia to look for work, afraid to tell his parents of his misfortune. However, his father eventually found him and convinced him to finish his studies at the University of Prague, where he made great progress on his alternating-current theories.

After his father's death in 1879, Tesla moved to Budapest to work for the American telephone exchange, where he began to study Thomas Edison's inventions. He would take the machines apart and improve them, although he never bothered to obtain patents on any of his inventions. He also pursued the alternating-current problem with such intensity, denying himself any rest or leisure, that he suffered a nervous collapse. He experienced severe oversensitivity to sound and light, claiming that the sound of a fly landing on a table would cause a thud in his ear and that the sun's rays would stun him. His condition must have been quite serious because his doctor warned that he might not recover. Relief came in a surprising way. Anthony Szigeti, Tesla's former classmate and closest friend, managed to convince him to join him in outdoor exercise, and it was while walking in the park with Szigeti and reciting a passage from Goethe's *Faust* that the solution to the alternating-current problem suddenly crystallized: "As I uttered these inspiring words the idea came like a flash of lightening and in an instant the truth was revealed. I drew with a stick on the sand, the diagram shown six years later in my address before the American Institute of Electrical Engineers. . . . Pygmalion seeing his statue come to life could not have been more deeply moved. A thousand secrets of nature which I might have stumbled upon accidentally I would have given for that one which I had wrestled from her against all odds and at peril of my existence."[20] Put simply, Tesla conceived of using two circuits that generated dual currents ninety degrees out of phase with each other. A receiving magnet, by means of induction, would rotate in space and continually attract a steady stream of electrons, whether the charge was positive or negative.

This revelation seemed to free Tesla. As he later wrote, "It was a mental state of happiness as complete as I have ever known in life. Ideas came in an uninterrupted stream and the only difficulty

I had was to hold them fast. . . . In less than two months, I evolved virtually all the types of motors and modifications of the system now identified with my name."[21] He designed dynamos, motors, transformers, and other devices needed for complete alternating-current systems. His ability to visualize equipment perfectly enabled him to create and test everything in his mind and then implement it in the machine shop, without ever having drawn up blueprints. When he was actually able to test his devices and see if his theory and mental images had been correct, they worked perfectly. This gave Tesla a tremendous sense of confidence, highlighting the role of "early wins" in creating self-efficacy, as discussed in the previous chapter. As biographer John O'Neill describes, "From these results he drew an unbounded sense of self-confidence; he could think and work his way to any goal he set. There was good reason for Tesla's self-assurance. He had just passed his twenty-seventh birthday. It seemed to him only yesterday that Professor Poeschl had seemingly so completely vanquished him for saying that he could operate a motor by alternating current. Now he had demonstrably accomplished what the learned professor said could never be done."[22] Tesla's alternating-current system would go on to revolutionize the use of electric power. As Marc Seifer notes in his biography of Tesla, "Before his invention, electricity could be pumped approximately one mile, and then only for illuminating dwellings. After Tesla, electrical *power* could be transmitted hundreds of miles, and then not only for lighting but for running household appliances and industrial machines in factories. Tesla's creation was a leap ahead in a rapidly advancing technological revolution."[23]

While working on several power plant projects in Paris and Germany (for which he was never fairly paid), he met Charles Batchelor, who was the former assistant to Thomas Edison. Batchelor encouraged Tesla to go the United States to work with Edison. Tesla decided to follow his advice, and in 1884 he sold most of his belongings and moved to America. He brought with him a letter to

Edison from Batchelor that read, "I know two great men and you are one of them; the other is this young man."[24] With this glowing recommendation, he was readily received by Edison. Tesla was thrilled to meet Edison, who was hailed as the "Napoleon of invention." He was in awe that Edison had been able to accomplish so much with so little education, and it made him wonder if perhaps he had wasted his time pursuing education rather than more practical pursuits: "I was amazed at this wonderful man who, without early advantages and scientific training, had accomplished so much. I had studied a dozen languages, delved in literature and art, and had spent my best years in libraries . . . and felt that most of my life had been squandered."[25] Eventually, however, Tesla realized that Edison was at a great disadvantage by not having mathematical and engineering training: "If he had a needle to find in a haystack he would not stop to reason where it was most likely to be, but would proceed at once with the feverish diligence of a bee, to examine straw after straw until he found the object of his search. . . . I was almost a sorry witness of his doings, knowing that just a little theory and calculation would have saved him 90 per cent of the labor. . . . Trusting himself entirely to his inventor's instinct and practical American sense . . . the truly prodigious amount of his actual accomplishments is little short of a miracle."[26]

Edison was an advocate and promoter of DC (direct-current) power transmission and had little interest in Tesla's AC system. Tesla soon fell out with Edison and quit the company because Edison refused to pay him for a solution for which he had been promised $50,000 (Edison mockingly told Tesla the offer had been a joke). The young man of limited means felt cheated, but he believed his time at Edison's laboratory had not been without value: he could see clearly how and why Edison's DC electrical system was inferior to his own AC system, and he learned the importance of patenting and commercializing his technological inventions. Thus, in 1885 he began setting up his own company, and he met with a patent attorney, Lemuel Serrell, who helped him apply for Tesla's first patent, an improved design of an arc lamp that prevented flickering.

The 1885 patent application marked the beginning of an intense period of invention for Tesla that would last for more than fifteen years. He would keep a grueling schedule, working around the clock and often driving himself until he collapsed. Although he spent every waking hour working on his inventions, he noted that he found "exquisite enjoyment" in his pursuit of innovation, "so much, that for many years my life was little short of continuous rapture."[27]

He developed entire systems of alternating-current machinery but was inept when it came to commercializing these important inventions. Unwittingly, Tesla had stepped into the middle of a major battle between the electrical inventors and entrepreneurs of the day. Thomas Edison, Elihu Thomson, George Westinghouse, William Stanley, and others were all embroiled in a fierce race to offer the world's leading electrical technology and win contracts to light America's cities.

Tesla was poorly suited to win such a battle; his nature was that of the intellectual scientist, not the cunning businessman. Comparing Tesla with Edison illustrates this point. Both men were independent, unconventional, and possessed an exceptional sense of self-efficacy. Both were widely renowned as geniuses and had maniacal work habits of long hours and fierce persistence. However, their differences were also stark. Edison had a more practical nature, building commercial extensions to technologies he was already working on: from working in a telegraph station he built a multiplex telegraph, which led to creating early telephones; the process of mastering the conduction of sound in telephones led, in turn, to Edison's creation of phonographs. His work on DC electrical systems led to his work on light bulbs and storage batteries. Tesla, on the other hand, was driven by far-reaching, often grandiose ideas of what could be done, such as a flying machine or a giant waterwheel under Niagara Falls. He wanted to free mankind of physical work so that people could focus on creative endeavors: "If we want to reduce poverty and misery, if we want to give to every deserving individual what is needed for a safe existence of an intelligent being, we want to provide more machinery, more power. Power is our mainstay, the primary source of our many-sided energies."[28] This led also to marked differences in their entrepreneurial spirit: whereas Edison was keenly motivated to patent and sell his inventions (and started his first business at the age of twelve), Tesla was motivated to publish ideas as theoretical advances and was often uninterested in or ineffective at commercializing many of his inventions.

The shrewd entrepreneurs of the day were keenly aware of both Tesla's technological sophistication and commercial naïveté. They thus sought to obfuscate Tesla's contributions and maneuver him out of a position to capitalize on his inventions. Edison tried to convince the public that alternating current was more dangerous than his own direct-current electrical systems by using alternating current to electrocute dozens of dogs, two calves, and a horse.[29] Elihu Thomson tried to gain patent priority over Tesla's system by suggesting that his own (inferior) alternating-current system predated Tesla's system. George Westinghouse shrewdly surmised that Tesla's system was superior to the other electrical systems available and was likely to be awarded priority dating, and thus in 1888 he proposed to buy Tesla's patents. The pricing scheme he proposed was complicated—it included cash outlays, Westinghouse stock, and royalties with minimums that changed over the years—and there is some disagreement about how much the entire proposal was worth. O'Neill reports that the proposal was for a million dollars in cash plus a one-dollar-per-horsepower royalty. Biographer Marc Seifer calculates the value of the deal to be roughly $255,000, and a PBS program reported the deal to be $5,000 in cash, 150 shares of Westinghouse stock, and a $2.50-per-horsepower royalty.

If $255,000 is the correct amount, it would be worth just over $6 million in today's dollars. Whatever the deal was, it evolved over time, and although Tesla probably did not get what he deserved for inventions that would turn out to be worth billions, he generally felt that Westinghouse treated him fairly. Tesla noted, years later, that "George Westinghouse was, in my opinion, the only man on the globe who could take my alternating current system under the circumstances then existing and win the battle against prejudice and money power. He was a pioneer of imposing stature and one of the world's noblemen."[30]

In 1891 Tesla agreed to present his findings on high-frequency phenomena at a symposium organized by the American Institute for Electrical Engineers. His lecture was so advanced, and the demonstrations that he made during it were so remarkable, that it was marked as a historic moment by all who saw it. As described by Joseph Wetzler in *Harper's Weekly,* "[With] lucid explanations in pure nervous English, this stripling from the dim border-land of Austro-Hungary . . . [had] not only gone far beyond the two distinguished European scientists Dr. Lodge and Professor Hertz in grasp of electro-magnetic theory, but . . . he had actually made apparatus by which electrostatic waves or 'thrusts' would give light for ordinary every-day uses." Wetzler went on to remark that Tesla had "eclipsed" Edison in his refinements of the incandescent lamp, and "He had set himself no less a task than to create a lamp which, without any external connection to wires . . . would glow brightly when placed anywhere in the apartment."[31] For audience members such as Elihu Thomson and Mihajlo Pupin, who competed with Tesla for both commercial and academic primacy in the development and application of electricity science, the revelation of how far advanced Tesla was must have been simultaneously awe inspiring and gut-wrenching.

In 1893 Tesla's dream of harnessing the power of Niagara Falls was finally realized. The International Niagara Falls Commission, headed by famous British physicist Lord Kelvin, created a competition that solicited proposals from around the world for ways to tap the waterfall's seemingly inexhaustible supply of power. However, the commission ended up rejecting all of the proposals that were submitted as unworkable. Then Lord Kelvin, who had begun following Tesla's work, concluded that only an AC system based on Tesla's design would be adequate to the task. He asked Westinghouse to build a power station based on Tesla's alternating-current technologies next to Niagara Falls. On November 16, 1896, the first power from the system reached Buffalo, New York, accompanied by cheers and a twenty-one-gun salute.[32] The completed system was a monumental achievement—a revolution in the generation and transmission of electrical power.

In recognition of Tesla's stature as a "wizard genius," he was elected to the Royal Society of Great Britain and was awarded honorary doctorates from Columbia and Yale. Reporters began to stream to his door seeking to profile the inventor, and he was featured in numerous prestigious periodicals. One of the earliest major profiles was provided by T. C. Martin, editor of *Electrical World* (and later a coauthor of the most definitive biography of Thomas Edison), who wrote that Tesla had "eyes that recall all the stories one has read of keenness of vision and phenomenal ability to see through things. He is an omnivorous reader, who never forgets; and he possesses the peculiar facility in languages that enables the educated native of Eastern Europe to talk and write in at least half a dozen tongues. A more congenial companion cannot be desired . . . the conversation, dealing at first with things near at hand and next . . . reaches out and rises to the greater questions of life, and duty, and destiny."[33] As another lengthy article in the *New Science Review* noted, "In this age of practical endeavor, when everything is turned to its immediate use with the least delay possible, a life like that of Tesla, devoted to scientific research for the love of it, stands out in peculiar and interesting prominence."[34] A profile of the inventor in the *New York Times* commented,

"A notable faculty of Tesla's mind is that of rushing intuition. As with Edison, you begin to state a question or proposition to him, and before you have half formulated it he has suggested six ways of dealing with it and ten of getting around it."[35]

Over the course of his life, Tesla created more than two hundred astonishingly important breakthrough innovations, yet because he was not particularly good at the strategic side of being an innovator, other inventors and investors of the time (notably Guglielmo Marconi, Mihajlo Pupin, George Westinghouse, J. P. Morgan, and Elihu Thomson) harvested much of the credit and commercial value of his achievements. For example, although Edison is often thought of as the most important innovator in electricity, it was Tesla, not Edison, who created the electric power distribution system now used throughout the world, as well as the polyphase electric motor, the bladeless steam turbine, the radio-guided torpedo, and numerous phosphorescent and fluorescent lighting systems. It was Tesla, not Guglielmo Marconi, who invented the first radio, although the issue would be contested for more than forty years.[36] In fact, Tesla had received the first patents from the US Patent and Trademark Office for long-distance radio in 1900 (the applications were filed in 1897).[37] On the basis of these patents, the USPTO turned down Marconi's 1900 applications, citing Tesla's prior claim: "Many of the claims are not patentable over Tesla patent numbers 645,576 and 649,621, of record, the amendment to overcome said references as well as Marconi's pretended ignorance of the nature of a 'Tesla oscillator' being little short of absurd . . . the term 'Tesla oscillator' has become a household word on both continents [Europe and North America]."[38]

Later, however, for mysterious and unknown reasons (often attributed to Marconi's greater financial backing), the USPTO reversed its decision in 1904, awarding Marconi the patents for radio. Tesla was devastated. In 1943, a few months after Tesla's death, the US Supreme Court would reverse the decision yet again, reinstating

Tesla's patents. In addition to the inventions mentioned above, Tesla created lasers, early robots, advancements in X-ray devices, and more. Tesla's contributions to science were equally numerous and profound, and his book *The Inventions, Researches and Writings of Nikola Tesla* was a "veritable bible" for engineers in the field of electricity.[39] It explained alternating-current motors, the rotating magnetic field, rotating field transformers, polyphase systems, and more. Yet because of academic jealousy, he was not credited with much of the work that would build upon his contributions. For example, Charles Steinmetz omitted any reference to Tesla's work in his 1897 text, *Theory and Calculations of Alternating Current Phenomena,* despite the fact that Tesla was overwhelmingly responsible for the foundational discoveries in the area. He makes the following excuse in the foreword: "Many of the investigations of the book apply to polyphase systems circuits [with chapters] on induction motors, generators, synchronous motors, [etc.]. . . . A part of this book is original, other parts have been published before by other investigators. . . . I have, however, omitted altogether literary references, for the reason that incomplete references would be worse than some, while complete references would entail expenditure of much more time than is at my disposal. . . . I believe that the reader . . . is more interested in the information than in knowing who first investigated the phenomenon."[40] Steinmetz repeated his snub of Tesla in his second text, *Theoretical Elements of Electrical Engineering,* written in 1902. Because later texts would build on the work of these two early texts, many generations of engineers would be trained without ever reading or hearing the name Tesla.[41]

Huge fortunes were made on Tesla's AC polyphase electrical system, his induction motors, and his wireless communications designs, but Tesla received almost nothing for them. Tesla never became rich, and even more disappointingly, he never amassed enough funding to complete his Wardenclyffe Tower—a 600-foot-tall wireless transmission tower in Shoreham, Long Island—with which he hoped to achieve global wireless telephony. In 1917, in a tragic confluence of bad management and bad luck, the tower, in which Tesla had invested hundreds of thousands of dollars, was torn down for scrap before ever being completed by a landlord to whom Tesla owed $19,000 in back rent.

By most accounts, Tesla was a lifelong celibate. Although rumors have often circulated that perhaps he was a closeted homosexual, most researchers of Tesla's history now conclude that it was more likely a form of self-denial in pursuit of preserving his focus on his calling. Once, when someone inquired about his celibacy, he responded, "I do not believe an inventor should marry, because he has so intense a nature, with so much in it of wild, passionate quality, that in giving himself to a woman he might love, he would give everything and so take everything from his chosen field. . . . I do not think you can name many great inventions that have been made by married men."[42] Indeed, it was a relatively common belief that sublimation of the libido would help to preserve the creative energy—Sigmund Freud (whom Tesla knew) championed this idea and was himself celibate from the age of forty onwards.[43] Sir Isaac Newton is also believed to be a lifelong celibate.

Throughout his life, Tesla continued to have neurological disturbances. Once, for example, he had the "sensation that my brain had caught fire. I saw a light as [though] a small sun was located in it and I [passed] the whole night applying cold compressions to my tortured head." He also continued experiencing flashes of light, particularly at moments of fear or exhilaration. He believed their intensity peaked when he was about twenty-five years old but never entirely disappeared, and he noted in 1919, while writing his autobiography, that "these luminous phenomena still manifest themselves from time to time, as when a new idea opening up possibilities strikes me."[44] He also had extremely good eyesight and hearing, and during periods of stress his hearing, and sensitivity to vibration generally, could become so acute that it caused him great discomfort. These disturbances point to the possibility of a dopamine imbalance that might have simultaneously enhanced his creativity, made him acutely sensitive to stimuli, and provoked manic episodes. Notably, Tesla's mania and obsessive compulsive disorder also continued throughout his life. He often worked around the clock—in fact, he preferred working at night to avoid distractions. Even during periods when he did sleep, he claimed to work from three in the morning until eleven in the evening every day. His capacity for self-control and self-denial was extreme. He ate sparsely, keeping his weight to 142 pounds (despite being over six feet tall!) his entire adult life. He had germ phobias, a strong aversion to spherical objects, and an obsession with the number three. In fact, in the latter part of his life he would often calculate the cubic mass of the food on his plate and could not eat it if it were not divisible by three, and he would often walk around buildings three times before entering.[45]

Tesla exhibits separateness and self-efficacy in their extremes. He was also profoundly idealistic (the topic of Chapter 4), and he benefited from the opportunities of his era (the topic of Chapter 6). However, perhaps more than anything else, Tesla's story highlights the powerful interaction between genius and mania, two traits that are common among breakthrough innovators.

How Much Does Intelligence Matter?

A PERSON CAN BE intensely creative without being a genius, and a genius isn't necessarily intensely creative, but the traits of genius and creativity are not entirely independent. For example, it is rare to find individuals among the ranks of people who appear on lists of the "most important innovators" who are not noted for being exceptionally intelligent. Every innovator whose life and work I researched was repeatedly described by biographers and others as a "genius." For example, Steve Jobs tested at the tenth-grade level when given an IQ test in fourth grade, suggesting that his

IQ may have been roughly 160, placing him in the 99.99th percentile of IQ distribution. Einstein's intellect is legendary, estimated by various sources to have been between 160 and 190, and Marie Curie was described by every biographer as exceptionally gifted intellectually—a "genius," whose outsized intellectual capability was matched by a monumental determination. Elon Musk, affectionately called "genius boy" by his family when he was a child, is today described by those who know him as "brilliant." Kevin Watson, a SpaceX engineer, captured what many in that company feel about their boss:

> He's involved in just about everything. He understands everything. If he asks you a question, you learn very quickly not to go give him a gut reaction. He wants answers that get down to the fundamental laws of physics. One thing he understands really well is the physics of the rockets. He understands that like nobody else. The stuff I have seen him do in his head is crazy. He can get in discussions about flying a satellite and whether we can make the right orbit and deliver Dragon at the same time and solve all these equations in real time. It's amazing to watch the amount of knowledge he has accumulated over the years. I don't want to be the person who ever has to compete with Elon. You might as well leave the business and find something else fun to do. He will outmaneuver you, outthink you, and out-execute you.[46]

Benjamin Franklin was another exceptional intellect. His scientific contributions were remarkable by any measure, but all the more so because he had almost no academic training. The diversity of his scientific contributions was also incredible. For example, when his brother John was seriously ill and had trouble urinating, Franklin invented the first urinary catheter used in America. Through his observation and improvised experiments he was able to name and chart the Gulf Stream, and navigators were able to use this new information to decrease the amount of time it took to travel on the Atlantic Ocean.

Thomas Edison is also a fascinating example of intellect. Although his entire education consisted of only three months of grammar school followed by homeschooling by his mother after his teacher implied that perhaps he was slow, his precocious intelligence soon became evident. He began reading very early at his own initiative, and as noted earlier, he became a voracious reader who insatiably pored through science books at the library. By the age of twelve he was asking questions about physics that stymied his parents and others.

There are numerous possible relationships between intelligence and innovativeness. Exceptional intelligence helps an individual to more quickly and easily acquire a broad range of knowledge, providing more fodder for generating creative ideas if one has the propensity to do so. Intelligence can also help creative people to implement their ideas and get them adopted. As I will show, integrating research on creativity, working memory, executive control, and neurotransmitters yields yet another possibility: some of the same biological mechanisms that give rise to exceptional intelligence can also give rise to creativity, if one has other traits or experiences that promote the generation and pursuit of unusual ideas.

Biological Processes in Creativity

The earliest work in psychology and creativity emphasized the importance of unstructured, visual mental activity called "primary process thinking."[47] Because of its unstructured nature, primary process thinking can result in combining ideas that are not typically related, leading to what has been termed "remote associations" or "divergent thinking." Sigmund Freud noted that primary process thinking was most likely to occur just before sleep or while dozing or daydreaming; others have observed that it might also be common when distracted by physical exercise, music, or other activities. For example, when Elon Musk was asked how he comes up with his new ideas, he responded "It's somewhat cliché, but it happens a lot in the shower. I don't know what it is about showers. . . . "[48] Einstein played the violin to help himself think, noting that "Mozart's music is so pure and beautiful that I see it as a reflection of the inner beauty of the universe itself. . . . Of course, like all great beauty, his music was pure simplicity."[49] As his son Hans Albert observed, "He would take refuge in music and that would solve all his difficulties."[50] A friend added, "He would often play his violin in his kitchen late at night, improvising melodies while he pondered complicated problems. Then suddenly, in the middle of playing, he would announce excitedly, 'I've got it!' As if by inspiration, the answer to the problem would have come to him in the midst of music."[51]

Other psychologists built on these ideas about the role of primary process thinking by positing that some people are more prone to using it or have more control over the primary thinking process. For example, the noted creativity researcher Dean Simonton argues that some creative people may make their minds more open to random associations. They then mentally sort through these associations, selecting the best for further consideration. Other lines of research have also found evidence that highly creative people make more or better use of primary process thinking.[52] They fantasize more, remember their dreams more clearly, and are more vulnerable to hypnosis.[53] However, while much of this work implies that creativity is a process of random association, subsequent studies (including my own work on cognitive insight) pointed to another explanation more directly connected with intelligence: long paths of association. In my work modeling cognitive insight as a network process, I showed that individuals who are more likely or more able to search longer paths through the network of associations in their mind can arrive at a connection between two ideas or facts that seems unexpected or strange to others.[54] What appears to be random may not be random at all—it is just difficult for other people to see the association because they are not following as long a chain of associations. Consistent with this, studies by professors Mathias Benedek and Aljoscha Neubauer found that highly creative people usually follow the same association paths as less creative people, but they do so with such greater speed that they exhaust the common associations sooner, permitting them to get to less common associations earlier than others would.[55] Benedek and Neubauer's research argues that highly creative people's speed of association is a product of exceptional working memory and executive control. In other words, the ability to hold many things in one's mind simultaneously and maneuver them with great facility enables a person to rapidly explore many possible associations.[56]

Tesla and Musk are excellent examples. Both men had such extraordinary cognitive power that they were able to process a long path of calculations almost instantly in their heads. Their conclusions appear to arrive almost by magic! There is a path to the conclusions they make, but they fly down that path so fast that others don't see the route they have taken. Something that seems obvious to them may seem far-fetched to people who have not already followed all of the steps and have not done all the math. When Musk first announced that he wanted to build reusable rockets and colonize Mars, for example, many people dismissed him as just another millionaire space cowboy who would waste a lot of money on a fantasy fueled by little more than ego. However, Musk had already worked out that human extinction was likely if we did not become a multi-planetary species. He had also worked out that the biggest obstacle to space travel was cost and that the biggest obstacle to reducing that cost was single-use rockets. He had deduced—correctly, it turns out—that rockets could be made reusable and vastly reduce their cost, thereby making space travel far more practical. It was obvious to him, even before he picked up a rocket science textbook, and he subsequently proved it. There are many similar examples from Tesla's story. One of the clearest was his immediate intuition that the production of electricity could be made vastly more efficient by eliminating the commutator. Although he did not know the specifics of how to do it when he first had the insight and although the existing textbooks of the time said that it was impossible, he deduced—correctly, it turns out—that it could be done. Within a few years he had proven it.

Although there is much we do not yet understand about intelligence, we do know that a significant component of intelligence is memory. Memory is usually divided into (at least) two interdependent types: working memory and long-term memory. Working memory is what keeps information temporarily available for immediate access and use; it includes executive functions that control what information is attended to, how it is manipulated, and how it is acted upon. For example, working memory is what enables you to retain partial results of an arithmetic problem while you solve it. It is limited in capacity, and the number of "chunks" of information a person can hold in her working memory depends on both the person and the nature of the "chunks." Typically, fewer words than digits can be held in short-term memory, fewer longer words than shorter words, and so on. However, individuals can learn to combine chunks into higher-level chunks that enable them to retain impressive series of information. This is where long-term memory comes in. A subset of information that enters working memory is encoded into long-term memory, where information can be stored indefinitely. The brain decides what is important to save, and a person can influence that process by rehearsing an association. For example, you can memorize the quadratic formula by practicing it over and over. Although an individual can have a vast amount of information stored in long-term memory, the amount of it that can be activated (thought about) at one time is limited by working memory. Furthermore, long-term memory can influence the capacity of working memory by creating "chunking" rules. For example, it is very hard to remember a random sequence of numbers such as 1–8–5–6–1–9–4–3, but it may be very easy to remember these numbers if you have studied Nikola Tesla and combine these digits into two chunks, 1856 and 1943, the years of Tesla's birth and death. Exceptional long-term memory can thus enhance the capacity and efficiency of working memory, and exceptional working memory enables more of long-term memory to be rapidly accessed. Measures of working memory, rather than long-term memory, tend to better predict many measures of intelligence,[57] but both types of memory are complementary pieces of the intelligence puzzle.

Many of the breakthrough innovators were specifically noted for having exceptional memories. Edison would often stun people when he remembered their names and personal details despite having met them only briefly decades prior. Curie could recite substantial poems or passages after hearing them only a couple of times. There is considerable evidence that Tesla, as noted earlier, possessed an eidetic memory—the ability to recall images and sounds with great precision after only a few exposures. Intriguingly, it seems highly likely that Musk also has an eidetic memory. His photographic memory as a child would amaze his family and classmates when he recited huge quantities of information from the encyclopedia. Later he realized he could visualize and manipulate objects in his mind with remarkable clarity. Musk speculates, "It seems as though the part of the brain that's usually reserved for visual processing—the part that is used to process images coming in from my eyes—gets taken over by internal thought processes." Musk adds, "I can't do this as much now because there are so many things demanding my attention but, as a kid, it happened a lot. That large part of your brain that is used to handle incoming images gets used for internal thinking." He also notes, "For images and numbers, I can process their interrelationships and algorithmic relationships. . . . Acceleration, momentum, kinetic energy—how those sorts of things will be affected by objects comes through very vividly."[58] As noted by biographer Ashley Vance, Musk's combination of extraordinary intelligence and memory gives him an ability "to absorb incredible quantities of information with near-flawless recall."[59]

Working memory provides an interesting connection between creativity and intelligence. Superior working memory and executive control are extremely valuable in general cognitive functioning. Measures of working memory are strongly correlated to comprehension, problem solving, and general measures of intelligence.[60] If working memory aids remote association and is also associated with general intelligence, this may explain at least in part the frequent finding of an association between intellect and creativity.[61] This does not mean that all extremely intelligent people will be innovative, but it does suggest that exceptional creativity might be more common in the presence of high intelligence.

The Personality Factor: "Openness to Experience"

IN THE EXTENSIVE RESEARCH on personality, there is a dominant classification system called the "Big Five Personality Traits" of *neuroticism, agreeableness, extraversion, conscientiousness,* and *openness to experience.* These "traits" are actually broad dimensions of personality that comprise many other more-specific traits. Personality characteristics that are in the same "big five" dimension tend to be highly correlated and consistently reported within individuals, while the dimensions themselves are basically independent and nonoverlapping. Of the big five, openness to experience is the one most commonly associated with creativity.

Openness to experience reflects an individual's use of active imagination, aesthetic sensitivity (the appreciation for art and literature, for example), attentiveness to emotion, a preference for variety, and intellectual curiosity. It is assessed by asking individuals to rate their degree of agreement or disagreement with statements such as "I have a vivid imagination," "I enjoy hearing new ideas," "I have a rich vocabulary," "I rarely look for deeper meaning in things" (negative), "I enjoy going to art museums," "I avoid philosophical discussions" (negative), and "I enjoy wild flights of fantasy." Individuals who score high on the openness to experience dimension tend to have great intellectual curiosity, are interested in unusual ideas, and are willing to try new things. They are also typically more tolerant of complexity and ambiguity than the average person. People with low scores on this dimension hold more-conventional beliefs and may be uncomfortable with novelty, complexity, and ambiguity.

A considerable amount of research suggests that openness to experience is associated with divergent thinking and creativity. Certainly, having a broader range of interests and experiences to mix in the combinatorial hopper should lead to more unusual associations. Furthermore, a tolerance for complexity and ambiguity could prompt heterodox thinking and enable more sophisticated abstraction. However, the evidence for this trait among the breakthrough innovators studied here is mixed. Einstein definitely exhibited aesthetic sensitivity, noting about himself, "Personally, I experience the greatest degree of pleasure in having contact with works of art. They furnish me with happy feelings of an intensity that I cannot derive from other sources."[62] Tesla was noted for his great love of poetry and literature, and he could recite passages from Goethe, Shakespeare, and Voltaire from memory. It was, as noted earlier, while reciting stances from Goethe's *Faust* that he had his great insight about how to achieve alternating-current electricity. Furthermore, most of the breakthrough innovators were avid and omnivorous readers, and some were polymaths with skills in numerous areas (for example, Franklin is generally described as a polymath). However, some of them were also so intensely focused on their objective that their lives were lived rather narrowly. For example, Tesla's work consumed him so completely that he spared himself little time to explore the world or pursue diverse adventures. Curie was similarly consumed by her work and found it uncomfortable to travel to new places and did so only reluctantly. Jobs's spiritual pursuits and travel are consistent with the typical descriptions of "openness," but it is harder to see "openness" in the maniacal work habits of Edison, Kamen, or Musk. It may turn out that openness to different intellectual ideas is a somewhat different trait than the pursuit of variety in real-world experiences. It is also possible that while "openness" helps creativity, maniacal focus is required to bring an exceptional innovation to fruition. The unusual combination of these traits may be a key to understanding exceptional breakthrough innovators.

What was more notable about these people than their *range* of interests was their drive to find *fundamental principles,* whether they be in physics, math, virtue, or social progress. For instance, Einstein was driven to find the fundamental principles of the mechanics of the universe, which led him to study gravity and light and to seek generalized solutions for his theories (i.e., theories that are robust to a wide array of contexts and applications, such as his General Theory of Relativity): "In this field, I soon learned how to scent out that which was able to lead to fundamentals and to turn aside . . . from the multitude of things which clutter up the mind and divert it from the essential."[63] Similarly, Tesla sought to understand and harness the fundamental dynamics of waves and oscillation on a grand scale. From the moment he understood how to transmit communication wirelessly, he was no longer content to transmit it between cities or even between countries. He wanted to wirelessly transmit communication globally and beyond. He spent a considerable period of his career, in fact, attempting to communicate with Mars. Similarly, from the moment he had demonstrated methods of transmitting electricity wirelessly, he began to envision global-scale wireless energy transmission. His tendency to immediately abstract the fundamental principles of a phenomenon and envision how it could be scaled up to vast proportions is a big part of why he often faced skepticism from the public and his investors—they had a hard time following his leaps of cognition, and because the scale of his ideas was intimidating, others were prone to label them as absurd. This drive to seek fundamental principles is also apparent in Jobs's search for truth through Zen and his concept of the computer as a "bicycle for the mind," in Franklin's relentless pursuit of more-efficient or welfare-enhancing ways of social organizing, and in Curie's identification of radioactivity as a fundamental property of elements.

Atypical Brain Chemistry

Although intelligence, memory, and "openness" are all characteristics that have long been associated with creative genius, the breakthrough innovators here—particularly Tesla—highlight a more unusual and less understood ingredient of creative genius: atypical brain chemistry. As neuroscientists have gained capabilities to explore the activities of the brain in greater detail, they have started to pay more attention to the relationship between the neurotransmitter system and creativity. Evidence is amassing about the relationship between dopamine and/or glutamate and divergent thinking. Dopamine has been shown to reduce latent inhibition: the automatic preconscious process whereby stimuli thought to be irrelevant are blocked from conscious awareness.[64] In a related line of research, psychologists have found that highly creative people typically have lower levels of latent inhibition and thus tend to respond to stimuli that others would ignore.[65] Highly creative people are often highly sensitive to physiological stimuli, such as auditory tones, electric shocks, or lights,[66] illustrated in the extreme by Tesla, who wrote in his autobiography about his senses during periods of nervous strain:

> I could hear the ticking of a watch with three rooms between me and the time-piece. A fly alighting on a table would cause a dull thud in my ear. A carriage passing at a distance of a few miles fairly shook my whole body. The whistle of a locomotive twenty or thirty miles away made the bench or chair on which I sat, vibrate so strongly that the pain was unbearable. The ground under my feet trembled continuously. . . . The sun's rays, when periodically intercepted, would cause blows of such force on my brain that they would stun me.[67]

Elevated dopamine levels can also cause individuals to attend to and retain cognitive stimuli that others would dismiss. Dopamine levels that are modestly higher than normal might thus enable more defocused attention and unusual associations, resulting in creative outcomes. Interesting evidence for this emerged when a number of studies found that drugs like L-DOPA that increase the body's level of dopamine and are used to treat patients with Parkinson's disease sometimes awaken or accelerate creative tendencies.[68] Initially, researchers thought that Parkinson's itself somehow induced big surges in creativity. Stories emerged like that of Tsipi Shaish, who worked at an insurance company and lived a "routine life" until she was diagnosed with Parkinson's disease in 2006. She had never taken art lessons, nor had she any particular interest in art. But after her diagnosis and commencing treatment, she began to feel "an uncontrollable urge" to create vivid abstracts on canvas, and by 2011, Shaish had major art exhibitions in Paris and New York City. Her works are described as exhibiting "startling symbolism" and "bold colors and pastels in a 'gleeful pandemonium.'"[69] Shaish could not explain what was happening to her and believed that the disease itself had made her more creative, but researchers now understand that the treatment for Parkinson's disease can unlock the creativity within an individual. Prior to treatment, Parkinson's patients have progressively less dopamine produced in their brains—the disease causes dopamine-producing cells in the brain to die off. Patients begin to feel increasingly less motivated, less verbal, and less physical. Dopamine is the brain's primary reward drug, and without it, many aspects of life lose their luster. Furthermore, because dopamine is a crucial ingredient for motor function, patients may have trouble moving, a symptom known as "hypokinesia." L-DOPA treatment jolts these patients back to life, making them more aware and interested in things around them, and more mobile. When L-DOPA is at its peak levels in the body, they may even be too mobile—experiencing jittery or jerky movements known as "dyskinesia."

While moderately elevated dopamine may aid divergent thinking and retention of cognitive stimuli, too much dopamine might make it impossible for a person to screen stimuli at all. In such a situation a person may find it extremely difficult to accurately perceive the world around her, leading to something that looks more like psychosis than creativity. Not coincidentally, an extensive line of research implicates dopamine and dopamine receptors in schizophrenia, and a range of antipsychotic drugs work by blocking dopamine receptors. Numerous psychologists note that schizophrenia (which psychoanalytic theory describes as a primary process state) appears to be significantly related to creativity. First, highly creative people are overrepresented among the families of schizophrenics, suggesting a genetic link.[70] Second, schizophrenics and highly creative people score similarly in a range of creativity tests,[71] and creative people score quite highly on tests of psychoticism.[72]

An overly active dopamine system (or administration of drugs that increase the production or availability of dopamine) also produces symptoms resembling mania. Mania is a state of abnormally elevated or irritable mood, elevated arousal, and elevated energy levels. It is typically associated with feelings of grandeur, a reduced need for sleep (and nocturnal hyperactivity), indulgence in enjoyable behaviors with a high risk of negative outcomes, and a possibility of hallucinations or preoccupying thoughts.[73] Both mania and elevated dopamine are also associated with an increased likelihood of addictive behavior. As noted previously, dopamine is one of the brain's primary reward system drugs; cocaine and amphetamines act by artificially inducing dopamine "highs," and people with elevated dopamine levels (e.g., individuals with naturally elevated dopamine or Parkinson's patients on L-DOPA therapy) may also experience an amplification of the "highs" reaped from such activities as gambling, sex, and exercise.[74] Nearly all of these patterns were repeatedly observed in Tesla. In his youth he suffered from visions that were akin to hallucinations. He struggled with a gambling addiction in college. Ideas often came to him in an overwhelming rush, causing him to engage in periods of frenzied work where he neglected all other aspects of his life. He slept very little, averaging less than two hours a night, and tended to work through the night. Finally, he pursued such grandiose ideas that people were inclined to ridicule him as a dreamer even though his track record for success was exceptional.

"Hypomania" (basically a mild form of mania), which may be caused by moderately elevated levels of dopamine, has been repeatedly linked to creativity. It thus may be no surprise that many of the most prolific innovators exhibit characteristics that resemble some degree of mania. Nearly all of the innovators, as we've seen, were noted for having exceptional self-efficacy, the self-confidence that they could do things others would deem impossible. Many (though not all) of the breakthrough innovators also did not sleep very much. Curie noted in a letter to her cousin that she slept five hours a night. Edison wrote in 1921, "For myself I never found need of more than four or five hours' sleep in the twenty-four,"[75] and multiple accounts suggest that he slept only three to four hours a night, and then frequently on a table in his laboratory. Franklin recounts in his autobiography that he slept five hours a night. Jobs was noted for sleeping erratically and often working at night. Kamen has told reporters that he sleeps about three to four hours a night. Musk has told reporters that he sleeps between six and six-and-a-half hours a night. By contrast, Einstein noted that he slept ten hours a night. A 2009 international study habits found that Americans sleep for an average of 8.5 hours a night, and in Japan (the advanced-economy nation with the lowest average hours of sleep), people average seven hours and fourteen minutes of sleep a night. Thus, all of the innovators except Einstein slept less than the current population average, and several slept very much less.

Unusual levels or fluctuations in the dopamine system may provide a crucial link among working memory, creativity, mania, obsessive/addictive behaviors, and schizophrenia. Research in neuroscience suggests that neurotransmitters such as norepinephrine and dopamine directly affect the functioning of working memory and cognition. For example, elevated norepinephrine speeds up neuronal activity, resulting in a burst of brain activity that can lead to the streaming of images in the brain,[76] perhaps explaining Tesla's eidetic images. Studies have also found evidence that dopamine activity in the prefrontal cortex is positively related to the personality trait "openness to experience" and to novelty-seeking behaviors.[77]

In sum, if modestly elevated dopamine or norepinephrine can promote creativity but excessive levels can lead to psychopathology, this sheds light on the legendary—and controversial—association between madness and genius. Genius does not require madness, nor does madness imply genius, but because both can be influenced by similar neurotransmitters, it is not surprising that people have long intuited a connection between them. It also elucidates why activities such as exercise or playing music, or a mild stimulant like coffee, might aid creative thinking: by modestly elevating dopamine they reduce latent inhibition and may enhance working memory, helping the individual to make unusual associations. Neurotransmitters such as dopamine and norepinephrine thus help to connect many of the threads of research on highly creative individuals. Many of the seemingly disconnected strands of research on creativity—personality, intelligence, patterns of association, psychopathology—are likely to be tightly connected once we better understand the chemical and physiological processes of the mind.

I didn't really think Tesla would be successful. I thought we would most likely fail. But if something's important enough, you should try even if the probable outcome is failure.

—Elon Musk, in an interview with
Scott Pelley, March 30, 2014

Being the richest man in the cemetery doesn't matter to me. . . . Going to bed at night saying we've done something wonderful—that's what matters to me.

—Steve Jobs, in an interview with
CNNMoney/Fortune, 1993

4

"Once she had recognized a certain way as a right one, she pursued it without compromise. . . ."

A Higher Purpose

It almost goes without saying that the great success of the innovators lay with their tackling huge problems. As important, though, is the fact that they tackled them with extraordinary fervor and tenacity. They worked excruciatingly long hours, often neglecting family, friends, and health. They often endured harsh criticism by those who doubted them, and yet on they still charged. What gave them this nearly superhuman commitment to their endeavors? All of the innovators studied here—with the notable exception of Thomas Edison—exhibited an intense idealism and an intense focus on a superordinate goal, and this sense of purpose profoundly shaped their behavior.

Idealism is the pursuit of high or noble principles and goals. Idealists prioritize ideals and values over the current reality. They focus on the world as they believe it *should be* rather than how it actually is.[1] Idealism pushed the innovators to pursue important goals, even if doing so required them to break with established norms or incur great personal cost or risk, as was the case with Benjamin Franklin.

Franklin was an intensely intelligent child with an unquenchable thirst for reading. Raised in a devout home where all of the available reading was about Puritan religion and ideals, he began to seriously engage with moral reasoning and ideals at a very early age. In fact, his father, noting his son's potential for spirituality, initially intended him for the ministry. Although Franklin did not pursue that path in part because his family could not afford to pay for the education required, he remained intensely interested in moral philosophy and would go on to develop his own set of beliefs and ideals that departed somewhat from Puritan orthodoxy. These beliefs and ideals were very central to his character and would drive him to spend his entire life pursuing social problems with vigorous and tenacious effort.

Franklin was born in Boston on January 17, 1706, into a family of craftsmen. The name Franklin is itself an icon of the middle class that Benjamin Franklin would idealize—it derives from the Anglo-Franco "fraunclein," which means a landowner of free but not noble origin. Thus, a Franklin is neither a serf nor landed gentry. Generations of the Franklin family were known for being avid readers, religious dissenters, and nonconformists who were willing to defy authority yet were still able to always remain woven into the fabric of civic life.[2] His grandfather, Thomas Franklin II, was a gregarious tinkerer who practiced several trades and professions, including blacksmith, gunsmith, and surgeon. Josiah Franklin, Benjamin's father, had emigrated to America in 1682 with his wife and their first three children. Landing in Boston, he set up shop as a tallow chandler, creating soap and candles from animal fat. A Puritan, his favorite piece of wisdom was a passage from the Proverbs of Solomon that affirms the importance of both industriousness and egalitarianism: "Seest through a man diligent in his calling, he shall stand before Kings." "Diligence in thy calling" was even inscribed on his tombstone when he passed.[3] Josiah's industriousness and diligence extended to his family life: he fathered a total of seventeen children (seven by his first wife, ten by his second). Benjamin was the third-youngest child and the youngest son.

Josiah Franklin's plan for Benjamin's entry into the clergy led him to send his son to Boston Latin School at the age of eight. A year later his father transferred him to another school for writing and arithmetic that was less expensive. In his autobiography, Franklin recalls that he excelled at writing but failed at arithmetic, so when he was ten his father took him home to help at the tallow shop and began searching for a trade for him. After that point Franklin continued his education through reading any books he could obtain. Most were devotional texts from his father's library, but by borrowing books from others with more-extensive libraries, he was able to read a great range of thought-provoking works, including Plutarch's *Lives,* Cotton Mather's *Essays to Do Good,* Locke's *On Human Understanding,* and Arnauld and Nicole's *Logic, or the Art of Thinking.*

Because Benjamin's keen love of books was obvious, Josiah determined that his son should become a printer and so indentured him (at the age of twelve) to Benjamin's older brother, James, who had a printing business. Benjamin excelled at the trade and discovered also a talent for writing. Fueled by his reading of great works in philosophy, rhetoric, and logic, Franklin began to hone his methods of writing, oration, and argumentation. As he notes in his autobiography,

> While I was intent on improving my language, I met with an English grammar (I think it was Greenwood's), at the end of which there were two little sketches of the arts of rhetoric and logic, the latter finishing with a specimen of a dispute in the

> Socratic method; and soon after I procur'd Xonophon's Memorable Things of Socrates, wherein there are many instances of the same method. I was charm'd with it, adopted it, dropt my abrupt contradiction and positive argumentation, and put on the humble inquirer and doubter. And being then, from reading Shaftesbury and Collins, become a real doubter in many points of our religious doctrine, I found this method safest for myself and very embarrassing to those against whom I used it; therefore I took a delight in it, practis'd it continually, and grew very artful and expert in drawing people, even of superior knowledge, into concessions, the consequences of which they did not foresee, entangling them in difficulties out of which they could not extricate themselves, and so obtaining victories that neither myself nor my cause always deserved. I continu'd this method some few years, but gradually left it, retaining only the habit of expressing myself in terms of modest diffidence; never using, when I advanced any thing that may possibly be disputed, the words certainly, undoubtedly, or any others that give the air of positiveness to an opinion; but rather say, I conceive or apprehend a thing to be so and so; it appears to me, or I should think it so or so, for such and such reasons. . . . This habit, I believe, has been of great advantage to me when I have had occasion to inculcate my opinions, and persuade men into measures that I have been from time to time engag'd in promoting. . . .[4]

Franklin's skill in persuasive writing and oration would turn out to be very important in his role as a diplomat and in his success at convincing people to cooperate in the social innovations that he initiated such as street lighting and sweeping programs, a volunteer fire department, and America's first public lending library.

However, his rebellious side also began to be more apparent during his time as an apprentice. When Franklin's letters appeared under the pseudonym of Silence Dogood in the *New England*

Courant, the newspaper published by his brother James, he revealed something of himself: "I am . . . a mortal enemy to arbitrary government and unlimited power. I am naturally very jealous for the rights and liberties of my country; and the least appearance of an encroachment on those invaluable privileges is apt to make my blood boil exceedingly."[5] He would also express his belief in education and egalitarianism by quoting passages extracted from an essay titled "The Education of Women," written by Daniel Dafoe in 1719 (although he does not identify Dafoe and attributes the passages only to "an ingenious writer"):

> I have (says he) often thought of it as one of the most barbarous Customs in the World, considering us as a civiliz'd and Christian Country, that we deny the Advantages of Learning to Women. We reproach the Sex every Day with Folly and Impertinence, while I am confident, had they the Advantages of Education equal to us, they would be guilty of less than our selves. One would wonder indeed how it should happen that Women are conversible at all, since they are only beholding to natural Parts for all their Knowledge. Their Youth is spent to teach them to stitch and sew, or make Baubles: They are taught to read indeed, and perhaps to write their Names, or so; and that is the Heighth of a Womans Education. And I would but ask any who slight the Sex for their Understanding, What is a Man (a Gentleman, I mean) good for that is taught no more? If Knowledge and Understanding had been useless Additions to the Sex, God Almighty would never have given them Capacities, for he made nothing Needless. What has the Woman done to forfeit the Priviledge of being taught? Does she plague us with her Pride and Impertinence? Why did we not let her learn, that she might have had more Wit? Shall we upbraid Women with Folly, when 'tis only the Error of this inhumane Custom that hindred them being made wiser?

Franklin began to resent the harsh authority of his brother, and at the age of seventeen he managed to escape his apprenticeship and flee to New York City and then Philadelphia, in search of employment. Gregarious and charming, Franklin soon found work with a printer and a few years later opened his own printing house. His industriousness earned him both success as a printer and the admiration of the community. A prominent local merchant even noted, "The industry of that Franklin is superior to anything I ever saw of the kind; I see him still at work when I go home from club, and he is at work again before his neighbors are out of bed."[6] Soon Franklin had also started his own newspaper, the *Pennsylvania Gazette,* which would rise to become one of America's most prominent newspapers and would continue to be published until 1800, ten years after Franklin's death.

During this time Franklin continued to read and ponder religion. He had abandoned the Puritan dogma of his childhood, and although he had been educated as a Presbyterian, he had little interest in organized religion. He described himself as a deist—believing that reason and observation of the natural world were sufficient to determine the existence of a divine creator, accompanied with the rejection of authority as a source of religious knowledge. He wrote a series of religious essays, as much for the purpose of establishing his own moral code as for influencing others. He ended up developing his own Thirteen Virtues of Life:

1. Temperance. Eat not to dullness; drink not to elevation.
2. Silence. Speak not but what may benefit others or yourself; avoid trifling conversation.
3. Order. Let all your things have their places; let each part of your business have its time.
4. Resolution. Resolve to perform what you ought; perform without fail what you resolve.
5. Frugality. Make no expense but to do good to others or yourself; i.e., waste nothing.

6. Industry. Lose no time; be always employ'd in something useful; cut off all unnecessary actions.
7. Sincerity. Use no hurtful deceit; think innocently and justly, and, if you speak, speak accordingly.
8. Justice. Wrong none by doing injuries, or omitting the benefits that are your duty.
9. Moderation. Avoid extremes; forbear resenting injuries so much as you think they deserve.
10. Cleanliness. Tolerate no uncleanliness in body, cloaths, or habitation.
11. Tranquility. Be not disturbed at trifles, or at accidents common or unavoidable.
12. Chastity. Rarely use venery but for health or offspring, never to dullness, weakness, or the injury of your own or another's peace or reputation.
13. Humility. Imitate Jesus and Socrates.[7]

Franklin then set about trying to achieve "moral perfection" by mastering each of these virtues. He noted that people are creatures of habit, which made it quite difficult to change their behavior and adhere to every virtue, but he devised a strategy whereby he would focus on mastering one virtue per week. He presumed that after focusing intensely on adhering to a virtue for a week it would have largely been ingrained into habit, making it easier to sustain thereafter. He listed his virtues in a table next to the days of the week and would note each day when he violated a virtue and would aspire to correct it. His progress in his table assured him that he was becoming more virtuous.

He was already well practiced in frugality and temperance. For example, as a young man of eighteen he had already concluded that money spent on beer was wasted. He recounts an illustrative example in his autobiography:

> We had an alehouse boy who attended always in the house to supply the workmen. My companion at the press drank every

> day a pint before breakfast, a pint at breakfast with his bread and cheese, a pint between breakfast and dinner, a pint at dinner, a pint in the afternoon about six o'clock, and another when he had done his day's work. I thought it a detestable custom; but it was necessary, he suppos'd, to drink strong beer, that he might be strong to labor. I endeavored to convince him that the bodily strength afforded by beer could only be in proportion to the grain or flour of the barley dissolved in the water of which it was made; that there was more flour in a pennyworth of bread; and therefore, if he would eat that with a pint of water, it would give him more strength than a quart of beer. He drank on, however, and had four or five shillings to pay out of his wages every Saturday night for that muddling liquor; an expense I was free from. And thus these poor devils keep themselves always under.[8]

The virtue of sincerity prompted him to refuse all submissions to his paper that he perceived as libelous or abusive. When the writers would plead that freedom of the press demanded he print their submissions, he replied that he would print as many copies as they desired for them to distribute on their own, but he would not spread detractions, noting, "having contracted with my subscribers to furnish them with what might be either useful or entertaining I could not fill their papers with private altercation."[9]

The virtue that would turn out to most define Franklin's character and shape his life was industry. Franklin believed very deeply in the value of hard work, and he also believed that to be seen as industrious was a mark of good character. He thus strove not only to be industrious but to *be seen* being industrious:

> In order to secure my credit and character as a tradesman, I took care not only to be in reality industrious and frugal, but to avoid all appearances to the contrary. I drest plainly; I was

> seen at no places of idle diversion. I never went out a fishing or shooting; a book, indeed, sometimes debauch'd me from my work, but that was seldom, snug, and gave no scandal; and to show that I was not above my business, I sometimes brought home the paper I purchas'd at the stores thro' the streets on a wheelbarrow. Thus being esteem'd an industrious, thriving young man and paying duly for what I bought, the merchants who imported stationery solicited my custom; others proposed supplying me with books, and I went on swimmingly.[10]

Franklin initially had only twelve virtues on his list, but he added the last—humility—when a Quaker friend informed him that he was generally perceived as proud. Franklin struggled mightily with this last virtue. He disciplined himself to not correct others' mistakes, and he learned to avoid making dogmatic pronouncements, but he never considered himself to have truly won the battle with pride. As he noted wryly in his autobiography, "In reality, there is, perhaps no one of our natural passions so hard to subdue as pride. Disguise it, struggle with it, beat it down, stifle it, mortify it as much as one pleases, it is still alive, and will every now and then peep out and show itself; you will see it, perhaps, often in this history; for, even if I could conceive that I had compleatly overcome it, I should probably be proud of my humility."[11]

In 1727 Franklin, an innate social networker, a gift none of the other breakthrough innovators seemed to possess, created the "Junto," a club where like-minded young and enterprising workingmen could gather. The word *junto* is an alteration of the Spanish word for "joined" and began to be used in the seventeenth century to signify a group of people united for a common purpose. Franklin and his friends rented a house where they discussed current events, debated philosophy, and developed self- and civic-improvement programs. When the members devised a method of pooling their books to form a common library, this gave rise to one of the first subscription lending libraries in America. Franklin subsequently used the Junto to launch a voluntary fire brigade, a night watchman corps that would supplement Philadelphia's police force, and the Pennsylvania Militia (a military force independent of Pennsylvania's government).

In the 1740s Franklin began to turn his attention toward his scientific curiosity. He had long been an enthusiastic student of nature, having analyzed lunar patterns, weather, and water currents. Having prospered as a printer, he now had enough money to more freely indulge his scientific interests and pursued them with zeal. Despite his having had only two years of formal education, his scientific contributions were remarkable. For example, after pondering the mechanics of heat transfer and convection, he developed wood-burning stoves (initially called Pennsylvania fireplaces but later referred to as Franklin stoves), which could be built into fireplaces and greatly increase the amount of heat produced while reducing smoke and drafts. While he could have patented the stoves and profited from them, he declined to do so. Driven by his ideal to serve God and mankind, he chose to give the designs for the stoves to the public—as he would do with all of his inventions—so that all people could freely benefit from them. As he remarked in his autobiography, "As we enjoy great advantages from the invention of others, we should be glad of an opportunity to serve others by any invention of ours, and this we should do freely and generously."[12] As noted in the previous chapter, when his brother John was seriously ill and had trouble urinating, Franklin invented the first urinary catheter used in America. In 1747 he began studying electricity, tinkering with glass tubes to generate static electricity and devising experiments to better understand its properties. He ultimately concluded that the generation of a positive charge was accompanied by the generation of an equal negative charge—giving rise to the principle of conservation of charge and the single-fluid theory of electricity. This was a monumental scientific breakthrough that future scientists described as "of the same fundamental importance to physical science as Newton's law of conservation of momentum."[13]

Franklin's observation that lightning behaved similarly to electricity led to one of his most famous experiments—the collection of electrical charge from lightning by means of a kite with a wire protruding from its top—and to one of his most important inventions, the lightning rod for protecting buildings from the destructive effects of lightning. Soon buildings all across the colonies and Europe were being fitted with lightning rods. In recognition of his accomplishment, Franklin was awarded honorary degrees by both Harvard and Yale in 1753 (he would later also receive honorary doctorates from the University of St. Andrews and Oxford).

He also made studies of population growth over this period that led to his 1755 publication of a paper titled "Observations on the Increase of Mankind," a profound and fundamental work on population growth and resource economics that greatly influenced Adam Smith and Thomas Malthus, although Malthus and Franklin came to different conclusions about the implications of growth.[14] Malthus's famous 1798 work, "An Essay on the Principle of Population, as It Affects the Future Improvement of Society," warns that unless actively curtailed, a human population tends to grow until it exceeds the resources available to support it. When food production or other aspects of well-being were increased, the population would grow and diminish per capita production, potentially to the point of catastrophe. Mankind, he argued, tended to not have the discipline to use excess resources to increase the standard of living; instead, its population would grow until people began to suffer famine or other destruction—a view that became known as the "Malthusian trap." Franklin, on the other hand, had a more optimistic view on population growth. He saw land in America as an underused resource. He argued that England should actively seek to increase its population in America because that would result in growing the wealth and power of England. When Franklin published this essay, he had not anticipated the American colonies seeking independence from the rule—and taxation—of England.

Franklin believed that industrious youths would be better served by a practical nonsectarian education than by the elite colleges of the time (Harvard, Yale, William & Mary, Princeton), so in 1751 he founded an academy that would become the University of Pennsylvania. In the same year he accepted a seat in the Pennsylvania Assembly, determining that a political position would enable him to do more good in the world. One of his first projects was to create street sweeping and lighting systems. In keeping with a lifelong tendency to immerse himself in every minute detail of his projects, he even designed new lamps that would vent the smoke and thereby stay clean and bright longer.

It is worth taking a moment here to note that the vast majority of Franklin's innovations—including the public lending library, the volunteer fire brigade, the nonsectarian university, and street sweeping and lighting systems—did not profit him directly (at least not more so than they profited the general public). Although he was a shrewd and practical businessman who strove to be financially successful in his printing business and later in his political roles, it is also clear that financial gain was not his primary motive, and he invested considerable effort and expense in the more idealistic quest of improving social welfare.

By 1753, when the British had appointed him to the post of Deputy Postmaster for the colonies, Franklin was becoming increasingly embroiled in politics. He felt strongly that the colonies of America should be unified into a nation. In 1754 he published his famous cartoon of a snake cut into parts with the phrase "Join or die" to illustrate his argument that the colonies needed to unite if they were to stop the French advance in America. Although the French colonies were vastly outnumbered by the British colonies, the French had allied with the Native Americans in an effort to try to seize control of the land west of the Appalachians. Franklin, who was initially a loyalist to the Crown, envisioned America as a nation that would remain part of the British Empire, its citizens enjoying all of the rights and liberties of those in England. However, he would eventually realize that the government in England had no intention of enabling the American colonies to achieve that kind of parity. In fact, the English actively suppressed development of manufacturing capabilities in America to forestall its economic independence. Franklin would ultimately be forced to choose between loyalty to England and pursuing what he thought would be best for the people of America.

It was a difficult and uncertain period. The British wanted to control the colonies and tax them, the French wanted to seize more swaths of American territory, the Native Americans wanted more restraint in the expansion of the colonies and better terms for their concessions, and the colonies themselves were not inclined to cooperate as a union. On top of this, although Franklin had considerable influence in the Pennsylvania Assembly, he was increasingly at odds with the Penn family, the Pennsylvania "proprietors" who had a charter from the Crown to govern Pennsylvania. As his battles with the Penns became more frequent and more heated, he frequently lost his carefully crafted temperament of calm and tolerance.

England's 1765 move to levy the "Stamp Act" tax on every newspaper, book, legal document, and deck of cards in the colonies set in motion a sequence of events that would eventually unite the colonies, but not as loyal members of the British Empire as Franklin had initially hoped. The tension among the colonists, the proprietors, and England increased over the next decade, fueled by multiple skirmishes over taxes and import duties. Franklin's role in arguing for the rights and liberties of the colonies increasingly put him at odds with leaders in England and with his son William, who, as a British loyalist, served as a royal governor in New Jersey. Franklin would ultimately choose loyalty to his ideals of a free and egalitarian America over any loyalty to his son, irrevocably severing their relationship.

On one occasion, while Franklin was living in England as an agent of the Pennsylvania Assembly, he was ordered to appear before the Privy Council, where British Solicitor-General Alexander Wedderburn accused him of being the "prime conductor" in stirring up agitation against the British government by illegally obtaining and releasing inflammatory letters from Massachusetts Governor Thomas Hutchinson filled with advice on how to subdue the Americans by restricting their liberties. Wedderburn spent a full hour launching an abusive attack upon Franklin in front of a jeering crowd of England's elite. However, Franklin stood stoic and silent. The proceeding led to him losing his postmaster position and facing threat of arrest. He had become a target for England's increasing anxiety about American rebellion, and most people expected that he would quickly leave England. But he did not leave, nor did he retire from public life. Instead, he continued to write biting satires that offered a critical look at how England was managing the relationship with America. He accrued many enemies during this time who mocked or slandered him in the press, sometimes accusing him of devious or lecherous behavior. But Franklin faced these difficulties with resolve; knowing that he was pursuing his duty to serve God and mankind gave him a moral high ground that helped make him resilient to such public attacks.

As the Revolutionary War unfolded, Franklin's extraordinary skills as a strategic thinker and diplomat became apparent to all. He realized that France could be persuaded to help America win independence from England, so he adroitly wooed the leaders and people of France in a way that appealed to both their idealism and pragmatism.[15] Franklin's portrayal of America as a virtuous young country battling against tyranny won the hearts of the people and leaders of France; Franklin's promises that a French-American alliance would benefit French trade at the expense of Britain won their minds and pocketbooks. Franklin became so esteemed in France that as his coach passed through the palace gates at Versailles, crowds gathered and shouted "Vive Franklin!"[16] With France's monetary support he was able to fund munitions to fight England on the battlefield, and with France's political support he was able to induce England to acknowledge America's independence.

During interludes in which he was not busy with politics, Franklin again turned to his scientific inquiries. His capacity for observation and deduction was remarkable, leading him to be the first to argue for such things as colds being transmitted from person to person (rather than from cold air), lead being poisonous, and ships being able to travel faster in deep water.[17] As a player of the violin, harp, and guitar, he had a great enthusiasm for music and in 1761 invented a musical instrument called a glass armonica.[18] In 1784, frustrated that he had to switch between different pairs of eyeglasses for reading versus seeing at distance, he invented bifocal glasses.[19]

Throughout his life Franklin would be guided and fueled by his ideals of egalitarianism, tolerance, industriousness, temperance, and charity. To know a problem existed was sufficient motivation for him to attempt to solve it, even if solving it did not contribute to his personal interests. Franklin's somewhat complicated relationship with slavery illustrates this point. For example, in 1787 he still owned slaves, but he recognized that egalitarianism must apply to all people. He became the president of the Pennsylvania Society for Promoting the Abolition of Slavery, but he did not actually support immediate abolition because he feared that turning all the slaves out into society without education or employment would spell disaster. He believed that abolition was a process that would take time and needed to be well thought out. Thus in 1789, the year before his death, he drew up a detailed charter called "Plan for Improving the Condition of the Free Blacks, 1789." The plan called for committees that would advise freed slaves and help them obtain education and employment. When Franklin died, in 1790, his will indicated that his slaves were to be freed (rather than inherited by his family, as was the custom of the time).

Franklin's early exposure to Puritan philosophy had sparked his quest to understand humanity's purpose in the world and later his pursuit of "moral perfection." However, it would be a mistake to conclude that Franklin's idealism was strictly a result of obedience to a particular religion. Franklin's beliefs did not adhere closely to any branch of orthodox Christianity; instead, he cultivated his own more general principle around the value of living a virtuous life. Franklin's ideals were centered on constructing a better, more humane society because moral behavior served the public good.[20] Religion played a valuable role, in Franklin's view, by helping people pursue a virtuous life who might not otherwise do so. As he noted in a letter to Thomas Paine,

> You yourself may find it easy to live a virtuous life, without the assistance afforded by religion; you having a clear perception of the advantages of virtue, and the disadvantages of vice, and possessing a strength of resolution sufficient to enable you to resist common temptations. But think how great a portion of mankind consists of weak and ignorant men and women, and of inexperienced, inconsiderate youth of both sexes, who have need of the motives of religion to restrain them from vice, to support their virtue, and retain them in the practice of it till it becomes habitual, which is the great point for its security. . . . If men are so wicked with religion, what would they be if without it?"[21]

Shortly before Franklin's death, Ezra Stiles, the Calvinist president of Yale College, wrote to him and asked if he would clarify his religious position. Franklin responded with the following:

> Here is my Creed. I believe in one God, Creator of the Universe. That He governs it by His Providence. That he ought to be worshipped. That the most acceptable Service we render to him, is doing Good to his other Children. That the Soul of Man is immortal, and will be treated with Justice in another Life respecting its Conduct in this. . . . As for Jesus of Nazareth . . . I think the system of Morals and Religion as he left them to us, the best the World ever saw . . . but I have . . . some Doubts to his Divinity; tho' it is a Question I do not dogmatise upon, having never studied it, and think it is needless to busy myself with it now, where I expect soon an Opportunity of knowing the Truth with less Trouble.[22]

Franklin would continue to work until his death at the age of eighty-four. During his lifetime he was known as the greatest American writer, scientist, and diplomat.

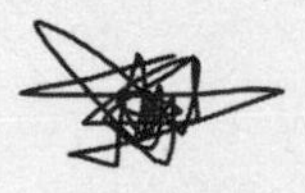

FRANKLIN'S STORY ILLUSTRATES SEVERAL different functions that idealism serves in the innovator's pursuit of her ideas. One of the most important is the powerful intrinsic motivation idealism can provide, inducing the innovator to exert exceptional effort toward solving problems even if she receives no obvious benefit from doing so. As noted previously, many of the projects in which Franklin invested considerable effort were to benefit society—he received no obvious rewards except perhaps an enhanced reputation. He donated even his technological inventions (such as Franklin stoves, lightning rods, and bifocals) to the public good instead of attempting to profit from them personally.

Although there are many books and articles on idealism as a philosophical concept, remarkably little research has been done on the role that idealism plays in human motivation. An exception is work by the psychologist Steven Reiss, who has made influential contributions to our understanding of intrinsic motivation (among other subjects). He developed a multifaceted theory of intrinsic motivation by conducting one of the first large-scale, cross-cultural empirical studies of this subject. By assessing survey responses from six thousand people from four continents, Reiss identified sixteen basic psychological needs that are deeply rooted in human nature. Every individual has these sixteen needs (or desires), but people differ in how they prioritize them. One need is idealism, which he defines as the need for social justice and the desire to help others or improve society.[23]

According to Reiss, individuals are motivated to seek a "set point," or what Aristotle called "a moderate mean," in the individual motives—that is, most people seek a moderate degree of status, a moderate degree of social contact, a moderate degree of idealism, and so on. However, people vary significantly about where each of those set points lie; some motives will be much more important to some individuals than others. For example, people who have a particularly high set point for idealism would be likely to pursue idealistic goals with greater frequency or intensity than people with a lower set point. They will, in all likelihood, expend considerable energy responding to this motive, occupying energy and time to such a level that it causes them to disregard motives that other people find more important, such as the desire to interact with one's family or the desire for tranquility or leisure. Franklin tended to neglect his family, his comfort, and even his health while pursuing his ideals. He spent long stretches of time away from his home and family, and even in his eighties, plagued with gout and kidney stones, went on numerous arduous trips on behalf of his nation.

Idealism as an intrinsic motivator is aptly illustrated by Dean Kamen's persistence in developing innovations that have social welfare benefits, even if they are unlikely to be profitable.

For example, Kamen developed a form of the Stirling engine that can generate electricity using any source of heat, such as burning methane from cow dung, and used it to run another of his inventions, the Slingshot, which can purify any liquid into clean drinking water. However, although both machines have been proven to work, Kamen has not found a commercial partner to manufacture them. As he notes, "The big companies long ago figured out—the people in the world that have no water and have no electricity have no money." Kamen adds, "If you include all the money we've spent on Stirling, and all the money we've spent on the water project, it probably is in the area of $50 million. And I'm a little company, and that's a lot of money. But I believe in it. I just believe in it. It might fail, but you've got to try. Look at the state of the world. . . . It's a mess. What if we can fix it?"[24]

Idealism also serves a role in helping innovators to maintain their focus on a long-term goal, helping them make choices among the demands competing for their attention. Such goals become an organizing structure, helping innovators to maintain a clear vision of the future and to prioritize their efforts. The goal is often more important to the individual than any personal benefit, explaining why individuals willingly sacrifice money, time, or comfort in their pursuit. For example, all of Elon Musk's seemingly disparate ventures are organized around his higher-order goals of addressing the problem of Earth's finite resources and making humans an interplanetary species. As he noted in a 2007 interview, "When I was in college and thought about what are the things that would most affect humanity, the three areas seemed to me to be the internet, transitioning to a sustainable energy economy, and space exploration. So after doing a few internet companies I basically turned to the other two elements, and decided to focus on the space exploration problem personally and fund some other folks to help solve the sustainable energy problem with Tesla and Solar City."[25] In Chapter 2 I described how Musk spent $100 million of his own funds to found SpaceX and continued to plow his own money into the company despite several spectacular rocket failures. He pursued the venture relentlessly, even when he was on the verge of bankruptcy, mired in a difficult divorce, and close to a nervous collapse. He has also resisted the urge to take SpaceX public, despite the fact that it would restore a massive amount of wealth to him personally, because the board of directors of a publicly held firm would undoubtedly force him to make changes in the company that would improve its profitability at the expense of its chances of reaching Mars. As he wrote in a letter to his SpaceX employees, "Creating the technology needed to establish life on Mars is and always has been the fundamental goal of SpaceX. If being a public company diminishes that likelihood, then we should not do so until Mars is secure."[26]

Anyone who thinks that Musk's fundamental goal is profits hasn't been paying attention. As Musk's mother puts it, "He's just determined to make things better."[27] Musk has risked his own wealth in pursuit of his goals multiple times, in ways that most profit-seeking entrepreneurs would never dream of. As Musk notes, "Most people, when they make a lot of money don't want to risk it. For me it was never about money, but solving problems for the future of humanity."[28] He explained the source of his motivation in a 2014 interview: "I'm much more inclined to say, 'How can we make things better?' And a lot of my motivation comes from me personally looking at things that don't work well and feeling a bit sad about how it would manifest in the future. And if that would result in an unhappy future, then it makes me unhappy. And so I want to fix it. That really is the motivation for me."[29]

Having lofty superordinate goals gave these innovators a drive and single-mindedness that helped them avoid getting caught up in other interesting problems. The archetypal creative person as described in many textbooks finds nearly every problem interesting and is at risk of accruing more projects and interests than can be realistically brought to fruition. Innovators such as Kamen are inordinately successful in part because of their extreme dedication to a particular cause. As Kamen put it, "I don't work on a project unless I believe that it will dramatically improve life for a bunch of people. . . . I do not want to waste any time. And if you are not working on important things, you are wasting time."[30] Kamen's work on the iBot, a unique wheelchair that would give rise to technology later used in the Segway, was motivated by his desire to positively transform the lives of the disabled. The iBot not only climbs stairs but it can also balance on two wheels and rise to bring the occupant face-to-face with others who are standing. As he explains, "People don't understand . . . when you lose the ability to walk, mobility is only a piece of what you're missing. You lose dignity, you lose respect, you lose access, because of stairs and curbs. Well, this thing will walk up and down stairs, up and down curbs, it lets you look people in the eye—it's a really big deal."[31] When people remark on the fact that he wears exactly the same clothes every day, he responds, "I always wear work clothes when I'm working. But if I'm awake, I'm working."[32] It comes as no surprise that Kamen, the rumor goes, has not taken a vacation since he was fourteen years old.

Even Franklin, who had broad talents and interests, and many opportunities to take on new roles, always returned to his focus on how he could best contribute to creating a prosperous and egalitarian nation. Notably, the innovator studied here who was least idealistic—Edison—was also noted for his *lack* of focus. As Randall Stross explains, "[B]y temperament, he tended to flit from project to project. Most were minor in ambition and were left in an incomplete state. This had been his pattern when he was working in the field of telegraphic equipment, and the phonograph's own serendipitous invention came from a tangential observation that had led away from the original project. He did not impose upon himself limits to his inventive excursions. He would strike off the main path, follow an interest, then branch off from that path, and then from that one too."[33] Stross notes that this is why Edison failed to commercialize the phonograph, one of his most important inventions.

The extreme focus of idealism also occasionally works against an innovator. Tesla's superordinate goals were to devise a mechanical means for doing away with all physical labor so that humans could spend more time in creative endeavors, and to create a global wireless communication system that he believed would end war. After all, if all people could talk to one another, he reasoned, they would be likely to work out their differences in less destructive ways. However, Tesla's projects required significant funding. Had he been more strategic in the development of his innovations, bringing his more readily commercializable inventions such as his numerous lighting systems or remote-control applications to market, revenue from these products might have helped fund his grander long-term ambitions. But "details" such as finance were distractions that Tesla could not be bothered with. Once on the scent of a meaningful step toward his superordinate goals, he was like a bloodhound and could not be deterred. An excellent example is Tesla's 1901 deal with J. P. Morgan. One of the wealthiest and most powerful financiers of the nineteenth and early twentieth centuries, Morgan was a large and imposing man, with piercing eyes and a beet-red, bulbous, lumpy nose, a problem caused by a condition known as rhinophyma. His appearance could be unsettling to people. He was also a terse and gruff man who did not suffer fools lightly and had little patience for small talk or flattery. Despite being wary of Tesla's reputation as a "visionary," a term not meant as a compliment in the early twentieth century, Morgan agreed to give Tesla $150,000 to build a ninety-foot-high tower to transmit communications across the Atlantic, and he also purchased a significant share in Tesla's lighting patents. Morgan wanted the tower to be able to report yacht races, signal incoming steamers, and send Morse code messages to England, but he also saw the more immediate commercial potential of the lighting technology. Tesla purchased a two-hundred-acre tract at a resort community known as Wardenclyffe-on-Sound in Shoreham, Long Island, to build his tower. The primarily wood-framed tower would extend 186 feet above the Earth and 120 feet below it. The design included a 55-ton steel dome-shaped top that made it look like a giant futuristic mushroom. A brick laboratory would stand at its base.

However, to achieve Tesla's true ambitions—develop global wireless communication, establish international peace, and defeat Guglielmo Marconi, who was also competing for primacy in wireless communication, albeit with lesser technology—required a much larger tower than the one required to fulfill the Morgan deal. Without consulting Morgan, Tesla abandoned the plan for the modest-sized transmitter and began designing a six-hundred-foot-tall tower that would be able to wirelessly transmit communications and energy around the world. The project that Tesla envisioned would cost $450,000—much more than what Morgan had agreed to. Eventually, Tesla believed, the tower would be at the center of a "World Telegraphy Center" that would include a model city with homes, stores, and buildings to house roughly 2,500 workers.[34] As Tesla told the newspapers, "Wardenclyffe will be the largest operation of its kind in the world."[35] Months later, Tesla went to Morgan to request more funds to complete his much larger tower. He began by pointing out that a plant with a radius of activity twice as large would cost twice as much but earn twelve times as much. When Morgan asked if Tesla had developed the lighting enterprise, Tesla responded that he had not. Then Morgan asked Tesla to verify that he had not, in fact, completed a transmitting tower and had run out of funds, which Tesla affirmed. The outraged Morgan then raised his voice to a dull roar: "Get out, Mr. Tesla!" Morgan was well-known for using expletives, so he continued the outburst with a torrent of curses.[36] The stunned inventor slipped quickly out of the office. As noted previously, Tesla would never raise enough money to complete the tower. Despite the fact that Tesla had invested hundreds of thousands of dollars in the project, it was torn down for scrap by a landlord to whom Tesla owed $19,000.

Curie understood the difficulty of pursuing science as a fervent idealist while attending to pragmatic concerns such as finances. She had little interest in material wealth and lived a moderate lifestyle. She repaid her scholarships, believing that the money should be available to others. She also gave away most of her first Nobel Prize money to friends, families, students, and research associates. She never patented the radium-isolation process so that the scientific community could advance it freely, telling Pierre that "Physicists always publish their research completely. If our discovery has a commercial future, that is an accident by which we must not profit. And radium is going to be of use in treating disease. . . . It seems to me impossible to take advantage of that."[37] She also insisted that monetary gifts be donated to the scientific institutions she was associated with rather than accepting any of it herself. She and Pierre also often refused awards and medals. As Einstein described her, "Marie Curie is, of all celebrated beings, the only one whom fame has not corrupted."[38] As she wrote in her autobiographical notes, "Humanity . . . surely needs practical men who make the best of their work for the sake of their own interests, without necessarily forgetting the general interest. But it also needs dreamers, for whom the unselfish following of a purpose is so imperative that it becomes impossible for them to devote an important part of their attention to material interest."[39]

ANOTHER POWERFUL ASPECT OF idealism is the way in which it provides a level of ego defense, helping the innovator to persevere in the face of harsh criticism that many people would find decimating. Idealistic innovators believe that the goals they are pursuing are extremely important and intrinsically honorable and valuable, so they are better able to disregard harsh judgment or failure as merely transitory burdens to be endured. Franklin's ability to withstand the Wedderburn attack, the possibility of being jailed, and slander in the press is one example. Einstein's story provides another. Einstein suffered discrimination both because his university professors did not like him (and thus did not support his efforts to get an academic job after his graduation) and because he was a Jew during a time when European society was rife with anti-Semitism. His ideas on relativity were initially ignored. However, Einstein was undeterred. He continued to write his pathbreaking articles in physics even though he did not have an academic post, and evidence eventually emerged that supported his ideas. As he wrote, "The ideals which have lighted me on my way and time after time given me new courage to face life cheerfully, have been Truth, Goodness, and Beauty. Without the sense of fellowship with men of like mind, of preoccupation with the objective, the eternally unattainable in the field of art and scientific research, life would have seemed to me empty. The ordinary objects of human endeavor—property, outward success, luxury—have always seemed to me contemptible."[40]

Jobs's intense beliefs about the importance of precise and beautiful design, reliability, and ease of use in computers led him into frequent conflict with those around him who thought that cost, compatibility with other computer systems, or other practical concerns were more important. But these intense beliefs are also what made Jobs so zealously pursue the exceptional design and intuitive user interfaces that made Apple's products remarkable and earned the company intense brand loyalty from its fans. Jobs's metaphor of the computer as a "bicycle for the mind" helps us gain insight into his vision:

> I remember reading an article when I was about twelve years old. I think it might have been *Scientific American* where they measured the efficiency of locomotion for all these species on planet earth. How many kilocalories did they expend to get from point A to point B? And the Condor 1 came in at the top of the list, surpassed everything else. And humans came in about a third of the way down the list which was not such a great showing for the crown of creation. And—but somebody there had the imagination to test the efficiency of a human riding a bicycle. A human riding a bicycle blew away the Condor, all the way off the top of the list. And it made a really big impression on me that we humans are tool builders. And that we can fashion tools that amplify these inherent abilities that we have to spectacular magnitudes. And so for me, a computer has always been a bicycle of the mind. Something that takes us far beyond our inherent abilities.[41]

He wasn't interested in complex and clunky computers that were machines for engineers; they had to be beautiful, intuitive machines for everybody. His mission was to create a computer that was no ordinary tool—it would be a revolution in how people think. As he stated, "The thing that bounded us together at Apple was the ability to make things that were going to change the world. That was very important."[42] When Steve Wozniak wanted to add extra ports to the Macintosh (like he had done with the Apple II) so that users could customize their computer with additional devices and features, Steve Jobs fought him. In Jobs's mind, extra ports were a threat to the seamlessness and reliability of the computer. When Apple CEO John Scully and others proposed licensing the Mac operating system to other manufacturers—akin to how Microsoft competed with Windows—Jobs furiously refused: other companies could not be trusted to create the kind of "insanely great" experience that the Macintosh was intended to provide.

Jobs even insisted that the factory be painted a stark white. Debi Coleman, Apple's manufacturing director, protested: "You can't paint a factory pure white. There's going to be dust and stuff all over." However, Jobs would not relent, saying that the aesthetics of the factory were important—they influence a company's sense of discipline in its engineering:

> I'd go out to the factory, and I'd put on a white glove to check for dust. I'd find it everywhere—on machines, on the tops of the racks, on the floor. And I'd ask Debi to get it cleaned. I told her I thought we should be able to eat off the floor of the factory. Well, this drove Debi up the wall. She didn't understand why. And I couldn't articulate it back then. See, I'd been very influenced by what I'd seen in Japan. Part of what I greatly admired there—and part of what we were lacking in our factory—was a sense of teamwork and discipline. If we didn't have the discipline to keep that place spotless, then we weren't going to have the discipline to keep all these machines running.[43]

When sales for the Macintosh were slower than expected, Jobs became increasingly tense and volatile, and was prone to casting blame on others around the company. Eventually Apple's board of directors pushed Scully to remove Jobs from the helm of the Macintosh division. Scully was reluctant, but Jobs forced a showdown between the two of them by telling Scully (and others) that it was Scully who should leave and that he should be made CEO. The board sided with Scully. Although they offered to keep Jobs on at the company in a research role, he stormed away from the company in a daze of fury and pain. In an interview with *Playboy*, he said, "I feel like somebody just punched me in the stomach and knocked all my wind out. I'm only 30 years old and I want to have a chance to continue creating things. I know I've got at least one more great computer in me. And Apple is not going to give me a chance to do that."[44]

Despite the sense of betrayal that he felt, and the humiliating sting of losing control of the company he had built, Jobs did not relent in his idealistic beliefs about what made computers—or any other product for that matter—great. As described in more detail in Chapter 7, he went on to found NeXT Computers with the same intense passion about what a great computer had to be. Although the company's hardware would not gain widespread adoption because of its high cost and a dearth of compatible software applications, its operating system, NeXTSTEP, was so exceptional that in 1996, Gil Amelio (by then the CEO of Apple) decided to cancel Apple's efforts to develop a next-generation operating system for the Mac and instead buy NeXT and bring Steve Jobs on as part-time adviser. Jobs would soon be reinstated as CEO of Apple, and he led the company to one of the most remarkable comebacks of all time.

Jobs recognized the key role that passion had played in his success: "I'm convinced that about half of what separates the successful entrepreneurs from the non-successful ones is pure perseverance. . . . Unless you have a lot of passion about this, you're not going to survive. You're going to give it up. So you've got to have an idea, or a problem or a wrong you want to right that you're passionate about; otherwise you're not going to have the perseverance to stick it through."[45]

Curie, Einstein, Franklin, Jobs, Musk, and Tesla all endured very difficult periods of public failure, ridicule, or discrimination. However, while each had moments of self-doubt, they were also so focused on a higher purpose that they measured their own success by a completely different metric than public affirmation. Thus, they pressed onward.

An innovator's idealistic goals can arise from a number of foundations such as spiritualism or nationalism. For example, Franklin's idealism was based in a sense of duty and virtue that had its origins in his Puritan upbringing but evolved with his increasingly sophisticated philosophical reasoning. Jobs's intense engagement with Zen Buddhism influenced his diet, his living environment, his sense of purpose, and his beliefs about product design. Zen teachings emphasized intense focus, intuition, and the filtering out of distractions. Jobs applied this to product design by insisting that products be simple, intuitive, and without unnecessary components. As Daniel Kottke, Jobs's college friend and one of the first employees at Apple noted, "Steve is very much Zen. . . . It was a deep influence. You see it in his whole approach of stark, minimalist aesthetics, intense focus."[46]

Curie's story, discussed more completely in Chapter 6, provides an apt example of idealism rooted, in part, in nationalism. Marie Curie was born during a period in which Poland was brutally suppressed by Tsarist Russia. The Tsar's agents attempted to erase Poland's heritage—its literature, language, culture, and even history. To save the Polish identity, Polish philosophers began arguing for a movement known as "Polish positivism," whereby Poland's identity would be preserved through the contribution of Poles to science, technology, and economic progress. Education was thus the key to Polish patriotism. Furthermore, Polish positivism emphasized equality among all members of society and argued strongly for increased access to education for women, Jews, peasants, and others. As Eliza Orzeszkowa, a famous Polish positivist, wrote, "[A] woman possesses the same rights as a man . . . to learning and knowledge . . . on the basis of her humanity."[47] The idealism at the heart of Polish positivism played a very significant role in what Curie would become.

Curie's family became passionately invested in self-education and in secretly educating others to preserve Polish nationalism and culture. The commonly held view at the time was that women were neither physically nor mentally suited for work outside the home. However, young female Poles inspired by Polish positivism began to proudly challenge the notion that women belonged only in the home: higher education was their right—their duty, in fact. It was Curie's intense interest in Polish positivism and social change that led her to become involved in the "Flying University," a secret, mobile academy that delivered a university curriculum to Polish women. She became heavily invested in educating herself and others, and that ultimately inspired her to overcome incredible odds to go to Paris for higher education. Much later in her career she would write, "I still believe that the [positivist] ideas which inspired us then are the only way to real social progress. You cannot hope to build a better world without improving the individuals."[48]

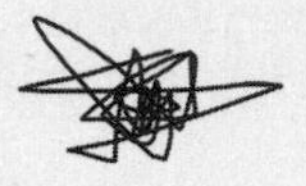

IDEALISM IS SIMULTANEOUSLY VERY fulfilling and very costly. On the one hand, idealists experience a sense of deep satisfaction and connection to something larger than themselves by holding and pursuing their ideals. On the other hand, the pursuit of ideals also often requires them to make sacrifices in other important areas of their lives. Many of the breakthrough innovators studied here kept extremely long hours, getting little sleep and forfeiting time with friends and family. Curie was known to work herself to exhaustion, frequently fainting at her laboratory bench and ultimately dying from radiation poisoning. Einstein spoke at the memorial given for her at the Roerich Museum: "Her strength, her purity of will, her austerity toward herself, her objectivity, her incorruptible judgment—all these were of a kind seldom found in a single individual. . . . Once she had recognized a certain way as a right one, she pursued it without compromise and with extreme tenacity."[49]

In her tenacity and refusal to compromise, she also turned over nearly all caregiving responsibilities for her children to her father-in-law. In the biography that Marie's daughter Eve would write after her mother's death, Eve expresses great admiration and respect for her mother. However, there are also overtones of sadness and longing—undeniable signs of the pain and sense of loss she felt by not having more of her mother. For example, in describing her grandfather, who took on a large share of the raising of Eve and her sister Irène, Eve wrote the following: "Without the blue-eyed old man their childhood would have been stifled in mourning. He was their playmate and master far more than their mother, who was ever away from home—always kept at that laboratory of which the name was endlessly rumbling in their ears."[50] As she continues,

> The struggle against sorrow, active in Irène, had little success in my case: In spite of the help my mother tried to give me, my young years were not happy ones. . . . It is not without apprehension that I have striven to grasp the principles that inspired Marie Curie in her first contacts with us. I fear that they suggest only a dry and methodical being, stifled by prejudice. The reality is different. The creature who wanted us to be invulnerable was herself too tender, too delicate, too much gifted for suffering. She, who had voluntarily accustomed us to be undemonstrative, would no doubt have wished, without confessing it, to have us embrace and cajole her more. She, who wanted us to be insensitive, shriveled with grief at the least sign of indifference.[51]

Self-denial is another pervasive theme. Jobs held to an extremely restrictive diet (often fruitarian) in pursuit of his ideals during many periods of his life. Both Franklin and Einstein strived to adhere to a vegetarian diet at various points in their lives to align more closely with their moral principles, although both struggled with such adherence because of the lack of support for vegetarianism at that time. As Einstein noted in a letter to Hermann Huth in 1930, "Although I have been prevented by outward circumstances from observing a strictly vegetarian diet, I have long been an adherent to the cause in principle. Besides agreeing with the aims of vegetarianism for aesthetic and moral reasons, it is my view that a vegetarian manner of living by its purely physical effect on the human temperament would most beneficially influence the lot of mankind."[52]

All of this raises an important question: do we want to nurture idealism in ourselves and others? Idealism played an important role in the achievement of great things by these innovators, but it should also be clear that idealism is not uniformly positive. Many of these individuals led difficult lives and imposed difficult lives on those around them because of their intense focus on an ideal. It is also important to note that idealism poses yet another risk not illustrated by the innovators here—the risk that the superordinate goal pursued by the individual leads to actions that most of us would consider ignoble or even evil. Many of the most atrocious acts of history were perpetrated by people who sincerely believed they were acting on a moral ideal. Nationalism has inspired many instances of war, terrorism, and even genocide. Religious differences have been used to justify repression, persecution, and even massacre throughout the ages. In fact, historical evidence suggests that holy wars can be the most ruthless and bloodiest of them all.[53] "Ordinary wars" (in the words of Roy Baumeister, who has written extensively on the causes of evil) often have pragmatic concerns—a city that is captured is more economically valuable, for example, if its inhabitants continue to live and work—whereas in a holy war such pragmatism may be dismissed in pursuit of a purer ideal. Adolf Hitler's racially motivated ideology led to the murder of at least 5.5 million Jews and millions of others he deemed *Untermenschen* ("subhumans"). The Khmer Rouge's communist ideals and a belief in the superiority of an agrarian society led to the Cambodian genocide, whose death toll has been estimated in the vicinity of two to three million.[54] It should thus be clear that idealism is very powerful, but like many powerful things, it can be used for both good and evil. In fact, good and evil, many would argue, are in the eye of the beholder. Idealism, if nurtured, must be nurtured with great care.

Dean Kamen with the DEKA prosthetic arm, 2009. *Photograph by Connor Gleason.*

Albert Einstein in his office at University of Berlin, 1920.

Photograph originally appeared in Scientific Monthly, *photographer unknown.*

Albert Einstein, 1921.

Photograph by F. Schmutzer.

Albert Einstein and his second wife, Elsa, 1921.

Photograph by Underwood and Underwood.

Elon Musk at unveiling of Dragon v2 inside SpaceX, 2014.

Photograph by Dimitri Gerondakis.

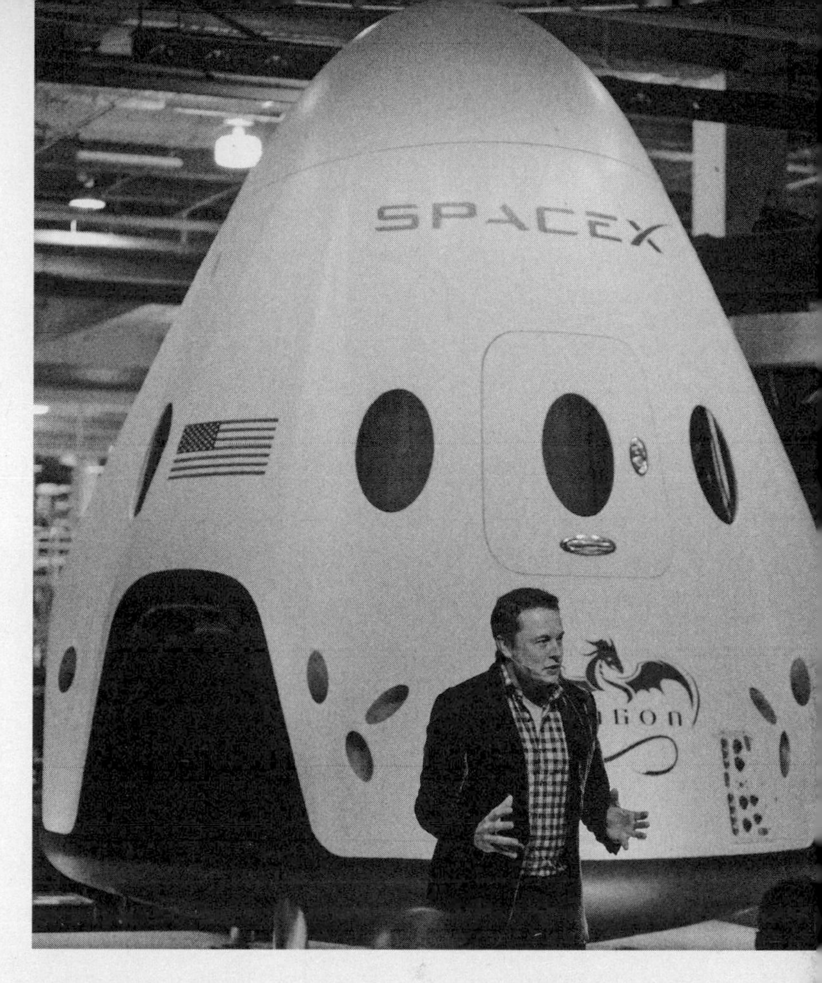

Elon Musk with Model S at the Fremont Tesla factory, 2011.

Photograph by Maurizio Pesce.

Nikola Tesla retouched photo, circa 1893.

Photograph by Napoleon Sarony.

Nikola Tesla, double exposure photo in his Colorado Springs laboratory, 1889.

Photograph by Dickenseon V. Ailey.

Marie Curie, 1898.

Photograph by Underwood and Underwood.

Marie Curie in mobile X-ray unit, 1915. *Photographer unknown.*

Thomas Edison, 1922.

Photograph by Louis Bachrach, restored by Michel Vuijsteke.

Thomas Edison and phonograph, 1877.

Photograph by Levin C. Handy.

Steve Jobs, 1984. *Photograph by Norman Seeff.*

Steve Jobs with Bono at unveiling of new iPod, 2004.
Photograph by Paul Akuma.

Steve Jobs with iPhone, 2010. *Photograph by Matthew Yohe.*

5

"Work made the Earth a paradise for me."

Driven to Work

Whereas idealism helped fuel the vigorous effort and persistence of breakthrough innovators such as Benjamin Franklin, Nikola Tesla, Elon Musk, and Marie Curie, there were no outward signs that Thomas Edison was pursuing some idealistic superordinate goal. Once when asked "What is life?" by a newspaper reporter, Edison responded, "My mind is not of a speculative order. It is essentially practical, and when I am making an experiment I think only of getting something useful, of making electricity perform work. I don't soar. I keep down pretty close to the earth. Of course, there are problems in life I can't help thinking about, but I don't try to study them out. It is necessary that they should be studied, and men fitted for that work are doing it. I am not fitted for it."[1] As biographer Randall Stross notes, Edison did not "see his work as a noble enterprise in service of humanity"; rather, his point of view was "unabashedly commercial."[2]

Although Edison was not driven by idealistic goals, he *was* driven—in fact, he was known for working so hard that those around him could barely fathom it. For example, one of Edison's assistants at the laboratory, Francis Upton (whom Edison affectionately nicknamed "Culture" because of his introspective nature and talent at playing the piano), once noted, "I have often felt that Mr. Edison never could comprehend the limitations of the strength of other men, as his own physical and mental strength have always seemed to be without limit."[3] Rather than idealism, Edison's vigorous effort and persistence were fueled by different motivators: a very high need for achievement and a pleasure derived from the process of work itself (or what Mihaly Csikzentmihalyi would call "flow," as I'll discuss in greater detail later in the chapter). Edison loved to work hard. He hammered away at problems until they bent to his will. He was relentless, and he enjoyed the challenge of a tough problem because it was all the more satisfying when it eventually succumbed to his effort.

Thomas Alva Edison (known as "Al" as a child) was born on February 11, 1847, in Milan, Ohio. His mother, Nancy, was an attractive and highly educated woman who had taught high school before marrying. His father, Samuel, was an innkeeper by trade in Canada, but after supporting a failed uprising against the Ontario provincial government, he had to flee to the United States, arriving in the canal town of Milan two years before Thomas was born. Known for having a mercurial and restless nature, Samuel dabbled in wood shingle manufacturing, land speculation, and truck farming. He prospered as regional trade grew and then lost nearly everything when railroads took away most of the canal trade.[4] He moved the family to Port Huron, Michigan, in 1854, where he earned a living lumbering, investing in land, and carpentry.

Thomas Edison was the youngest of seven children in his family, although only three of his siblings survived beyond age six. Edison was considered a fragile child. He was often sick, and he had an "abnormally large though well-shaped head"[5] that prompted doctors to fear that he might have some type of problem with his brain. Because of his presumed delicacy, he was not initially sent to school, and when at age seven he was permitted to attend grammar school, he was hyperactive and highly distractible. One day Edison heard his teacher refer to him as "addled" (an expression meaning that he was incapable of thinking clearly), and he burst into tears. When his mother learned what had happened, she marched indignantly to the school and informed the teacher that her son "had more brains than he himself."[6] She promptly took him out of school, ending his grand total of three months of formal education. Loving, ambitious, and highly capable, she began homeschooling him.[7]

Nancy Edison avoided the authoritarian style and rote memorization used at the grammar school and instead made an effort to engage her son's interest by exposing him to great books. Observing his keen interest in physical phenomena, she brought him R. G. Parker's *School of Natural Philosophy,* which carefully explained how to perform chemistry experiments at home. Edison delighted in this book, later recalling that it made learning fun and that he had performed every experiment in the book. His father also encouraged him to read the classics and rewarded the young boy ten cents for each that he completed. Edison became a voracious reader, and by the age of twelve, with his mother's help, he had read Gibbon's *Decline and Fall of the Roman Empire,* Hume's *History of England,* Sears's *History of the World,* Burton's *Anatomy of Melancholy,* and the *Dictionary of Sciences.*[8] He also had an extraordinarily retentive memory and could remember the exact page and position of facts or passages he had found interesting. He asked questions incessantly about how things worked, wearing his father down to exhaustion. Although some attributed his multitude of questions to a dullness of intelligence, his mother knew this was not the case. He famously stated later, "My mother was the making of me. She was so true, so sure of me; and I felt I had something to live for, someone I must not disappoint."[9]

Edison became obsessed with chemistry. Spurning the play that other boys his age engaged in, Edison spent all of his free time in a laboratory he had set up in the cellar of his parents' home. He would spend what little pocket money he had on chemicals (he had at least two hundred small bottles lined up on the shelves of his laboratory) and conducted experiments that replicated findings he had read about in books. It was to finance his purchases of chemicals (and obtain access to fresh reading) that Edison, at the age of twelve, became a newsboy. He persuaded his mother to let him take a job selling newspapers and candy on the Grand Trunk Railway train between Port Huron and Detroit.

Edison found his entrepreneurial spirit very early in life. He quickly realized that he could buy produce at a low price in Detroit and resell it for a profit in Port Huron. So at the age of twelve, he opened two stores—a newsstand and a produce stand—and even hired two boys to work for him. By fifteen he was publishing his own newspaper, the *Weekly Herald*, which he printed in the baggage car of the train during its sixty-three-mile journey from Port Huron to Detroit, using a small printing press that had formerly been used to print hotel bills. He also began conducting his own chemistry experiments in the baggage car. One day a stick of phosphorous fell and started a fire on the train, and Edison, his newspaper, and his chemistry lab were all forcibly thrown from the train by the enraged conductor.[10]

One day in the summer of 1862, while the train was stopped at the Mount Clemens platform, Edison noticed that the station agent's three-year-old son was playing on the tracks in the path of an oncoming freight train. Edison made a running dive for the child and scooped him up just in time. It was such a close call, in fact, that Edison's heel was struck by the train, and both Edison and the toddler suffered cuts on their faces and hands from the gravel ballast on which they fell. The station agent, in his gratitude, offered to teach Edison Morse code, which soon enabled Edison to become a telegraph operator at the Western Union Office—all before he turned sixteen.

In the years that followed, Edison worked at several telegraph posts, and in his free time he tinkered with telegraph equipment and similar electrical projects. In 1869, at the age of twenty-two, he was awarded his first patent, for an electronic vote recorder that would speed up the voting process in state legislatures.[11] Edison's device would enable legislators to vote by flipping a switch that would transmit information by electric current to a main recorder. After the voting was complete, a clerk could feed a piece of chemically treated paper through the machine that would "print" the votes for all to see.[12] Being awarded a patent must have been a thrill for the young Edison, who would apply for (and be granted) patents at a frenetic pace throughout his life, garnering 1,093 in the United States and more than 1,200 internationally. His record would stand until 2003, when it was surpassed by Shunpei Yamazaki of Japan, who in turn, was passed in 2008 by Kia Silverbrook of Australia.

The vote recorder would not turn out to be a commercial success—as it turns out, faster vote counting was not the kind of breakthrough in efficiency that politicians were looking for because it eliminated the time for the politicking needed to change votes. However, the invention and its patent marked an important turning point for Edison. He loved to tinker and experiment, and he knew that if done well, inventing might afford him the luxury of being independent—an extremely attractive option for the individualistic young man. Within the year he had quit his job as a telegraph operator and became a full-time inventor. His primary goal at that time was to have his own shop and make enough money to work on his projects autonomously. Over the next few years he hopped from one venture to the next, moving from Boston to New York City to Newark, each time finding a partner who would fund him to develop and manufacture small lots of completed telegraph instruments. In 1870 he founded American Telegraph Works, and he proudly wrote his parents to joke that he had become a "Bloated Eastern Manufacturer."[13]

The success of his early ventures waxed and waned, and when the twenty-four-year-old Edison went prematurely gray, he claimed it was from the long working hours and the stress of having to pay the bills. His lifelong habit of losing himself in his work and staying at the laboratory late into the night was already apparent. For example, in 1871 he married sixteen-year-old Mary Stilwell (a worker at his company), and on the day of his wedding a friend visited his laboratory to find him dozing at his desk. When his friend woke him and told him it was past midnight, Edison replied, "By George. I must go home, then. I was married today."[14] Although Edison often left Mary alone days at a time while he worked in the laboratory, she did not openly complain about it. In fact, she recounted about herself (in the third person), "[S]he never feels neglected when her husband shuts himself up at Menlo Park for the purpose of making experiments or for invention, and she just waits until he has emerged from his seclusion, only taking pains to see that he has his meals properly."[15]

Edison's business during the 1870s primarily developed telegraph systems that provided information to businessmen in the financial sector. While the firm was sometimes profitable, cash flow was vulnerable to the volatility of an economy that experienced frequent panics. For example, the panic of 1873 nearly wiped Edison out and also forced him to sell his house at a loss. Edison thus began considering ways to diversify and in particular to tap the much larger consumer markets. In 1874 he and his partner Joseph Murray invented a device for inducing electric shocks that they called the Inductorium. Advertisements exhorted that the device should be in every home "as a specific cure for rheumatism, and as an inexhaustible fount of amusement."[16] The device was surprisingly successful and whetted Edison's appetite for developing more products that could be marketed to mass-market consumers.

Edison preferred to be deeply involved in developing rather than manufacturing products and to work without a partner. Thus, in 1876 he moved to a site in rural New Jersey about thirty miles from New York called Menlo Park, where he could build a much larger laboratory at a more reasonable cost. Over the next couple of years Edison and his assistants would develop a variety of electronic products—an electric drill, an electric sheep-shearing device, some electronic toys—that were sold through American

Novelty Company, a separate firm that Edison had established. In that same year, Alexander Graham Bell, a professor of vocal physiology at Boston University, obtained a patent for an "apparatus for transmitting vocal or other sounds telegraphically."[17] This was only a short-range telephone, but it spurred Edison and another electrical engineer of the day, Elisha Gray, to race to introduce better telephones that were capable of long-distance voice communication.

The earliest sound transmission devices did not convey speech clearly and were better suited to transmitting music. Bell, Edison, and Gray thus all held concerts to demonstrate to the public that their devices could transmit recognizable music from a location miles away. As the competition heated up, it became the subject of quite a bit of attention in the newspapers. For example, an 1877 article in the *Newark Daily Advertiser* reported that "Mr. Edison has so often been scoffed at, that it has no other effect upon him than to stimulate him to increased study and labor," and, adding a dose of humor, it noted that if Edison succeeded in creating a device that would transmit voice, "what an instrument of torture it would be in the hands and at the mouth of a distant and irate mother in law."[18] The *New York Times* was more critical, noting that "This evening Prof. Edison gave a public rehearsal of his telephone, which consists of a musical instrument not nearly as loud in tone as that of Prof. Gray of Chicago. . . . "[19] Alexander Graham Bell won the race and was ultimately awarded the most important patents. However, Edison created a carbon transmitter that greatly enhanced a telephone's functionality. Furthermore, Edison's work on capturing and relaying sound waves using a diaphragm led to an invention where his primacy could not be disputed: the phonograph.

Edison expected his assistants to work the same long hours that he worked, and this often meant staying through the night at the laboratory. He had established a tradition of ordering a midnight dinner for the workers at the laboratory on such occasions, and it was one of the only times when he permitted himself to relax. The men would enjoy the feast, banter, and tell jokes until Edison rose and signaled it was time to go back to work. During one of these late nights, on July 18, 1877, Edison and his assistants had been trying out a range of materials to use as diaphragms that would vibrate when receiving sound waves. After the midnight dinner had been consumed but not yet cleared, Edison was toying with one of the diaphragms, speaking in one side and feeling the vibrations on the other. He casually noted to Charles Batchelor, one of his most valued assistants, "Batch, if we had a point on this we could make a record on some material which we could afterwards pull under the point, and it would give us the speech back."[20] It was sheer genius. Instantly the men jumped up to test it. Within the hour, they had demonstrated that Edison was correct. As Edison would later describe it,

> From my experiments on the telephone I knew of the power of a diaphragm to take up sound vibrations. . . . I reached the conclusion that if I could record the movements of the diaphragm properly, I could cause such record to reproduce the original movements imparted to the diaphragm by the voice, and thus succeed in recording and reproducing the human voice. Instead of using a disk, I designed a little machine using a cylinder provided with grooves around the surface. Over this was to be placed tinfoil, which easily received and recorded the movements of the diaphragm. A sketch was made, and the piece-work price, $18, was marked on the sketch. . . . The workman who got the sketch was John Kruesi. I didn't have much faith that it would work, expecting that I might possibly hear a word or so that would give hope of a future for the idea. Kruesi, when he had nearly finished it, asked what it was for. I told him I was going to record talking, and then have the machine talk back. He thought it was absurd. However, it was finished, the foil was put on; I shouted "Mary had a little lamb," etc. I adjusted the reproducer, and the machine reproduced it

> perfectly. I was never so taken aback in my life. Everybody was astonished. I was always afraid of things that worked the first time. Long experience proved that there were great drawbacks found generally before they could be got commercial; but here was something there was no doubt of.[21]

When the creation of the phonograph was described in the October–December 1877 edition of *Scientific American,* Edison suddenly became famous. The article, titled simply "The Talking Phonograph," gives a detailed technical explanation of how the phonograph worked and then provides the following commentary:

> No matter how familiar a person may be with modern machinery and its wonderful performances, or how clear in his mind the principle underlying this strange device may be, it is impossible to listen to the mechanical speech without his experiencing the idea that his senses are deceiving him. We have heard other talking machines. The Faber apparatus for example is a large affair as big as a parlor organ. It has a key board, rubber larynx and lips, and an immense amount of ingenious mechanism which combines to produce something like articulation in a single monotonous organ note. But here is a little affair of a few pieces of metal, set up roughly on an iron stand about a foot square, that talks in such a way, that, even if in its present imperfect form many words are not clearly distinguishable, there can be no doubt but that the inflections are those of nothing else than the human voice.[22]

At the time it was incomprehensible that a device could record the human voice and play it back in different places and times. People noted with awe that the device would enable one to hear the voices of the dead (presuming their voices were captured before death!). Reporters and visitors began to stream to the Menlo Park laboratory, eager to see the "wizard" and his inventions. The *New*

York Sun dubbed him the "Napoleon of Invention." Commercial applications of the phonograph seemed endless, and Edison helped to whip excitement over the product into a frenzy by speculating on its many potential uses: it could be used to record songs by famous singers, executives could dictate letters, books could be read into it and played back, or it could be mounted into the wall of politicians' office to record political secrets. He also often alluded to other inventions that were near completion—a talking foghorn and a hearing aid—stoking the public's curiosity and enthusiasm.

Strangely, however, whereas Edison had been comfortable releasing telegraph inventions that were not quite finished and letting the "sharps" (the vernacular for men in suits at the time) finish the fine tuning, he was reluctant to release the phonograph until he thought it was perfected. The public would just have to wait. They would wait for a long time, in the end, because Edison was prone to getting distracted by other projects and by all the attention of well-meaning visitors to the laboratory. Although he was repeatedly extolled to bring the phonograph to market, Edison's fierce independence, evident even as a child when he would "involuntarily challenge" everything he read and insist on testing its veracity himself, meant that it was nearly impossible for others to rush him or to influence the direction of his efforts. As Randall Stross notes in a compelling biography of Edison, "Edison was not receptive to guidance from others, whether its nature was technical, strategic, or business."[23] Like most of the innovators studied here, Edison was stubborn, individualistic, and would not often take direction from others. Pressing him would only make him more defiant.

Partially deaf since his youth (usually attributed to a bout of scarlet fever), Edison refrained from speaking publicly. Social situations could make him feel awkward, although he claimed that deafness was an advantage that gave him uninterrupted time to "think out my problems."[24] Edison fueled the enthusiasm of the public by dangling out ever-more-exciting promises of invention but also found the public's demands to be a burden. There is a great paradox in the fact that Edison masterfully created his own celebrity by playing the part of the "wizard" yet by all appearances did not enjoy the attention. At a reception to show off the phonograph to the National Academy of Sciences he was described as "shy and shrinking," and he admitted to a reporter that he did not like crowds and had not enjoyed the academy president's welcome because he had not heard a word that was said.[25]

Edison also retreated almost completely from domestic life with his wife and children, spending most of his time in the laboratory. According to his assistant Edward Johnson, from 1868 to 1878 Edison averaged eighteen hours a day at his desk and often did not go home for days at a time. His chief assistant, Charles Batchelor, added that when working on something that interested him, "Edison hardly stops to eat even if they send his meals to him."[26] As described by another of his assistants, Mr. Jehl, at the Menlo Park laboratory, "It often happened that when Edison had been working up to three or four o'clock in the morning, he would lie down on one of the laboratory tables, and with nothing but a couple of books for a pillow, would fall into a sound sleep. He said it did him more good than being in a soft bed, which spoils a man."[27] Another worker at the lab, Mr. Upton, pointed out that "He could work continuously as long as he wished, and had sleep at his command. His sleep was always instant, profound, and restful. He has told me that he never dreamed."[28] Working long hours and sleeping on a laboratory table were lifelong habits for Edison.

In late 1878 the project that interested Edison was not completing a phonograph machine that could be sold to the mass market but instead perfecting an incandescent light bulb that could burn for more than the few minutes that platinum filaments would burn. Finding a filament that would enable a bulb to burn for many hours proved challenging, but Edison was like a bloodhound on a trail. Many details of this search are provided in a comprehensive document that is Edison's only authorized biography, aided substantially by Edison's own dictation. The authors of this work, Frank Lewis Dyer, a patent lawyer and Edison's personal attorney, and Thomas Commerford Martin, an electrical engineer who served as editor of *Electrical World,* wrote that "Continuing these experiments with most fervent zeal, taking no account of the passage of time, with an utter disregard for meals, and but scanty hours of sleep reluctantly at odd periods of the day or night, Edison kept his laboratory going without cessation."[29] By late 1879, he had concluded that the answer would lie in a carbon filament, and he began carbonizing anything he could lay his hands on: tissue paper, cardboard, paper saturated with tar, cotton thread, fishing line, lamp wick, twine, celluloid, boxwood, coconut hair, spruce, hickory, baywood, cedar, maple, rosewood, punk, cork, flax, grasses, canes, and more.

By 1880, he had finally demonstrated a long-lasting incandescent bulb using a carbon filament that produced the soft light needed for indoor use (arc lights, which had already been established, shone too brightly for use indoors), for which he was granted US patent 223,898.[30] The patent describes any number of substances that may be used for the carbon filament, but shortly after the patent was granted, Edison and his team discovered that a particular type of bamboo filament enabled the bulb to burn for 1,200 hours. Edison described this period to Dyer and Martin for the 1910 biography:

> I speak without exaggeration when I say that I have constructed three thousand different theories in connection with the electric light, each one of them reasonable and apparently to be true. Yet only in two cases did my experiments prove the truth of my theory. My chief difficulty, as perhaps you know, was in constructing the carbon filament, the incandescence of which is the source of the light. Every quarter of the globe was ransacked by my agents, and all sorts of the queerest materials were used, until finally the shred of bamboo now utilized was settled upon. Even now . . . , I am still at work nearly every day

> on the lamp, and quite lately I have devised a method of supplying sufficient current to fifteen lamps with one horse-power. Formerly ten lamps per horse-power was the extreme limit.[31]

At just thirty-three years old, Edison had revolutionized lighting and was now the most famous inventor in all the world. With the bulb technology established, Edison turned to creating a centralized power plant in Manhattan. Lighting, after all, could be used only by people with electricity, and the race was now on to determine supremacy in electrification. By the time Edison's company began placing electrical lines underground based on direct current, Charles Brush, another Ohio-born inventor, already had a head start installing lines based on alternating current (the technology invented by Nikola Tesla) that powered the arc lighting systems he was providing to several parts of the city. Although Edison was offered many opportunities to build isolated lighting systems for particular businesses that would operate their own onsite power plants, he turned most of them down and instead focused on developing a centralized system that could power an entire city.

Edison successfully began lighting districts of Manhattan by 1882, but growth of the installations inside and beyond the city was slower than he had expected, and the thirty-five-year-old "Wizard of Menlo Park" began to get bored and impatient. Although he could not bring himself to relinquish managerial control over Edison Electric, he began searching for some new intellectual challenge to stimulate him. Friends encouraged him to return to completing the phonograph, but Edison did not consider the phonograph to be either important or exciting. It was not until the threat of competition emerged—in the form of a company called American Graphophone that marketed a product invented by his rival Alexander Graham Bell—that Edison was inspired to return to the phonograph.

Edison's competitive nature was brought out in an interview with the *New York Tribune:* "I don't care so much for a fortune as I do for getting ahead of the other fellows."[32] The idea that Bell would steal the limelight for the phonograph—an invention he had referred to as "his baby"—was infuriating. Unfortunately, Edison's deafness meant that he did not see the phonograph from the perspective of a typical consumer. Edison was convinced that the phonograph's best purpose was for recording the human voice (as in recording speeches or as a dictation machine for businesses); he could not imagine the mass appeal of music played for entertainment purposes. This is understandable when one considers his impairment. After all, as Edison's daughter Madeleine noted, Edison often had to resort to putting his teeth on a piano—literally biting it—in order to hear the music by having it vibrate through his skull bones![33] (Phonographs currently displayed in the Edison Museum in Fort Myers, Florida, show Edison's teeth marks.) Unfortunately, the machine's ability to play back intelligible speech was limited, and most of the early devices were scrapped. It would be several years until Edison introduced his "improved" phonograph and built manufacturing facilities next to his new laboratory (now in Orange, New Jersey) to produce both phonographs and recorded cylinders.[34]

Edison's personal life also took an unexpected turn. Mary, now mother of Edison's three children, was having unexplained health problems: constant headaches, panic attacks, and fatigue. She died in 1884 at the age of twenty-nine. Her exact cause of death is unknown, but her death certificate states that she died from "congestion of the brain," a description often given by doctors of the time for morphine overdose (morphine was readily available without prescription and was widely taken for a range of ailments). Edison was distraught and floundered briefly, but by the summer of 1885 he had become infatuated with nineteen-year-old Mina Miller, and they were married the next year. Unlike Mary, Mina came from a wealthy family and was educated and cultured. Whereas Mary likely suffered from being left alone so often by Edison, Mina excelled in her role of managing Edison's life (she even referred to herself as the "home executive") and was also busy serving leadership roles with the Chautauqua Association and the Daughters of the Revolution. Edison adored Mina, and she brought great comfort to his life, which he would need in the hard years to come.

By this time the "current wars," a public battle between supporters of AC versus DC, were well under way. Alternating current had the advantage of being capable of transmitting much larger amounts of power greater distances, making it much more economical. Direct current had the advantage of being perceived as safer—an attribute that Edison vigorously reinforced by comparing the length of time it took to electrocute dogs with AC versus DC. Ultimately, however, economy won out: AC was the overwhelming winner. Thus, in 1890 Edison was willing to sell his stake in the electric light business and his various manufacturing businesses to a group of investors led by Henry Villard, who formed the Edison General Electric Company. Edison, who received shares worth $3.5 million, was eager to have more ready access to cash and to focus more on his work in the laboratory, which he assumed would continue to be funded by Edison General Electric. He quickly sold 90 percent of his shares. Much to his dismay, however, the new company, now free from Edison's controlling hand, slashed the budget it would pay to the laboratory and demanded that Edison's laboratory develop an alternating-current system. J. P. Morgan also arranged for the company to be merged with longtime competitor Thomson-Houston, and its executives filled out nearly all of the new company's leadership positions. The new company also shed Edison's name—in 1892 it became General Electric Company.

Edison was shocked. The "sharps" had maneuvered him right out of his central role in the industry, much as they would later do to Nikola Tesla. In an unusual moment of personal candor and humility, he admitted "I am not business man enough to spend time" in the power and lighting business.[35]

However, letting go of lighting allowed Edison to do what he did best: throw himself completely into something entirely new.

He was convinced that he had conceived of a novel way to extract iron from ore by magnets. New York, New Jersey, and Pennsylvania had large repositories of low-grade iron ore, but mining it by conventional means was too expensive to attract investors. Edison believed that he could develop a system of magnetic concentration that would make mining low-grade ore much easier and thus economically competitive. Determined that this would be "so much bigger than anything I've ever done before,"[36] he committed himself fully to his new venture. Rather than enjoy the comfortable life that the proceeds from his sale of the electric company would have afforded, Edison now spent most of his time in stark conditions at the Ogden mine he had purchased in northern New Jersey. He couldn't ask Mina to move up to the mine, so instead he would take the train up on Monday mornings and return on the last train on Saturday nights. For five years Edison continued in this way, working in freezing winters, scorching summers, and air that was heavy with dust. Despite such hard conditions, Edison's letters to his wife paint the picture of a man who was having fun. Edison enjoyed hard work, and even as his money ran out and his colleagues became dejected, Edison thrived with the pleasure of novel technical problems to solve. The mining venture was a failure, and soon Edison had spent all of the money he had made in the sale of his lighting business. When told his shares in General Electric would have been worth $4 million if he had kept them (over $108 million in 2017 dollars), he paused and then responded, "Well, it's all gone, but we had a good time spending it."[37]

While Edison was busy at the mine, W. K. L. Dickson was working on a kinetoscope—the precursor to modern movie projection—back at Edison's laboratory. As with the phonograph, Edison did not see the enormous potential value of the kinetoscope as an entertainment device and did little to advance or promote the product. However, others did see its potential, and soon inventors were developing machines that would enable viewers to watch short films by peering into a tiny box. Luckily for Edison, when

C. Francis Jenkins and Thomas Armat invented a machine that would enable projecting films onto a large screen, the distributors that Armat approached (Raff & Gammon, which distributed Edison's kinetoscope) insisted that it would be very beneficial to convince Edison to lend his name to the venture. Edison agreed, and the "Vitascope" was widely attributed to Edison's genius, even though he contributed almost nothing to its creation. Edison's company went on to develop numerous improvements to motion picture projectors and to produce a large number of films until Edison left the business in 1918.

In 1900, after having conceded defeat in the mining operation and shutting down the ore-milling plant, Edison decided to set about inventing a better storage battery. Automobiles had recently been introduced, and most were steam powered or electric. However, the lead-acid batteries used by electric cars were very heavy and short lived because the acid inside them corroded the metalwork. Edison believed it would be possible to develop batteries that were lighter, less expensive, and powerful enough to be the foundation of a successful electric car. As he noted to a friend, R. H. Beach of General Electric, "Beach, I don't think Nature would be so unkind as to withhold the secret of a GOOD storage battery if a real earnest hunt for it is made. I'm going to hunt."[38] Edison set about searching for a better battery design with characteristic zeal and multitudes of experiments. As Edison's friend and associate Walter S. Mallory recounted,

> About 7 or 7:30 A.M. he would go down to the laboratory and experiment, only stopping for a short time at noon to eat a lunch sent down from the house. About 6 o'clock the carriage would call to take him to dinner, from which he would return by 7:30 or 8 o'clock to resume work. The carriage came again at midnight to take him home, but frequently had to wait until 2 or 3 o'clock, and sometimes return without him, as he had decided to continue all night. This had been going on more than

> five months, seven days a week, when I was called down to the laboratory to see him. I found him at a bench about three feet wide and twelve feet long, on which there were hundreds of little test cells that had been made up by his corps of chemists and experimenters. I then learned that he had thus made over nine thousand experiments in trying to devise this new type of storage battery, but had not produced a single thing that promised to solve the question. In view of this immense amount of thought and labor, my sympathy got the better of my judgment, and I said: "Isn't it a shame that with the tremendous amount of work you have done you haven't been able to get any results?" Edison turned on me like a flash, and with a smile replied: "Results! Why, man, I have gotten lots of results! I know several thousand things that won't work!"[39]

Edison would never succeed in developing a reliable and economical battery for automobiles, despite being given several loans from Henry Ford, who saw Edison as a hero and a close friend. Ford famously wrote in his autobiography that Edison was "the world's worst businessman" and that he "knows almost nothing of business," although it is clear that Ford's respect and affection for Edison never wavered.[40] Most of Edison's businesses struggled, and other people would profit much more from his inventions than he did himself (as happened also to Tesla), but in general he expressed little remorse or discouragement about unprofitable projects. The work itself was his primary joy. "I never intend to retire," he stated. "Work made the Earth a paradise for me."[41] Furthermore, despite the spotty nature of Edison's commercial success, his name would be indelibly associated with a remarkable array of technologies. In 1928 Congress estimated the value of his contribution to the world at $15.6 billion (about $220 billion in 2017 dollars) when it awarded him the Congressional Gold Medal. Edison's personal estate at his death in 1931 was worth $12 million ($180 million in 2017 dollars).[42]

In 1910 Frank Dyer and T. C. Martin, the biographers who knew Edison well, speculated about the characteristics that had led to his inordinate success as an inventor. They concluded that in addition to his clarity of thought, well-developed imagination, and physical vigor and stoicism, he had

> an intense, not to say courageous, optimism in which no thought of failure can enter, an optimism born of self-confidence, and becoming—after forty or fifty years of experience—more and more a sense of certainty in the accomplishment of success. In the overcoming of difficulties he has the same intellectual pleasure as the chess-master when confronted with a problem requiring all the efforts of his skill and experience to solve. To advance along smooth and pleasant paths, to encounter no obstacles, to wrestle with no difficulties and hardships—such has absolutely no fascination to him. He meets obstruction with the keen delight of a strong man battling with the waves and opposing them in sheer enjoyment, and the greater and more apparently overwhelming the forces that may tend to sweep him back, the more vigorous his own efforts to forge through them.[43]

In a 1921 interview Edison would aptly illustrate his self-efficacy and tenacity when he described his attitude toward failure:

> I never allow myself to become discouraged under any circumstances. I recall that after we had conducted thousands of experiments on a certain project without solving the problem, one of my associates, after we had conducted the crowning experiment and it had proved a failure, expressed discouragement and disgust over our having failed "to find out anything." I cheerily assured him that we had learned something. For we had learned for a certainty that the thing couldn't be done that

> way, and that we would have to try some other way. We sometimes learn a lot from our failures if we have put into the effort the best thought and work we are capable of.[44]

In Edison we see a man who worked incredibly hard, not because he was driven by the zealous idealism of Franklin (or, for that matter, Musk, Kamen, Curie, Jobs, or Tesla) but rather because he had a strong working ethos, had a high need for achievement, and found the work rewarding in and of itself. He enjoyed the process of achieving things, he was competitive by nature, and the physical and mental activity of work gave him pleasure.

Working Ethos

THE STRONG BELIEF IN the importance of working hard is a characteristic running through the lives of all of the innovators who are examined here. For example, Franklin valued industriousness as one of his most important ideals. Edison, according to Dyer and Martin, was "conscientiously afraid of appearing indolent, and in consequence subjects himself regularly to unnecessary hardship."[45]

This working ethos was readily visible in the parents of the innovators and the values with which they were raised. Although all were from families with sufficient resources so that food and adequate housing were not concerns, there was never so much as to foster complacency. The innovators were encouraged to work and earn money relatively early in life. For example, Franklin was indentured at the age of twelve. Edison was also working by age twelve and owned his own business within the year. Kamen was making $60,000 per year on his inventions before he finished high school. Nearly all had working mothers, and both Edison and Tesla described being strongly influenced by their mothers in their work habits. Edison said that "My mother was the making of me." Tesla similarly attributed his work habits—and his mechanical ingenuity—to the influence of his mother. In his autobiography, Tesla states, "My mother was an inventor of the first order and would, I believe, have achieved great things had she not been so remote from modern life and its multifold opportunities. She invented and constructed all kinds of tools and devices and wove the finest designs from thread which was spun by her. She even planted the seeds, raised the plants and separated the fibres herself. She worked indefatigably, from break of day till late at night, and most of the wearing apparel and furnishings of the home were the product of her hands."[46]

Tesla would follow his mother's example when he started at the Polytechnic in Graz. He worked tirelessly, from 3 A.M. to 11 P.M. seven days per week, and successfully completed nine final examinations—more than any other former student. As noted previously, Tesla worked so obsessively at his studies that his teachers wrote to his father warning him that Nikola was at risk of injuring his health by his long and intense hours of study. He did not graduate from the Polytechnic, having become as obsessive about gambling as he had been about studying, but later, after getting his first patent in 1887, he began an intense period of invention that would last for decades. As noted by biographer Marc Seifer, "Tesla began a vigorous schedule that frightened those around him. On many occasions, he drove himself until he collapsed, working around the clock with few breaks."[47] Alone or with one or two assistants in his laboratory on South Fifth Avenue (now Laguardia Street) in Greenwich Village in New York City, he worked seven days per week, often stopping only for occasional dinners or to freshen up. During this period he developed three complete systems of AC machinery (for single-phase, two-phase, and three-phase currents) with dynamos, motors, transformers, and devices for automatically controlling them. An 1893 *New York Herald* article observed that "Mr. Tesla is such a hard worker that he has little time for social pleasures, if indeed he has any taste in that direction." Seifer adds, "Monastic by choice and compelled by an all-consuming desire to be a major player in the burgeoning new age, the wizard preferred working through the night, when distractions could be minimized and concentration could be intensified."[48]

Part of Tesla's motivation to adopt such an aggressive work schedule was his desire to obtain patent priority on his electrical and communication systems, highlighting the need for achievement, another driver that motivated Tesla and all the other innovators. The *need for achievement* is a personality trait associated with a strong and consistent concern about setting and meeting high standards and accomplishing difficult tasks. Early work by psychology researchers Henry Murray and David McClelland on motivation and personality identified a set of human psychic needs related to achievement: a need for power over people or things, a need for recognition and approval, and a need to overcome obstacles or achieve something difficult as well and as quickly as possible.[49] McClelland observed that some people have higher needs for achievement than others and that this is reflected in their approach to goal-directed activities. McClelland also noted that children often exhibit meaningful differences in need for achievement very early—often as young as five years of age.[50]

McClelland and others argued that individuals with a high need for achievement would tend to select activities and roles of moderate risk that were more likely to offer a combination of potential for recognition and high likelihood of success. Later research overturned this view, however, finding that people with high need for achievement tended to choose challenging, riskier goals with only moderate chance of success and that they would not only persist in the face of negative feedback but would also increase their efforts. That is, rather than being discouraged by negative feedback or obstacles, they would double down on their effort, tenaciously sticking with the problem. Here is the interesting part that turns our negative connotation of risk on its head: for people with very high need for achievement, the difficulty and risk of a task become a signal of its potential for *reward*—the powerful thrill that will accompany the task's achievement. This association between difficulty and reward inoculates them from the frustration of initial difficulties.[51] For individuals with high need for achievement, difficulty is an indicator of opportunity for gain rather than a threat of failure.

McClelland also noted that people with a high need for achievement often exhibit a strong desire for knowledge of their results and feedback, and they are prone to becoming exceptionally absorbed in their work.[52] Each of these characteristics can be seen in all of the innovators here, particularly in Edison. He took great pleasure in amassing patents, being much more motivated to win patents than to accumulate material wealth. Patents offered tangible evidence of his inventive accomplishments even if he did not successfully commercialize all of them. In reading of Edison's long hours at the laboratory or his self-imposed isolation at the Ogden mine, it would be tempting to conclude that he did not enjoy home life and was not that close to his wife, Mina. However, the tender and affectionate letters that Edison wrote to her while away at the mine portray a man who loved his wife deeply and missed her company. He wrote her with unabashed affection (e.g., addressing her as "Darling Sweetest Loveliest Cutest" and telling her that "There can't [be] 1 woman in 20,000 that is really as smart as yourself") and would note that he sometimes felt blue without her. However, Edison loved his work *more*. Even when it was clear that the mine was a failure and all the money invested in it had been lost, Edison described himself in a letter to Mina "as bright and cheerful as a bumble bee in flower time."[53]

Research on the need for achievement is mixed on the role of intrinsic versus extrinsic rewards. On the one hand, individuals with a high need for achievement might experience strong intrinsic rewards from mastering skills, excelling at activities, and completing tasks. On the other hand, they can also be very sensitive to extrinsic rewards such as praise and prestige, and they may show a tendency for being extremely competitive.[54] As a result, the need for achievement is often described in conjunction with a need for recognition, approval, and prestige. In other words, it is typical to presume that people who want to accomplish things do so, in part, because they want others to recognize their accomplishments and think highly of them. The innovators studied here also exhibit some mixed evidence about the importance of recognition and praise. In some instances, it is clear that peer approval was important to them. For example, Curie had been stoic when faced with discrimination for being a woman of science, but after the scandal broke regarding her affair with Paul Langevin, she had a nervous collapse and long bouts of depression, suggesting that she suffered in response to the intense criticism she faced at that time. Similarly, although Tesla was, by any measure, a very unconventional person, comments written by him in his letters and articles convey a man who believed that eventually the public would see that his visions of the future had been correct, and it was important to him that his efforts and tactics would be vindicated. However, it is also clear that most of these innovators were willing to defy social norms and bear significant disapproval in pursuit of their goals. For some of them—notably Jobs, Edison, and Musk—external evaluations were almost meaningless because they believed few, if any, people were qualified to really understand and judge their performance.

Where does the need for achievement come from, and can it be taught? Early work in sociology and philosophy argued that attitudes toward work and achievement were rooted in deep cultural and religious belief systems. As early as 1904, Max Weber argued that frugality and entrepreneurial spirit were some of the consequences of Protestant asceticism. Later work by psychologists such as David McClelland extended this view and argued that cultures differ in their need for achievement and that such differences could, in part, explain differences in economic development across populations and societies.[55] McClelland (and others) believed that factors such as religion, social class, and childhood parenting practices affect an individual's development of need for achievement.

Furthermore, McClelland believed that need for achievement could, to some degree, be taught and that this offered important opportunities to improve economic development. His classic—and controversial—1961 book, *The Achieving Society*, drew considerable criticism for the ways that it generalized concepts from individuals to whole cultures, nations, or tribes. In fact, in his review of the book written for the *Journal of Economic History*, economist Julius Rubin described it as "one of the most fascinating and irritating, one of the most valuable and misleading books I have ever had the pleasure and displeasure of reading."[56] However, one of McClelland's findings that appears to have withstood the scrutiny of several decades of subsequent research is that high-achieving individuals typically have parents who set high standards for them yet were not excessively restrictive or authoritarian. For example, parents who did not let children make decisions for themselves did not tend to rear high-achieving children. Recent work, including studies by Oliver Schultheiss and Joachim Brunstein, draws a similar conclusion. In their review of three studies that explored childhood antecedents of high need for achievement, they conclude that individuals are more likely to have a high need for achievement if their parents emphasize early (but age-appropriate) self-reliance and mastery of basic skills, and encourage them to set challenging goals for themselves.[57]

Energy and "Flow": The Pleasure of Work

We have seen that part of a breakthrough innovator's motivation to work is tied to *outcomes* such as fulfilling ideals, pursuing superordinate goals, amassing achievements, and earning recognition and praise. However, many of the breakthrough innovators also exhibit another driver of hard work not related to these outcomes: pleasure in the feeling of work itself. The process of being fully engaged in a task—either mental or physical—can be extremely pleasurable or satisfying. An apt description is offered by psychologist Mihaly Csikszentmihalyi in his concept of *flow:* "the state in which people are so involved in an activity that nothing else seems to matter; the experience itself is so enjoyable that people will do it even at great cost, for the sheer sake of doing it."[58]

Csikszentmihalyi was born in Hungary in 1934 and spent time in an Italian prison as a child during World War II. Surrounded by misery and loss, he began to understand a phenomenon he would later call "flow" by losing himself in chess: "I discovered chess was a miraculous way of entering into a different world where all those things didn't matter. For hours I'd just focus within a reality that had clear rules and goals."[59] People in a state of cognitive flow may intensely focus on a task and lose all sense of time or self-awareness. Csikszentmihalyi also discusses flow in the realm of physical activity, such as the pleasure an individual might feel while dancing, completely lost in the rhythm of music, or the feeling of one's muscles being exerted or stretched to their limit in running or yoga.

One cannot help but notice the parallels in Csikszentmihalyi's analysis of flow and Dyer and Martin's 1910 description of Edison when they note his "same intellectual pleasure as the chess-master when confronted with a problem" or the way he "meets obstruction with the keen delight of a strong man battling with the waves."[60] According to Csikszentmihalyi, flow is most likely to occur when there is an appropriate match between an individual's capability level and the challenge she is facing. If the challenge is below her capability level, the individual will be bored; if the challenge is above her capability level, she will experience anxiety. However, in many realms an individual's capability level increases with experience; thus, the challenges she takes on must also be increasingly difficult in order to experience flow. This is illustrated perfectly in Kimbal Musk's description of Elon's need to constantly move on to bigger and more important challenges, such as his intention to send humans to Mars: "His mind needs to be constantly fulfilled.

The problems that he takes on therefore need to be more and more complex over time to keep him interested."[61]

Csikszentmihalyi's observation that flow is more likely to occur when an individual's capability level matches the challenge she is facing highlights another interesting point that helps us to better understand the behavior of Edison and others like him. Although we tend to focus on the exceptional *cognitive* abilities of innovators, Edison appears to have also had exceptional *physical* capabilities. His colleagues frequently noted his seemingly boundless energy, strength, and stamina. This may have had a biological foundation. Research on humans, rodents, and other species has shown that individuals vary tremendously in their amount of voluntary daily energy expenditure. For example, studies have shown that humans not only make widely different choices about voluntary exercise (which is to be expected given their diverse objectives and cultural influences) but also exhibit significant differences in spontaneous physical activity (e.g., fidgeting) or, more generally, "non-exercise activity thermogenesis" ("NEAT"). NEAT is the energy expended by an organism for everything that is not sleeping, eating, or sports-like exercise. It includes things like working, playing, grooming, and fidgeting. Although differences in NEAT are definitely influenced by lifestyle and cultural norms, there are also biological reasons for such differences that may include differences in energy metabolism and in neurotransmitter patterns.[62]

Humans make awkward research subjects for studies of energy expenditure because it is difficult to standardize their living environment and diet, and harder still to control for their motivations (such as wanting to fit into skinny jeans). Mice, with few known concerns about how they look in jeans, make much better research subjects in these respects. In one study, for example, thirty-five three-week-old male mice (sets of siblings from ten families of an ordinary house mouse strain) were put into cages with running wheels, Purina rodent chow, and water. Their voluntary running was recorded by instruments that counted the revolutions of the wheel. Remarkably, the mice exhibited very large individual differences in their voluntary running activity. The least active mice ran an average of twenty-four revolutions per day; the most active ones ran almost 14,000 revolutions daily. Furthermore, although there was great variation across individuals, there was a strong correlation in activity over time for a given mouse. That is, some mice ran consistently less, others consistently more, despite being closely related, having identical resources, and being in identical habitats.[63] These findings were subsequently replicated by dozens of studies that identified significant individual variation in energy expenditure within an animal species, including mice, rats, dogs, fish, birds, deer, and lizards. Most of these studies attributed the variation in voluntary energy expenditure to a combination of biological and psychological factors, including differences in personality traits such as "boldness" or "aggressiveness."[64] For example, mice that quite aggressively attack and eat crickets also exhibit higher levels of voluntary exercise. Intriguingly, constant fidgeting, which is a form of NEAT, is also often cited in mania, ADHD, and obsessive-compulsive disorder. Furthermore, elevated dopamine (as discussed in more depth in Chapter 3) is linked to both creativity and hyperkinesia (an increase in muscular activity that can result in excessive abnormal movements). Could extreme innovators like Edison be similar to mice who run significantly more revolutions on a wheel—in other words, could they have vastly higher voluntary energy expenditure caused by biological or psychological factors? Those who knew Edison certainly seemed to believe that he was bold and fearless, exerted a remarkable amount of effort, and had more physical stamina than an average man. I know of no existing studies relating NEAT to innovation, but it is an intriguing area for future research.

Anyone who has raised or closely observed a border collie intuitively understands the points of this chapter about being driven to work. Bred to herd sheep, the border collie is an extremely energetic dog with seemingly unlimited stamina and an intense need for physical and mental stimulation. The border collie's drive to work is so strong, in fact, that if the dog is not given an outlet for its physical and mental energy, it can become aggressive or neurotic. In dog breeding circles there is a saying that "A border collie needs a job, and if you don't give him one, he'll come up with his own, and you won't like it." All of the innovators here, but none more so than Edison, resemble border collies in their behavior. We don't yet completely understand why some individuals want or need to expend more energy than others, but it suffices to say there could be both biological and psychological reasons that individuals such as Edison exhibit physical and mental strength that "seemed to be without limit."

I feel incredibly lucky to be at exactly the right place, in Silicon Valley, at exactly the right time historically where this invention has taken form.

—Steve Jobs, in an interview
with Robert X. Cringely, 1995

6

“The sixties produced an anarchic mind-set. . . ”

Opportunities and Challenges of an Era

How much does being in the right place at the right time matter in the making of serial breakthrough innovators? The short answer is that it definitely matters but it's not enough. Being in the right place at the right time is what economists would call a “necessary but insufficient condition.” Moments of technological or cultural change—such as the industrial revolution, the countercultural movement, or the rise of information technology—create rich periods of opportunity that increase innovation, and this opportunity may be crucial for the emergence of a serial breakthrough innovator. However, it is also clear that even in such periods, the emergence of this type of innovator is rare—most people inventing during even such fertile periods will not go on to become famously important innovators. In this chapter and the next we will look at how the place and time influenced the innovators' success for better or worse. In this chapter we will focus on the role of timing—opportunities and challenges created by the era. In the next chapter we will focus on the role of resources, including which resources matter and why. The two are often inextricably entwined: the resources you have access to will depend, in part, on when and where you are, as will be illustrated by the account of Steve Jobs growing up in Silicon Valley during the computer revolution.

Few stories illustrate the opportunities and challenges of an era as poignantly as that of Marie Curie, whose parents and community were passionately dedicated to the education of women at a time when formal education for women was extremely rare. She was born Maria Salomea Skłodowska on November 7, 1867, in Warsaw. In the late eighteenth century, Russia had invaded Poland and seized territory in three successive partitions that eliminated sovereign Poland for 123 years. The Polish people suffered greatly under the ruthless suppression of Tsarist Russia. The tsar's agents vigorously enforced a "Russification" that attempted to erase all traces of Poland's literature, language, culture, and other aspects of its heritage. Children could not be taught Polish history or literature, nor could they be taught in Polish—they had to learn and use Russian instead. Many Polish educators (like Marie Curie's parents) and other Poles in influential positions lost their posts or were demoted to less influential roles.

Initially the Polish people had fought back, but two uprisings by Poles in November 1830 and January 1863 were catastrophic and led to increased efforts to Russify Poland and the exile or imprisonment of hundreds of thousands of Poles.[1] After the failure of the uprisings, many in Poland, including Curie's parents, Władysław and Bronisława Skłodowska, concluded that their country could not be saved through military means. Instead, education, science, and hard work were the only ways to preserve Poland.[2] Both parents were from the lower aristocracy of Poland known as the *szlachta* class. The *szlachta* were legally privileged nobles, but they had lost most of their land and wealth under Russian rule. All members of this class were considered socially and legally equal, even if they had far less wealth than the richest *szlachta* (the "magnates"), and they were typically disdainful of using titles and other forms of hierarchical distinction. They valued intellectual achievement over materialistic goods.

Władysław was a math and physics teacher who gave his children a broad education in both the sciences and the forbidden Polish literature. Later, after Marie Curie moved to France, he continued being engaged in her education by working on advanced math problems with her through the mail. Bronisława was also a teacher and at the time of Marie's birth was the headmistress at Freta Street School, a private girls' academy in Warsaw.

Around the time Marie was born, Bronisława began to exhibit signs of tuberculosis. The foreboding shadow of her illness haunted the family. When Marie was four years old, Bronisława began taking "rest cures" in the mountains or in other locales with a mild climate, in hopes of recovering her health. For two years, Bronisława spent most of her time away from home, taking her oldest daughter, Zofia (who was ten years old when the trips began), to help care for her. When Bronisława finally returned home, six-year-old Marie rushed to embrace her, but Bronisława, wanting to protect the child, forbade it. Marie would later note that she remembered her mother raising her palm up sharply and warning her to stay away in order to avoid infection. There would be no warm embraces between mother and child. Instead, Marie would crouch at her mother's feet and gaze at her with intense adoration, while her mother would carefully and lightly touch the child's forehead. It was the only physical gesture of affection she would receive.[3]

Throughout Marie's childhood, her parents fought to keep the spirit of Polish nationalism alive in their children. When Marie was nine years old and her mother was too sick with tuberculosis to educate her children at home, Marie and her sister Hela were sent to a school run by Madame Jadwiga Sikorska, a kind and intelligent woman who was also a Polish patriot. Sikorska operated a double schedule: one taught the official Russian curriculum, and the other taught a secret curriculum of Polish language, history, and geography.[4] "Home economics" on the official schedule actually meant Polish history, for example. The school was subject to regular inspections, so all of the students had to be alert to the sound of a bell that meant they needed to quickly hide their Polish work, and both teachers and students would then switch to speaking Russian.[5]

Marie's exceptional intelligence was apparent very early. Though the youngest and smallest of her class, she was also the brightest and had the best command of Russian. Thus, she was often the student called upon to recite something in Russian when the dreaded inspector visited the school. She was also often asked to help her classmates with their math and other subjects. Although all of the Skłodowska children were very bright, Marie was easily the brightest.

In a cruel twist of fate, while Bronisława continued to weaken from tuberculosis, Zofia and another of Marie's sisters, Bronia, contracted typhus. Bronia recovered, but Zofia, now fourteen years old, died. As described by Marie's sister Helena, the death "literally crushed our mother; she could never accept the loss of her oldest child."[6] Bronisława lived for two more years and then succumbed to her tuberculosis. The ten-year-old Marie was devastated by the death of her mother and sister, and the grief would leave a deep and permanent impression on her nature. As noted in Chapter 1, she began to suffer from recurring bouts of deep depression—a pattern she retained throughout her life. Immediately after the deaths, Marie began to hide away and cry, but she would always attempt to conceal her emotions from her family and classmates. She focused obsessively on her schoolwork to push away her feelings. She rarely spoke, but she remained at the top of her class.

Despite Marie's efforts to hide her feelings, Sikorska noticed her suffering and emotional fragility. She suggested to Marie's father that perhaps his daughter should take a year off from school—she was, after all, already a grade ahead of her age. Instead, her father enrolled her in the much stricter and less nurturing Russian gymnasium. The Russian gymnasiums were more selective schools for academically talented children and were the only path to higher education. For the Skłodowskas, education always came first. Although Marie hated her teachers at the gymnasium and hated the curriculum that demonized Poland, she graduated first in her class at the age of fifteen and received a gold medal for being the best student of 1883.

Her education for the time being completed and thus no longer able to hide from her feelings in her schoolwork, Marie suffered a complete nervous collapse. Sinking into despair, she hid away in her darkened room. She did not speak, and she hardly ate. Władysław now seemed to finally recognize the depth of his daughter's suffering and sent her to stay with relatives in the country. At first the broken Marie could only rest, but she gradually began to recover. Surrounded by nature and the playful warmth of family members, her spirits began to lift.

Marie returned to Warsaw in the fall of 1883, mostly recovered. Her father, who like many Polish educators had been demoted and had his salary reduced, fretted over how his children would secure a future when he had no money to send them to college. In the meantime, he continued his intense effort to further their education at home. A man of wide intellectual interests and expertise, he kept up with developments in chemistry and physics and continued his extensive reading in literature and poetry. He could speak five languages and would read aloud to the children every Saturday evening, often simultaneously translating from the text's native language. As Marie's daughter Eve would later write about her mother, "Thanks to her father she lived in an intellectual atmosphere of rare quality known to few girls of her age."[7]

Despite the importance that Polish positivism placed on education as the key to patriotism and the nation's eventual success in reemerging as an independent country, Polish universities were not open to women. Because Marie and her sisters had little money to travel elsewhere to pursue their educational ambitions, Marie, as noted in Chapter 1, began to focus on self-education, reading science, politics, literature, and poetry, while she developed a plan for furthering her educational career. She became involved in the "Flying University," a clandestine academy started by Jadwiga Szczasinska-Dawidow in 1882 that delivered a university curriculum to Polish women who met secretly in supportive institutions around Warsaw. Marie described their ideals in a letter written forty years later: "We cannot hope to build a better world without improving the individual. Towards this end, each of us must work toward his own highest development, accepting at the same time his share of responsibility in the general life of humanity—our particular duty being to help those to whom we feel we can be most useful."[8] Education and patriotic fervor were thus tightly interwoven.

Marie used her earnings as a governess in Szczuki to support her sister Bronia, who would go to study in Paris at the Sorbonne. Then, when Bronia's studies were complete, she would support Marie's education in turn. While a governess, Marie sought other ways to support the cause of Polish positivism, which considered Polish peasants to be an untapped resource that could be empowered through education. Embracing these ideals with her typical intensity, Marie created and taught a class to ten Polish peasant children during the hours that she was free from her governess duties. This kind of project was forbidden by the government—and dangerous—but by this point in her life Curie already fully embraced education as a form of nationalistic resistance to Russian oppression.

When Bronia had completed her studies in Paris (one of only three women out of a student body of one thousand to graduate from the Sorbonne's Faculty of Medicine), it was finally time for Marie to take her place in Paris. Initially she hesitated. Although she had an intense desire for education, depression and fear of a new environment proved difficult for her to overcome. Furthermore, she felt a sense of duty to her father, who was now living alone in Warsaw, so she decided to return and join him there.

Fortunately, her cousin Józef Boguski was serving as the director of the Museum of Industry and Agriculture, a private, positivist-influenced institution in Warsaw. This gave Curie access to a chemistry laboratory, much to her delight. A brief taste of running experiments in the lab quickly reaffirmed her ambition of being a scientist. As later described by Eve, "When she took the test tubes of the Museum of Agriculture and Industry into her fine, clever hands, Manya [the family nickname for Marie] returned, as if by magic, to the absorbing memories of her childhood, to her father's physics apparatus, motionless in its glass case, with which, in the old days, she had always wanted to play. She had taken up the thread of her life again."[9] In November 1891, twenty-three-year-old Marie finally boarded a train bound for Paris to begin her studies at the Sorbonne.

Curie arrived in Paris with her clothes, a feather mattress, a little food and water, and a stool. She had almost no money and for twenty-five francs per month rented an unheated room where it could become so cold in the winter that the water in the washbasin would freeze. However, the apartment was close to the Sorbonne, and her solitary life afforded her time to focus intensely on her studies. She later referred to these years of "deprivation" as "one of the best memories of my life."[10]

At the Sorbonne, education was basically free—there were only small fees for qualifying tests and diplomas. Students could attend classes as frequently as they desired and could take exams if and when they chose. In many ways the Sorbonne perfectly empowered and reaffirmed Curie's habit of independent work. As she wrote, "The student who comes to France should not expect to find direction towards a utilitarian goal right at the start. The French system consists essentially of awakening the student's confidence in his own abilities and fostering the habit of using them . . . the goal of the teachers is to create large possibilities for free work rather than to form disciples. Required exercises and scholarly discipline don't play an essential role."[11]

Curie was one of only twenty-three women of the two thousand students in the School of Sciences at the Sorbonne, but she seemed unconcerned or unaware of the disadvantages of her gender. Obsessed with her studies, she worked to such a degree of fatigue and malnutrition that she once fainted in the library. She passed her examination for a master's degree in physics in 1893, ranking first in her class, and then in the following year received a master's degree in mathematics, ranking second in her class. Her tenacity and talent paid off as one of her professors, Gabriel Lippman, arranged for Marie to receive a stipend to study the magnetic properties of steel.

Marie's progress was hampered by a lack of sophisticated equipment; thus, a friend arranged to introduce her to Pierre Curie, a thirty-four-year-old physicist who had invented a number of instruments that might help her. By the time Pierre met Marie, he was already an accomplished scientist. Dyslexic as a child but with a profound capacity to visualize mathematical concepts, he had been homeschooled by his parents. By the age of sixteen he had achieved his science baccalaureate; unable to choose between physics and chemistry, he proceeded to study both. He studied physics at the Sorbonne and chemistry at the School of Pharmacy in Paris. Upon graduation he became an assistant to a professor at the Sorbonne and later formulated a general principle of symmetry related to magnetism. He and his brother then went on to create a state-of-the-art quadrant electrometer. As discussed further in the next chapter, this electrometer and Pierre's tutelage in its use would turn out to be very important to Marie's later discoveries.

Pierre had been generally indifferent to women, but after meeting the brilliant Marie, he was captivated and began to pursue her intensely. After a few years of persistent courtship, Marie agreed to marry Pierre, and they soon had a daughter, Irène. Although Marie initially tackled domestic life and parenthood with her characteristic diligence, she soon began to pine again for scientific work. Thus, in 1897 Pierre and Marie hired nurses to care for Irène.

Pierre's father also moved in with them to provide care for the girl so that both Marie and Pierre could go back to their work full time.

In 1895 the German physicist Wilhelm Conrad Röntgen had discovered that some type of mysterious ray could pass through various substances and create a fluorescent image on a piece of cardboard painted with barium platinocyanide. Using the mathematical meaning of "X" as unknown, he called them "X rays."[12] In the following year French physicist Antoine Henri Becquerel discovered that uranium salts also emitted radiation and could leave an image on a photographic plate.[13] Although most of the public focused on X-rays because they were easy to produce and yielded dramatic results, Marie decided to study the "Becquerel rays," which were relatively neglected because the rays were weaker and required uranium, which was almost impossible to obtain. Becquerel himself had used Pierre's electrometer to attempt to measure the energetic rays that he had inadvertently discovered, but he was unable to master the delicate and complicated instrument. Marie, on the other hand, had the advantage of being with Pierre, who worked intensely to modify the machine to improve its sensitivity for detecting currents. He added a piezoelectric quartz (another of his discoveries), which improved the measurement of low-intensity electrical currents. Finally, he spent twenty days training Marie in how to use the extremely difficult device to measure Becquerel rays.

Marie used Pierre's electrometer to measure the electric charge from pulverized uranium through a process that required exceptional persistence, focus, and dexterity. She soon noticed that other substances produced similar energetic rays and began to test a range of compounds. One of the compounds, pitchblende (a heavy black ore from which uranium has been extracted), produced rays four times as strong as pure uranium. The strength of the rays made her realize that there was a hitherto unknown element present in the pitchblende. With intense persistence and insatiable curiosity, she conducted experiment after experiment to attempt to identify what unknown element was generating the rays. It was during this process that she wrote a paper, the "Theory of Radioactivity," positing that measuring radioactivity could be used to discover new elements—a finding that would pave the way for atomic science.

With Pierre helping to secure laboratory space and supplies of pitchblende, Marie worked tirelessly, distilling and fractionating the substances over the course of four years. Ultimately, she isolated one substance that was four hundred times as strong as uranium (which she named "polonium" after her beloved homeland). However, upon successfully identifying polonium, she immediately began attempting to identify yet another radioactive substance in the pitchblende, which turned out to be ten million times more radioactive than uranium (which she named "radium," a name derived from the Latin for "ray"). In June 1903 she defended her work in a doctoral thesis titled *Recherches sur les substances radioactives* (translated as *Research on Radioactive Substances*), becoming the first woman in France to achieve this level of education. In the same year, a group of scientists (including Curie's former professor Gabriel Lippmann) nominated Pierre Curie and Henri Becquerel for the 1903 Nobel Prize in Physics for the discovery of radioactivity, even though it was well-known that the discovery was primarily a result of Marie's efforts. It was, after all, extremely unconventional for a woman in Europe to receive an education beyond the age of fourteen and virtually unthinkable for her to play serious roles in science or business. However, Pierre made it clear that the achievement was largely Marie's and that he would not accept the award if Marie was not included.[14] The committee relented and awarded half of the prize money to Becquerel "in recognition of the extraordinary services he has rendered by his discovery of spontaneous radioactivity" and jointly awarding the other half to Pierre Curie and Marie Curie "in recognition of the extraordinary services they have rendered by their joint researches on the radiation phenomena discovered by Professor Henri Becquerel."[15] Curie thus became the first woman Nobel laureate and would continue to be the only woman to receive the award until thirty-two years later, when her daughter Irène Joliot-Curie received it in 1935. The discovery of radium would turn out to be her most remembered accomplishment, but scientists note that her greatest achievements were actually the discovery of radioactivity as an atomic property, her methods for isolating radioactive isotopes, and her discovery of a range of uses for those isotopes.

Throughout all their work isolating polonium and radium, the Curies never realized that the radioactivity was affecting their health. Pierre Curie had severe unexplained bone pain and weakness, and Marie Curie lost a lot of weight and had symptoms resembling tuberculosis. There were also bright moments—newfound fame had brought the Curies better positions and more resources. The couple also had a second daughter, Eve. Then tragedy struck: on a rainy night in 1906, Pierre was hit by a horse-drawn carriage and died. Pierre's death was a devastating blow to Marie. As Eve would later write about her mother, "From the moment when those three words, 'Pierre is dead,' reached her consciousness, a cape of solitude and secrecy fell upon her shoulders forever. Madame Curie, on that day in April, became not only a widow, but at the same time a pitiful and incurably lonely woman."[16]

She returned to the laboratory the day after Pierre's funeral. Over the next ten months, she completed a six-hundred-page book on radioactivity and gravity that Pierre had begun. She isolated herself in the laboratory, driving herself relentlessly, often until two or three in the morning.[17] She avoided social contact. She even became emotionally isolated from her children, who fortunately had a close and warm bond with their jovial and affectionate grandfather, who continued to raise them. One of Eve's earliest memories was of her mother falling to the floor, fainting from exhaustion. In periods when the exhaustion became too acute to overcome, she retreated to her bed and allowed no one to see her.

Without Pierre at her side, she was even more vulnerable to the sexism of the time. Not only was it unusual in the early twentieth century for women to be highly educated; it was also considered somewhat distasteful for them to have professional positions. Thus, even though Marie was a Nobel Prize–winning scientist, many other scientists did not give her the respect she would have been given as a man. She was excluded from the Academy of Sciences, which permitted no women; her papers had to be read by others in her stead. Lord Kelvin, who had been an admirer of Pierre Curie's work and a supporter of the Curies in the earlier years, was now at odds with Marie over the age of the Earth and attacked her in the press. Kelvin had used thermal gradients to calculate the age of the Earth and concluded that it had to be somewhere between 20 million and 100 million years. He had assumed the Earth began as a molten object, and he based his calculations on the time it would take for the surface to cool to its current temperature. However, this was incompatible with Darwin's theory of evolution, which suggested that the Earth had to be much older. The disagreement sparked an intense debate among scientists about the age of the Earth and the assumptions upon which calculations should be based. Kelvin stuck to his original arguments, and as late as 1897 even declared that the Earth's age was probably much closer to the lower end of his estimate: 20 million years. Marie Curie's discovery of radium pointed to the flaw in Kelvin's logic: radioactivity meant that the Earth's heat was being continuously replenished. Furthermore, radioactivity itself provided a means of calculating the age of rocks because it decayed at a known rate, and her calculations indicated that the Earth was at least twice as old as Kelvin's calculations. In an unusually aggressive move that would normally be considered beneath the dignity of a great scientist, Kelvin wrote a letter to the *London Times* in 1906 in which he charged that radium was not an element at all, but rather a compound of helium. It was surprising that he had gone to the public press; the more typical action of a scientist would have been to publish a study in a scientific journal. It appeared that Kelvin wanted to publicly humiliate Curie and undermine the legitimacy of the science of radioactivity.

In her typical fashion, she did not engage in the debate in the press; instead, she went back to the lab and spent three years proving radium's atomic weight with extreme precision, dispelling all doubts about her methods and discoveries.[18]

Work was Marie Curie's primary shelter and solace, and she now turned to seeking ways that radioactivity could be harnessed for medical benefits. Noting that radiation killed tumor-forming cells faster than healthy cells, and having unique knowledge and skill in isolating radioactive isotopes, she began to conduct the world's first studies using radioactive isotopes to treat tumors. Curie had become a profound role model for women, and by 1910 twenty women scientists were working as unpaid volunteers in her laboratory. As noted in Chapter 4, 1911 would turn out to be a tumultuous year; the public became aware that Marie was having an affair with her friend and colleague Paul Langevin at exactly the same time that she was awarded her second Nobel Prize, this time in chemistry, "in recognition of her services to the advancement of chemistry by the discovery of the elements radium and polonium, by the isolation of radium and the study of the nature and compounds of this remarkable element."[19] Rather than being bathed in adulation for accomplishing the seemingly impossible as the first person to ever receive two Nobel prizes and for many years the only person to win Nobel prizes in two different fields, she faced vicious public attacks because of the scandal. Curie once again retreated from public life, losing herself in her work.

When World War I broke out, Curie heard that wounded soldiers were having their limbs amputated because field hospitals did not have X-ray equipment to find the location of bullets and shrapnel. She thus developed mobile X-ray units that she drove to field hospitals on the battlefront, and she set the units up with the help of her daughter Irène, who was now seventeen. She is attributed with saving the lives of over one million soldiers.[20] By the age of nineteen, Irène would be training women X-ray technicians at the Edith Cavell Hospital. Irène would develop into a profoundly talented scientist like her mother, discovering (among other things) a way to create artificial radioactivity and winning a Nobel Prize of her own.

The constant exposure to X-rays and radium took their toll, and in 1934 Marie Curie died at the age of sixty-seven from "aplastic pernicious anemia" caused by radiation exposure. As Eve Curie notes, "When her mission was accomplished she died exhausted, having refused wealth and endured her honors with indifference."[21]

Marie Curie exhibits many of the themes discussed in previous chapters. She was unconventional, was uninterested in social life, and lived in self-imposed isolation. She dedicated her life to a grand purpose and doggedly pursued her objectives. When obstacles and challenges arose, she did not falter—she just dug in her heels and worked even harder. The crucial role of Pierre and his electrometer in Marie's discoveries also aptly demonstrates how important access to resources can be, as will be discussed in the next chapter. However, perhaps more than anything else, Curie's story illustrates how large a role can be played by both the opportunities and challenges of an era.

On the one hand, Curie's story poignantly conveys the challenges of being a woman in science prior to the late twentieth and early twenty-first centuries. Women were not supposed to be in scientific and business domains, and many universities in Europe did not admit women. It was only through Curie's extraordinary effort and resourcefulness that she obtained higher education. Furthermore, even after her brilliance was acknowledged and her accomplishments were irrefutable, she was denied access to the Academy of Sciences and nearly denied a Nobel Prize—all because of her gender. Her success also required making a choice that would have been very difficult for many women: she relinquished nearly all of her caregiving duties for her children to others. This one story of a female breakthrough innovator does much to reveal to us why there is a paucity of women on lists of famous innovators.

On the other hand, Curie's story also exquisitely demonstrates the opportunities and positive effects that an era can offer. First, her birth into a time in which Poland was defending its cultural heritage by secretly educating its people meant that not only did Marie have access to education; she also thought of it as her patriotic duty. Her involvement in the Flying University meant that she interacted with some of the most intelligent and fearless women of Warsaw, giving her access to an intellectual community and to an ethos in which women should pursue intellectual and scientific advance with courage and fervor. The rise of Polish positivism during this time reaffirmed both of these factors: Polish positivism overthrew the idea that women should have lesser access to education and emphasized that diligent and pragmatic work was the key to Poland's future.

The events unfolding in Poland were not the only significant opportunities of the era affecting Curie. In Europe at the beginning of the 1800s, women had virtually no access to university education. By the mid-1800s, however, changes were under way. Several colleges in the United States had begun admitting women in the early 1800s, and by the middle of the century European women were pressing their case for access to university education. In 1865 the University of Zurich became the first European university to admit women, followed quickly by the University of Paris (the Sorbonne) in 1867. By the late 1860s and early 1870s, many other European universities were following suit. In 1878 the University of London became the first university in the United Kingdom to permit women to earn degrees (Oxford and Cambridge allowed women to take classes at this time but did not permit women to earn degrees until 1920 and 1947, respectively). Marie Curie started at the Sorbonne in 1891; if she had been born thirty years earlier, it is likely that no amount of resourcefulness or tenacity would have enabled her to pursue a career in science.

The rise of Polish positivism and the rise of women's access to education in Europe coincided to inspire Marie and Bronia to craft their plan to take turns going to the Sorbonne. It was a bold, unlikely, and resourceful scheme for two Polish girls without financial resources. The fact that it worked and both Marie and Bronia obtained university educations is quite remarkable. There were moments when, as a governess, Marie did not think they would have enough money to see each other through and succumbed to discouragement. Her description of an alternative future provides a sharp contrast to the one that actually transpired: "My plans for the future are modest indeed: my dream, for the moment, is to have a corner of my own where I can live with my father. . . . I shall install myself in Warsaw, take a post as a teacher in a girls' school and make up the rest of the money I need by giving lessons. It is all I want. Life does not deserved to be worried over."[22]

Finally, it must also be noted that Curie's discovery of radium and radioactivity occurred because of the unique confluence of her work studying the magnetic properties of steel, Pierre Curie's development of the electrometer, and the timing of the discovery of mysterious invisible energy rays by Röntgen and Becquerel. Given Curie's intellect and drive, we can speculate that she might have achieved amazing things even without this convergence of time and place, but we do not know what those achievements might have been or whether she would be remembered as one of the most important innovators of all time.

When the world is jolted by technological or economic shocks, there are often corresponding "blooms" of innovation and innovators as individuals respond to the changing needs or resources created by the shock. The rise of the personal computer and the development of the Internet are excellent examples. These shocks in information technology led to feverish innovation activity as people and organizations raced to exploit the new opportunities these technologies offered.[23] These shocks didn't just influence innovation in the computer and software industries; they also spurred innovation across almost every industry by enabling new types of products and production methods. Drug compounds could be automatically screened by computers, automated processes could be incorporated into industrial machinery, textbooks could be digitized and made modular and customizable, and products could be marketed and sold over the Internet. It is difficult to identify an industry that was *not* affected by the rise of information technology. Many famous innovators emerged during the period from the late 1970s (when the personal computer first emerged) to the mid-1990s (when the Internet became available to the general public), including Steve Jobs; Bill Gates, who cofounded Microsoft with Paul Allen; Linus Torvalds, who initiated the development of Linux; Tim Berners-Lee, credited with inventing the World Wide Web by writing the hypertext markup language and hypertext transfer protocol; Jeff Bezos, who founded Amazon; Marc Andreesen, who founded Netscape; and Larry Page and Sergey Brin, who cofounded Google.

Shocks that are not directly related to technology can also spur innovation by changing regulatory constraints, our access to resources, and our economic priorities. For example, in 1973 the members of the Organization of Petroleum Exporting Countries (OPEC) declared an oil embargo, causing oil prices to quadruple and creating an oil crisis. Politicians called for gas rationing, and President Nixon asked gas stations to voluntarily refrain from selling gasoline on Saturdays and Sundays, resulting in long lines at the pumps. Many states even asked citizens to not put up Christmas lights, with Oregon actually banning them! Although the embargo was lifted a few months later, the crisis had jolted governments, industries, and consumers, leading to a long-term effect on their behavior. For example, US auto manufacturers began to focus on developing cars that were more fuel efficient, and consumers began taking fuel efficiency into earnest account when choosing a new car. Both companies and individuals began to dramatically increase their efforts in developing renewable energy alternatives such as solar and hydroelectric power. Rapid innovation resulted in the fall of the cost of solar power from $100 per watt to about $20 per watt, and suddenly solar cells began to be used in a wide range of applications, from digital watches to residential power in remote locations. In a telling bit of irony, oil companies even started using solar cells to power the warning lights on offshore rigs.

Social movements also play a role in stimulating innovation by changing social priorities or norms of behavior. Consider, for example, Steve Jobs, whose life and career were deeply affected both by the technological shocks occurring in computing technology and by his strong identification with the sixties counterculture movement. In the 1960s, opposition to the Vietnam War and growing tension over sexual and racial discrimination led to a series of antiwar protests and intensification of social movements such as the civil rights movement, the free speech movement, and the women's liberation movement. These mostly peaceful movements were fueled by unprecedented levels of student activism and rejected the authority of "the establishment" in favor of a world characterized by peace, equality, and freedom of personal expression. Because the movements sought to overthrow social norms of the past, they collectively became known as the "countercultural movement."

The ethos of the counterculture movement played a big role in Jobs's beliefs about resisting authority and the constraints of social norms, and helped to nurture his vision of the personal computer as a tool of personal expression and liberation. The computer, in Jobs's mind, was not a mere tool for productivity; it was also a means of social revolution. The musician Bono, a friend of Jobs, explained why the hippies of the countercultural movement played such a big role in the creation of the personal computer industry: "The people who invented the twenty-first century were pot-smoking, sandal-wearing hippies from the West Coast like Steve, because they saw differently . . . the hierarchical systems of the East Coast, England, Germany, and Japan do not encourage this different thinking. The sixties produced an anarchic mind-set that is great for imagining a world not yet in existence."[24]

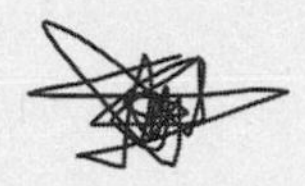

War also has a substantial impact on innovation, although the effect is double-edged. On the one hand, it removes people from their work in science and industry and puts them in uniform and on the battlefield, disrupting their pursuit of goals. It also leads to the widespread destruction of resources, including both physical assets as well as the intellectual and creative talent that is crucial for innovation. On the other hand, war can also spur innovation by inspiring a sense of urgency and idealism that leads individuals to pursue bigger projects. People break out of roles and routines that may have been preventing them from realizing their full innovative potential. War also tends to stir the social pot, bringing together people who might normally not come into contact by virtue of gender, race, or walk of life. Consider, for example, the role of women in industry during World War II. From 1940 to 1945, the percentage of women in the workforce rose dramatically—reaching 37 percent in 1945—as women filled the holes in the workforce left by men who went off to war. A US government campaign aimed at recruiting women to the munitions industry featured the muscle-flexing "Rosie the Riveter," who became a symbol of female strength, independence, and patriotism. Women were accepted into positions formerly closed to them, as in the aviation industry, for example. In 1943 women made up 65 percent of the workforce in aviation, up from a mere 1 percent prior to the war.[25] Hundreds of women were also enlisted as "computers" who used desk calculators to calculate long lists of equations used to target artillery on the battlefield. Women mathematicians were also involved in the development and programming of the ENIAC (electronic numerical integrator and computer), widely considered to be the first general-purpose computer. As a result, women gained unprecedented access to science and technology, and science and technology gained unprecedented access to women, vastly widening the pool of intellectual and creative talent employed in technological innovation.

Perhaps no one is a better example of radical new opportunity than Grace Hopper, born in 1906 in New York City. Her mother was an accomplished mathematician, and her father was an executive at a life insurance company.[26] Grace shared her mother's love of math and in 1934 became the first woman to receive a doctorate in mathematics from Yale. As Hopper notes, "I wanted to be an engineer. . . . My dad always made things, and I've always been fascinated with how things work. But there was no place at all for women in engineering when I graduated in 1928."[27] She thus accepted a position as a professor at Vassar and by 1940 was both a popular teacher and a highly respected member of the Vassar faculty.

Being a professor was one of the few professional roles considered appropriate for women at that time. She had a comfortable life. All of that changed in December 1941, when the Japanese bombed Pearl Harbor. Within the next six months Grace Hopper's husband, brother, cousins, and many of her friends had enlisted in the military. As soon as President Roosevelt signed the Navy Women's Reserve Act authorizing women to enter noncombat positions in 1942, Hopper decided she would enlist as well. At 36 years old and 105 pounds, she was considered too old and small for naval service; however, she was able to obtain a waiver as mathematics professors were highly sought after for the war effort.[28] Because of her math background, she was assigned to a project to develop a machine that could rapidly make difficult calculations for tasks such as laying minefields. After the war, many of the major technology firms (including IBM, Honeywell, and Eckert-Mauchly Computer Corporation) wanted to interview her. Although women were not generally accepted in either science or business at that time, her military rank (she would eventually attain the rank of admiral) and protocol neutralized the gender discrimination she would have normally faced, enabling her to be more influential. She went on to develop the first computer programming language and was, ironically, voted "Man of the Year" by the Data Processing Management Association. In her honor, in 1997 the US Navy named its newest guided-missile destroyer the USS *Grace Hopper.*

During wartime, governments and industries often vastly increase their efforts at developing communication, transportation, and munitions technologies, and these investments create pools of assets and expertise that continue to give rise to innovations even after the wartime needs recede. Although the fundamental science underlying the development of radar goes back at least to work on electromagnetics in the late 1800s, the big advances that made radar useful occurred during World War II. The governments of Germany, Japan, the United States, Britain, the Soviet Union, the Netherlands, France, and Italy all invested vigorously in trying to develop radar systems that would enable the detection and tracking of aircraft. Britain made major scientific advances in radar but lacked the money and other industrial resources needed to develop radar to its potential during the war. Thus in June 1940, when France had already fallen to the Nazis and fearing that Britain would be next, Winston Churchill decided to seek the help of the United States. Churchill brokered a deal to share Britain's radar technology with the United States in exchange for help with production and financing. A British magnetron that was developed by a team led by Henry Tizard and that was a thousand times more powerful than the best US transmitter of the time was sent by ocean liner to the United States in a secret operation known as the "Tizard mission."[29] Bell Telephone Laboratories immediately went to work putting the new transmitter into production.

A Bell Labs team that included John Bardeen, William Shockley, and Walter Brattain worked on developing pure germanium "crystal" diodes for use in the radar systems. It was this work on diodes that would give rise to transistors, invented in 1947 (Bardeen, Shockley, and Brattain were awarded the 1956 Nobel Prize in physics for the development of the transistor). In 1956 Shockley moved from New Jersey (where Bell Labs was located) to Mountain View, California, to help his ailing mother. There he founded Shockley Semiconductor Laboratory. Although Shockley was undeniably brilliant, he also had psychological problems, was a proponent of eugenics, and was—to put it mildly—difficult to work with.[30] It is perhaps not surprising, then, that only a year later eight of Shockley's top researchers left to form Fairchild Semiconductor. Over the next two decades, dozens of companies would be spawned by the intellectual talent at Fairchild Semiconductor, giving rise to Silicon Valley.

Let's take a moment to review that sequence of events: Churchill, fearing the fall of Britain to the Nazis, sends vastly superior radar technology to the United States. Bell Labs gets the contract to work on the radar and ends up also developing transistors. Shockley takes the transistor technology to Mountain View because his mother is ill, but because of his psychological problems, his research team leaves to found Fairchild. Fairchild subsequently spawns dozens of companies that give rise to Silicon Valley. It's an iconic example of "path dependence," a situation where the outcome is exquisitely sensitive to the sequence of events that led up to it. What if Churchill had not sent the British magnetron to the United States or if the Tizard mission had been thwarted? What if the contract to work on the magnetron had not been given to Bell Laboratories? What if Shockley had not moved to Mountain View to care for his ailing mother? Any change to this sequence of events could have led to an entirely different future where Silicon Valley did not emerge. What would the United States look like today if Silicon Valley never came to be? What companies and technologies would not exist? What companies and technologies might have arisen instead? Would we know who Steve Jobs was?

We can review a similar path for most of the innovators studied here: Thomas Edison was offered a job in a telegraph station because he had saved the stationmaster's child from an oncoming train. If he had not saved that child, he would not have been offered that job, and his career would have taken a completely different direction. Edison had a nearly insatiable appetite for chemical experiments, so it is probable that he would still have become a scientist or inventor, but perhaps not in electricity. Edison (and Tesla) lived during a period that was ripe for electrical invention. Work by Hans Christian Ørsted, André-Marie Ampère, and James Clerk Maxwell on electromagnetism, the development of the electric motor by Michael Faraday, and work on electric circuits by Georg Ohm had laid the necessary scientific groundwork upon which others such as Edison, Tesla, Bell, Kelvin, and Westinghouse would build.[31] Because the timing was right, we didn't just see a steady trickle of invention in electrical devices; we saw a huge surge in electrical inventions that would drive the second industrial revolution and radically transform our society's way of life.[32] If Tesla or Edison had come of age in a different time or chosen a path in something other than electricity, they may have still been inventors—possibly even famous inventors—but they would not be known for the things they are known for today. It is even possible that their names would have been lost to posterity.

The role of "right time, right place" is immensely important but is not *enough* to account for a serial breakthrough innovator. Thousands of people were working on electricity and electrical devices in the late 1800s, but only a very few of them continued to develop breakthrough innovations repeatedly throughout their lives with a similar impact on the world as that of Edison or Tesla. Similarly, although thousands of people have made individual important breakthroughs in computing, none became as synonymous with repeatedly creating life-transforming products as Jobs did. Röntgen and Becquerel identified radioactive rays ahead of Curie but did not pursue them with the intensity and persistence that enabled her to become one of the most famous scientists of all time. Although the opportunities of an era are important for almost every breakthrough innovation, they are not sufficient to account for a serial breakthrough innovator. This type of innovator also has a nature and a drive that help her capitalize on such opportunities in a way that others do not.

7

"It's not about the money. It's about the people you have, how you're led, and how much you get it. . . ."

Access to Resources

The previous chapter showed that timing matters—sometimes, technological, political, or cultural shocks foster a burst of innovative activity, such as how the invention of the transistor led to major improvements in computers. Timing isn't the only source of situational advantage that affects innovation, however. Another major source of "right time, right place" benefits is an innovator's access to resources.

When business and economics researchers study why a nation or region innovates—or fails to—they often focus on access to capital and education. That makes sense; surely, having money and spending it well on innovative ventures and training have proven to be important. Also, a strong capital market—a well-developed market of investors and lenders, along with strong financial reporting standards, financial analysts, and good contract law—is important for innovation and efficiency. It also goes without saying that education enhances the opportunities of people and helps advance an economy. But how much do financial resources and education matter for the emergence of a breakthrough innovator?

The answer is surprising and is more nuanced than the question. Each innovator studied here benefited from living and working in a well-functioning economy replete with capital resources and educated people, but the innovators themselves typically had scant financial resources of their own and far less formal education than you might expect. Most, in fact, had almost no financial resources when they began their careers. Benjamin Franklin famously arrived in New York with enough money for two rolls of bread, and his formal education was close to nonexistent. Thomas Edison, likewise with almost no formal education, bootstrapped his way up from a position as a newspaper sales boy to owning his own research laboratory. Elon Musk also began his career with almost nothing, having moved to Canada as a teenager with very little money and working odd jobs during his school years to keep himself afloat. Access to financial resources is not a necessary condition for being a breakthrough innovator. In fact, it is possible that *not* having significant financial resources provides benefits by giving the innovator little to lose and ensuring a strong work ethos. As Musk tersely put it in a 2013 interview, "If I couldn't make money I could run out of food and die." On the other hand, nearly every innovator's story illustrates the important role of access to other kinds of resources, especially *technological* and *intellectual* resources. Steve Jobs provides an apt example.

Jobs was born in San Francisco on February 24, 1955, to two University of Wisconsin graduate students. His father, Abdulfattah "John" Jandali, an emigrant from Syria, was a teaching assistant pursuing his doctorate in political science. His mother, Joanne Schieble, was studying speech pathology. When the twenty-three-year-old students realized they had conceived a child, they at first planned to marry. However, their plans were thwarted by Joanne's conservative father, who threatened to disown her if she married Jandali, a Muslim. Joanne thus traveled to San Francisco to have her child in secrecy and then gave him up for adoption. The family Joanne first chose was Catholic, well-educated, and affluent. However, at the last minute they decided to adopt a girl instead. The baby was then placed with Paul and Clara Jobs, who named him Steven Paul Jobs.

Joanne was dissatisfied with the Jobs family and took them to court to challenge the adoption. Although she ultimately agreed to drop the case under the condition that Paul and Clara Jobs commit to sending Steve to college, the court case had created an unsettling start for the new family. Chrisann Brennan, Jobs's first girlfriend, later recounted that one day when she and Steve were teenagers and had only recently begun dating, Clara suddenly confessed to her that "I was too frightened to love him for the first six months of his life. . . . I was scared they were going to take him away from me. Even after we won the case, Steve was so difficult a child that by the time he was two I felt we had made a mistake. I wanted to return him."[1] By many accounts, the knowledge that his birth parents had given him up weighed heavily on Jobs, a source of pain and bitterness he would wrestle with throughout his life.

The Jobs family lived in a modest home in the San Francisco suburb of Mountain View, right in the center of the area that would become known as Silicon Valley. Paul was an engine mechanic who had dropped out of high school and served in the Coast Guard during World War II. He was an industrious man who was constantly working. In his spare time, he would buy old cars and fix them up for resale. Paul had a well-stocked workshop in his garage with hundreds of impeccably organized tools, each with its proper place outlined on a pegboard in black marker. Steve's room was similarly meticulous in its organization; every item had been carefully assessed for its value, usefulness, and the space it took up—much like the set of priorities with which he would later design computers.[2] Clara was a good-natured woman whose parents had emigrated to the United States after fleeing the Turks in Armenia. She worked as a bookkeeper.

From early on it became clear that Steve was *very* smart. He was also very rebellious and was prone to getting in trouble at school, where he was frequently bored. When he was in the fourth grade, Steve scored at the tenth-grade level on intelligence tests, so his elementary school suggested having him skip two grades to keep him adequately stimulated. His parents wisely had him skip only one and moved to a new neighborhood in Los Altos, also in Silicon Valley, so Steve could attend a better school.

After work or on weekends, Paul would show Steve the cars he was working on, and the two would often go together to junkyards to look for needed parts, a skill that Steve would later use when he hunted through technology flea markets. His father also taught him to appreciate careful design—including the insides and backs of products that a user would not normally see—because these were important aspects of quality craftsmanship. This was also a lesson Steve would use later in life; the circuit boards of Apple computers had to look orderly, and even the inside of the computer cases had to be polished to perfection. Although Paul could be hard on Steve, and according to Chrisann Brennan would constantly berate him with criticism and disapproval, Steve responded with "sad smiles and painstaking patience."[3] He knew his adopted parents were devoted to him, and he loved them deeply.

Heathkits, from which one could build radios and television receivers, were an obsession for Jobs during his teenage years. The kits gave him confidence about his ability to understand electronics and build electronic products. As Jobs explained, "Heathkits came with all the boards and parts color-coded but the manual also explained the theory of how it operated. . . . It made you realize you could build and understand anything. Once you built a couple of radios, you'd see a TV in the catalogue and say 'I can build that as well,' even if you didn't. I was very lucky, because when I was a kid both my dad and the Heathkits made me believe I could build anything."[4]

The Steve Jobs we know as a serial breakthrough innovator may have emerged from just about anywhere, but his chances were enormously enhanced because of the San Francisco area's unique endowment of technological and intellectual resources. By the 1960s, Silicon Valley had already emerged as one of the largest and most important information technology clusters in the world. Its genesis had begun in the early 1900s, when the area became a site of significant US naval research and technology. Firms such as Federal Telegraph Corporation were creating wireless communication systems, and Lockheed was founded there to develop aerospace applications. In 1933 an air base in Sunnyvale became the Naval Air Station Moffett Field, which would later house the National Advisory Committee for Aeronautics. Silicon Valley was thus an early fertile garden for advanced electronic technologies. In the 1940s and 1950s, Frederick Terman (then Stanford's dean of engineering) began encouraging Stanford students and faculty to start up entrepreneurial ventures. He also leased land around the campus to high-technology companies in order to fund the university's growth. Soon Stanford had become the hub of a thriving technology center that included Hewlett Packard, Varian Associates, Intel, and, as noted in the previous chapter, Shockley Semiconductor and Fairchild Semiconductor. Nearly every household in Jobs's neighborhood was connected in one way or another to electronics and engineering. When many technology-based companies are in this type of proximity, clustering advantages emerge. As decades of research in economic geography have shown, employment opportunities multiply in technology clusters, and the region grows a large pool of highly skilled labor. Furthermore, employees from different companies will be neighbors and belong to the same clubs; their children will go to the same schools. Soon a web of personal relationships knits the organizations together and ensures that knowledge rapidly diffuses among them.[5] In the words of the famous economist Alfred Marshall, who wrote about such clusters,

"[T]he mysteries of the trade become no mysteries; but are as if it were in the air."[6] Breathing such heady air undoubtedly made any teenager growing up in this environment more likely to enter the information technology industry, but it was a particularly rich resource for a smart and enterprising kid like Jobs.

Having a father and a wide array of people in his neighborhood with expertise in electronics had an importance influence on Jobs's future, as did seeing what was going on in nearby organizations and companies. He described this early influence during an interview in 1990:

> I saw my first computer when I was twelve. And it was at NASA. We had a local NASA center nearby. And it was a terminal, which was connected to a big computer somewhere and I got a timesharing account on it. And I was fascinated by this thing. And I saw my second computer a few years later which was really the first desktop computer ever made. It was made by Hewlett Packard. It was called the 9100-A. And it ran a language called BASIC. And it was very large. It had a very small cathode ray tube on it for display. And I got a chance to play with one of those maybe in 1968 or '69. And spent every spare moment I had trying to write programs for it. I was so fascinated by this. And so I was probably fairly lucky.[7]

One engineer in the neighborhood was Francis Wozniak, a brilliant rocket scientist at Lockheed who taught engineering principles to his son Steve, known to his friends as "Woz." As Woz recounted, "He would explain what a resistor was by going all the way back to atoms and electrons. He explained how resistors worked when I was in second grade, not by equations but by having me picture it."[8] Woz was both extremely intelligent and extremely nerdy—he was much more comfortable with circuit boards and transistors than with people. When he and Steve Jobs met, however, they became immediate friends. Their shared passions included pranks, electronics, and music. As Woz noted, "We had so much in common. Typically, it was really hard for me to explain to people what kind of design stuff I worked on, but Steve got it right away. And I liked him. He was kind of skinny and wiry and full of energy."[9] It was a serendipitous meeting for both: while their commonalities brought them together, their differences made them a synergistic match. Jobs was the spiritual dreamer with vision and ambition; Woz was the gifted technical genius who could execute Jobs's ideas. Jobs had a domineering and mercurial nature that made him difficult to get along with, but Woz's unassuming and gentle disposition made him exceptionally tolerant of Jobs's difficult personality and sometimes hurtful behaviors. Soon the two young men were spending much of their time hunting down Bob Dylan bootlegs and coming up with complicated pranks together. One such prank, which ultimately became their first money-making venture, was creating the "blue boxes" that enabled them to fool the AT&T phone system into making long-distance calls for free, as discussed earlier.

When Steve Jobs graduated from high school in 1972, his parents honored their commitment to his birth mother, Joanne, by agreeing to send him to the college of his choice. Steve chose the very expensive and artistic Reed College, in Oregon. There, like many American college campuses, students were transitioning from the activism of the 1960s into the pursuit of enlightenment and personal expression of the 1970s. Jobs became increasingly involved in meditation, Zen Buddhism, and psychedelic drugs, and these things, in turn, would cause him to increasingly value intuition and a minimalist aesthetic. Minimalist design and an emphasis on intuitive interfaces would become the signature features of the products he would later design.

Jobs didn't like conforming to the curriculum requirements of Reed, and he also felt guilty about the financial burden it was imposing on his parents. He therefore made the rather remarkable decision to drop out of Reed but continue to audit the courses he found interesting. As Jobs later described, "I had no idea what I wanted to do with my life and no idea how college was going to help me figure it out. And here I was spending all of the money my parents had saved their entire life. So I decided to drop out and trust that it would all work out OK."[10] The dean of students at Reed, Jack Dudman, agreed because "He had a very inquiring mind that was enormously attractive. . . . He refused to accept automatically received truths, and he wanted to examine everything himself."[11] He rented a garage apartment for $20 per month and supported himself by returning soda bottles for the five-cent deposits. He would walk seven miles across town every Sunday evening to get dinner at the Hare Krishna temple. He enjoyed his Bohemian lifestyle and had little need for material goods. However, by February 1974, after eighteen months of hanging around Reed, he knew it was time to move on.

Jobs moved back in with his parents and, as noted earlier, took a job at Atari. It was during his time at Atari that he began working again with Woz. Nolan Bushnell, founder of Atari, had challenged Steve to develop a single-player version of Pong, with a catch: if the design used fewer than fifty chips, he would get a bonus for every chip under fifty used. Jobs recruited Woz to help him as Woz was by far the better engineer. Woz would work on the design while Jobs implemented it. The pair finished the project in four days, using only forty-five chips. This success reaffirmed what the blue box experience had taught the young men a few years earlier: Jobs's ambition and design skills paired with Wozniak's engineering genius made a powerful combination. Jobs was bold and visionary; Wozniak provided the exceptional intellectual and technological resources to deliver on that vision. They were primed to seize the next big opportunity, and they wouldn't have to wait long.

In January 1975, *Popular Mechanics* put the first personal computer kit, the Altair, on its cover. The Altair was invented by Henry Edward "Ed" Roberts, a computer engineer who had previously created and sold model rocketry and calculator kits. Although the Altair was little more than a series of switches that could be flicked in a sequence that would generate a pattern of lights, it was an object of desperate desire to hobbyists and would-be software programmers. Before 1975, unless you were a computer engineer working for a large company with a mainframe computer, you had no access to a computer of any kind. The Altair, as simple as it was, was *almost* a computer, and anyone could buy the kit for about $500. When that January issue came out, Roberts's company, Micro Instrumentation and Telemetry System (known as MITS), was flooded with orders and sold thousands of kits within the first month. The Altair was an inspiration to Jobs and Wozniak. Wozniak, in fact, knew he could do better than Roberts had done. The Altair used the Intel 8080 microprocessor, which at around $180 per unit was too expensive for Jobs and Woz. Instead, they found a $20 microprocessor made by MOS Technologies, the MOS 6502, which was nearly identical to the Motorola 6800—a $360 microprocessor. Woz immediately set about assembling and coding a computer based on this microprocessor, and just a few months later he had created a prototype that enabled him to type letters on a keyboard and have them show up on the monitor—the first time in history this had been achieved. Jobs made some calls to Intel and was able to obtain some dynamic random-access memory chips for free. Jobs also began accompanying Woz to the Homebrew Computing Club, a club at Stanford where many of personal computing's "firsts" got their start.[12] Woz's instinct was to give his schematics away for free: "It never crossed my mind to sell computers. It was Steve who said, 'Let's hold them in the air and sell a few.'"[13] There was no business plan or a hunt for investors. There was no rented office or manufacturing space, and no corporate logo—none of the trappings of business that today's would-be entrepreneurs assume are crucial for their start-up. It was just two guys building computers in the Jobs family garage with $1,300 raised by selling Woz's calculator and Jobs's Volkswagen bus.

The Apple I enjoyed a modicum of success—selling a few hundred units—but it was merely a computer circuit board and required hours of laborious assembly. Jobs soon realized that very few people wanted to assemble their own computer: "It was clear to me that for every hardware hobbyist who wanted to assemble his own computer, there were a thousand people who couldn't do that but wanted to mess around with programming . . . just like I did when I was 10. My dream for the Apple II was to sell the first real packaged computer. . . . I got a bug up my rear that I wanted the computer in a plastic case."[14] In September 1976, Wozniak and Jobs began developing the Apple II, placing it in an elegant molded plastic case so that it had the friendly aesthetic appeal of a high-end kitchen appliance rather than an industrial device. Jobs also insisted that it have a power supply that did not require a fan because the noise of a fan was *not* Zen. However, these design decisions required money, which Woz and Jobs didn't have. They also needed managerial expertise to help run the growing company. Fortunately, being in the heart of Silicon Valley, with its dense network of information technology companies and investors, gave them access to both. Jobs approached his former employer, Atari's Nolan Bushnell. Bushnell declined Jobs's offer to sell him a one-third stake in the company for $50,000 (Bushnell later remarked, "It's kind of fun to think about that, when I'm not crying"[15]) but referred him to Don Valentine, the founder of Sequoia Capital, a Menlo Park venture capital firm. Valentine also declined to invest, but he gave Jobs a referral to Mike Markkula Jr., a former marketing manager at Fairchild Semiconductor and Intel, who had made millions on stock options and retired at the age of thirty-three. Markkula agreed to join as a partner and provide capital, and in April 1977 they launched the Apple II, a $1,298 product that could be used straight out of the box. Markkula's time at Fairchild and Intel had given him deep insight into the pricing, marketing, and distributing of technology products. He also had a large network of personal connections in the industry and could help Jobs and Wozniak access the people, technology, and money they needed. He would prove to be an invaluable resource to Apple, and to Jobs personally, over the next two decades.

The Apple II was an unprecedented success; by the end of 1978, Apple's sales were about $15 million, but this was just the beginning.[16] By itself, the personal computer was still mostly a toy for hobbyists. The breakthrough to a much bigger market came in 1979, when Daniel Bricklin and Bob Frankston launched a software program called Visicalc (for "visible calculator"). This was a spreadsheet program that came to be known as the first "killer app" of the personal computer era.[17] Visicalc could do in an instant what would formerly take accountants hours to do by hand with a ledger and a desktop calculator, and it transformed the personal computer into a crucially important business tool. Luckily for Jobs and Woz, Visicalc had been created on, and for, Apple computers.

By 1980, Apple was generating over $100 million in annual revenues and had more than 1,000 employees. Just three years after its founding, Apple Computer went public, and when trading of its shares closed on the first day, Apple had a valuation of $1.8 billion—more than any other initial public offering since Ford went public in 1956.[18] Suddenly IBM, Hewlett Packard, and others realized they had seriously underestimated the potential role of the personal computer. This was particularly jolting for IBM, for decades the 800-pound gorilla of the computing industry. Respect for IBM bordered on reverence. A well-known piece of folk wisdom in the business world was that "nobody ever got fired for buying IBM." As IBM executive Jack Sams reminisced, "The worry was that we were losing the hearts and minds. . . . So the order came down from on high: 'Give me a machine to win back the hearts and minds.'"[19]

In its race to bring a personal computer to market quickly, IBM decided to use many off-the-shelf components from other vendors, including Intel's 8088 microprocessor and Microsoft's software. IBM was not worried about imitators because IBM's proprietary basic input/output system (BIOS), the computer code that linked the computer's hardware to its software, was protected by copyright. While other firms could copy the BIOS code, doing so would violate IBM's copyright and incur the legendary wrath of IBM's legal team. IBM thus believed its personal computer was protected from direct imitation. This couldn't have been more wrong. Getting around IBM's copyright turned out to not be so difficult after all. Copyright protected the written lines of code, but not the functions those codes produced. Compaq exploited this weakness by having a team of programmers document every function the IBM computer would perform in response to a given command, without recording the code that performed the function. This list of functions was then given to another team of "virgin" programmers who could prove they had never been exposed to IBM's BIOS code.[20] These programmers went through the list of functions and wrote code to create identical functions. As a result, Compaq was able to reverse engineer the BIOS in a matter of months without violating IBM's copyright. Compaq sold a record-breaking 47,000 IBM-compatible computers in its first year (it would go on to become one of the world's largest computer manufacturers and was acquired by Hewlett Packard in 2002). Once Compaq had reverse engineered the BIOS, other clones were quick to follow.[21] In order to perfectly emulate the IBM personal computer, the clones all adopted the operating system and microprocessor used in the IBM models: Microsoft's MS-DOS and Intel's 8088. So, while IBM had been ineffective in securing proprietary control of its own computer design, it had inadvertently created dominant positions for Microsoft and Intel.

Meanwhile, in December 1979 a group of Apple engineers, including Jobs, had been permitted to tour the fabled Xerox Palo Alto Research Center (PARC). Xerox knew that computers were a threat to its printing and copying business and had set up the center to find a way to dominate the paperless office of the future. Xerox thus gave a group of young, genius computer researchers free rein. According to former Xerox PARC researcher and later chief scientist at Apple Larry Tesler, "The management said 'Go create the new world. We don't understand it.'"[22] There Xerox had developed the Alto, the first computer with a graphical user interface (GUI) that enabled the user to interact with the computer with a mouse, and it was connected to other computers by means of the Ethernet, the first computer network. However, the Xerox executives were hesitant to move forward on any of the leading-edge technologies—they just didn't understand them. As put by former PARC researcher John Warnock, "There was a tremendous mismatch between the management and what the researchers were doing . . . they had no mechanisms for turning those ideas into real life products. That was really the frustrating part of it, because you were talking to people who didn't understand the vision."[23] However, Steve Jobs understood the vision. As he recalled,

> And they showed me, really, three things. But I was so blinded by the first one that I didn't even really see the other two. One of the things they showed me was object-oriented programming. They showed me that, but I didn't even see that. The other one they showed me was really a networked computer system. They had over a hundred Alto computers all networked, using email, etc. I didn't even see that. I was so blinded by the first thing they showed me, which was the graphical user interface. I thought it was the best thing I'd ever seen in my life. . . . Within ten minutes it was obvious to me that all computers would work like this someday."[24]

Being able to witness the stunning software that Xerox had created, before Xerox itself had figured out how to commercialize it, was yet another example of Jobs being at the perfect place at the perfect time. It is hard to overstate how important Jobs's exposure to the developments at PARC was to the success of Apple. PARC had hired an army of brilliant engineering talent that spent years creating revolutionary technologies and then, in a single afternoon, gave them away. From the moment Jobs saw those revolutionary technologies, he knew they would change the world. He picked up the ball that Xerox had dropped and ran with it.

Astounded that Xerox had not commercialized the GUI for the personal computer market, Jobs and his team immediately set about not only executing Xerox's ideas but also improving them. With Bill Atkinson as principal design engineer, they created a virtual desk where an individual could pick up a file by dragging the mouse over its icon or access other features from a menu bar at the top of the screen. People would no longer need to know commands or be taught how to use a computer—the computer would be intuitive.

The interface was first incorporated into the Apple Lisa, a high-end computer being developed for the business market. The computer was named after the daughter Steve Jobs had fathered with Chrisann Brennan. (This was an interesting choice given that he had initially denied that he was her father.) Unfortunately, Jobs's demanding and volatile nature led to frequent clashes on the team, so Mike Markkula and Michael Scott (who Markkula had insisted be hired to act as president of the company because neither Wozniak nor Jobs had the experience required) removed Jobs from his role of running the Lisa project. The frustrated Jobs responded by taking over the Macintosh project—a much more affordable personal computer being developed by Jef Raskin. He moved the Macintosh project into a separate building across the street from Apple, flying a pirate's flag overhead to signify the project's rebellious autonomy, and told his team "It's better to be a pirate than to join the Navy!"[25] Jobs instinctively understood that in order to create something really special, the Macintosh people needed to be both physically and psychologically distanced from the rest of Apple. This distance would enable them to have their own standards and norms and to create their own dream.

Jobs's perfectionism bordered on fanaticism. Fonts had to have perfect proportional spacing, and window icons had to have beautiful curves. According to one Macintosh team member, "He hounded the people on the Macintosh project to do their best work. He sang their praises, bullied them unmercifully, and told them they weren't making a computer, they were making history. He promoted the Mac passionately, making people believe that he was talking about much more than a piece of office equipment."[26] Perfectionism was part of Jobs's idealism; the Mac was supposed to revolutionize personal expression. Its designers weren't just engineers; they were artists as well. As Andy Hertzfeld recalled of his time on the Macintosh team, "The goal was never to beat the competition, or to make a lot of money. It was to do the greatest thing possible, or even a little greater."[27] Compromises were not to be tolerated.

Jobs demanded that the Mac launch by early 1982.[28] This was an inconceivable schedule, but Jobs insisted it was possible and bent others to this belief with his "reality distortion field," as described in Chapter 1. As Hertzfeld noted, "If one line of argument failed to persuade, he would deftly switch to another. Sometimes, he would throw you off balance by suddenly adopting your position as his own, without acknowledging that he ever thought differently."[29] It's worth noting that Elon Musk makes similarly "impossible" demands of his employees, although his style is more brute force than reality distortion field. On one occasion, for example, Musk gave a speech at Tesla noting that the team (including himself) would need to work Saturdays and Sundays, sleeping under their desks in order to meet a deadline. When an employee argued that everyone had been working very hard and needed a break to see their families, Musk fired back with "I would tell those people they will get to see their families a lot when we go bankrupt."[30]

The Macintosh ultimately launched in January 1984 at a price of $2,495. It was smaller and lighter than most personal computers, and during its hundred-day introductory period, it included a free word processing program and a graphics package.[31] It was a remarkable technical achievement that combined ease of use with advanced graphics capabilities that immediately secured it a stronghold position in desktop publishing. By now, however, it was facing significant competition from the IBM PC, IBM clones, the Commodore 64, the Atari 400/800, and others. Worse still, Bill Gates announced that Microsoft was developing a graphical user interface for IBM personal computers and IBM clones that would enable them to emulate the ease of use of the Macintosh. This interface would be known as Windows.

The Microsoft announcement infuriated Jobs, who felt betrayed. He had signed Gates on to develop graphical versions of a spreadsheet program and a word processing program, along with the BASIC programming language for the Macintosh; thus, Gates and his engineering team had frequent exposure to the Macintosh development project. Hertzfeld had begun to worry about it, noting that his contact at Microsoft had been asking many detailed questions about how the Mac's operating system worked: "I told Steve that I suspected that Microsoft was going to clone the Mac."[32] Gates had agreed that Microsoft would not develop graphical software for any other computer companies until after the Macintosh launched, but at that time the launch date was scheduled to be January 1983 (already a year past Jobs's initial launch date for the computer). The delay in launching meant that Gates had not actually violated the Apple agreement.

Jobs insisted Gates come down to face him; remarkably, he did. Hertzfeld recalled that Gates was in a room with ten Apple employees, including Steve Jobs, when Jobs assailed him: "You're ripping us off! I trusted you, and now you're stealing from us!" But Gates remained cool, looked Jobs directly in the eye, and responded, "Well, Steve, I think there's more than one way of looking at it. I think it's more like we both had this rich neighbor named Xerox and I broke into his house to steal the TV set and found out that you had already stolen it."[33]

As IBM personal computers and their clones rose, it put pressure on Apple to allow cloning of the Macintosh as well—that is, to license the Macintosh operating system and hardware specifications to other companies that would enable them to produce Macintosh-like machines. Without cloning, many feared that Apple would increasingly lose share in what was starting to look like a winner-take-all market. An operating system that has more users attracts more developers of complementary software applications. The operating system with the most compatible software applications, in turn, has an advantage in attracting users. It was a self-reinforcing cycle known as "network externalities" that could cause a single standard to rise to overwhelming dominance in a market. Licensing the Macintosh operating system to other computer hardware producers might result in lower-cost Macintosh-like products coming to the market, helping to increase sales of the Macintosh operating system and turning the tide back in Apple's favor.

However, Jobs was staunchly opposed to cloning. He believed strongly that the quality of the hardware and simplicity and beauty of the user experience could be protected only by keeping the entire computer proprietary and integrated. As he would later articulate, "We're the only company that owns the whole widget—the hardware, the software and the operating system. We can take full responsibility for the user experience. We can do things the other guy can't do."[34] He wanted to instead boost sales of the Macintosh by cutting its price. Unfortunately for Jobs, he no longer had the last word at Apple after the company went public. As disagreements became increasingly heated between Steve Jobs and John Scully, who had been brought in to help manage the firm, the board of directors sided with Scully. Jobs was ousted from his role of running the Macintosh team and given the ceremonial role of chairman. Feeling shocked and betrayed, he turned down the job and resigned from Apple:

> What had been the focus of my entire adult life was gone, and it was devastating. I really didn't know what to do for a few

> months. I felt that I had let the previous generation of entrepreneurs down—that I had dropped the baton as it was being passed to me. I met with David Packard [cofounder of HP] and Bob Noyce [cofounder of Intel] and tried to apologize for screwing up so badly. I was a very public failure, and I even thought about running away from the valley. But something slowly began to dawn on me—I still loved what I did. The turn of events at Apple had not changed that one bit. I had been rejected, but I was still in love. And so I decided to start over. I didn't see it then, but it turned out that getting fired from Apple was the best thing that could have ever happened to me. The heaviness of being successful was replaced by the lightness of being a beginner again, less sure about everything. It freed me to enter one of the most creative periods of my life.[35]

One of the most important traits of a successful breakthrough innovator, as we previously noted, is persistence in the face of criticism or failure. The most profoundly successful innovators are tenacious, persevering long after most other people would walk away. Jobs was such an innovator. Within a few months he founded a new computer company called NeXT, and the next year he also funded the spinoff of a computer animation division from George Lucas's Industrial Light & Magic that was led by Edmund Catmull and Alvy Ray Smith, and came to be known as the animated film company Pixar. NeXT made high-end workstations based on object-oriented software. The computers were technically extremely elegant and visually striking—black die-cast magnesium cubes, with each side exactly one foot long. The NeXT won accolades and awards for its innovative design, but with a $6,500 price tag and few compatible software applications, the hardware was doomed to commercial failure. Pixar, on the other hand, became one of the most successful film production companies of all time. Jobs's visionary perfectionism was a perfect fit for the ambitions of Catmull and Smith. Together, Jobs, Catmull, and Smith shared the dream of using computers to push the state of the art in animation as far as possible. The cutting-edge technology they developed made it possible to use computer animation to make full-length feature films with stunning graphics quality.

During the time with Jobs out of the company, Apple Computer didn't fare well. Scully had tried to gain share by introducing lower-cost products and initiated a program to develop a version of the Mac operating system that would run on Intel-based personal computers. However, with profit margins at their lowest ever, the board of directors decided to replace him in 1993 with Mike Spindler, who had been running Apple's international operations at the time and had formerly worked for Digital Equipment Corporation and Intel. Spindler didn't fare much better. He canceled the program to put the Mac operating system on Intel-based personal computers and instead licensed a handful of companies to make Macintosh clones. He also made efforts to slash costs, cutting 16 percent of Apple's workforce and reducing R&D spending.[36] Profits unfortunately continued to slide, and after posting a $69 million loss in early 1996, the board replaced him with Gilbert Amelio, a former CEO of National Semiconductor who had previously worked at both Bell Labs and Fairchild Semiconductor. Amelio decided to streamline Apple's product line and focus on higher-margin products. He also hoped that a new advanced operating system would restore Apple to a position of technological leadership. However, work on the next generation of the Mac operating system wasn't going well. The company had spent $500 million on R&D to develop the operating system, had incurred multiple delays, and still was far from where it needed to be. Scully, Spindler, and Amelio were all experienced and respected executives, but it appeared that none of them could revive Apple, and by the fall of 1996 it appeared to be months away from bankruptcy. *Wired* even ran an article titled "101 Ways to Save Apple," and among the ways were "Sell yourself to IBM or Motorola" and "License the Apple name to appliance manufacturers."[37]

In December 1996, in a truth-is-stranger-than-fiction moment, Amelio canceled the Macintosh operating system development program and announced his plan to buy NeXT Software instead.[38] Apple bought NeXT Software for $429 million in January 1997; its operating system, NeXTSTEP, would become the foundation for the new Mac operating system, and Jobs would be brought on as a part-time adviser.[39] Many in the industry had already been murmuring about the possibility of bringing Jobs back to run Apple. Despite the many criticisms one could levy against Jobs for his management style, many people had begun to realize that much of the "magic" that had made Apple special and had inspired a zealously loyal following had come from his intense idealism and passion. Amelio's decision to bring Jobs in as an adviser was a tacit admission of it, and years later Scully would state to the press that Jobs had been the greatest CEO of all time. Within nine months of the acquisition, the board asked Jobs to take the position of CEO. He declined, agreeing instead to serve as interim CEO to help get the company back on track until someone else could be found. He was, after all, already CEO of Pixar.

With Jobs as interim CEO, Apple began to turn around. First, he killed the Mac clone project. Then he slashed almost all of the fifty or so development projects that were under way. Apple would focus on making just four great products: a desktop and a notebook for consumers (the iMac and iBook) and a desktop and a notebook for businesses (Power Mac and Powerbook). As Jobs described the situation, "People think focus means saying *yes* to the thing you've got to focus on. But that's not what it means at all. It means saying no to the hundred other good ideas that there are. You have to pick carefully. I'm actually as proud of the things we haven't done as the things I have done. Innovation is saying no to 1,000 things."[40] Whereas companies like Sony and Nike had become famous for using incremental innovation to rapidly spawn hundreds of different versions of their products—a phenomenon referred to as "mass customization"—Jobs preferred to invest all of the company's money and energy on a few blockbuster products. In 1998, when UCLA strategy professor Richard Rumelt pointed out that it could be difficult to survive as a niche computer maker and asked Jobs what he planned to do next, Jobs just smiled and replied that he was "waiting for the next big thing."[41] As it turned out, he wouldn't have to wait very long.

All of the products were successful, but the most pivotal would be the iMac. Jobs had put industrial designer Jonathan Ive in charge of creating the look of the product, which would be remarkable for its rounded shape and boldly colored translucent case. Jobs, who always had a preference for simplicity, insisted that the iMac not have a floppy drive and that all the old input/output ports common on other personal computers be replaced with USB slots. The iMac turned out to be one of Apple's most successful products ever, selling two million units in its first two years.[42] The iBook, which had a similar design theme as the iMac, with rounded shapes and bold colors, and an attractive $1,599 price, was also a strong seller.[43] NeXTSTEP was also successfully integrated into a new Mac operating system called MacOS X. From 1997 to 2000, Apple went from posting a $1 billion loss to a $786 million profit, and in 2000 Jobs acknowledged what was already obvious to everyone—that he would stay at Apple—and he dropped the "interim" from his title.

If anyone had ever doubted the role that Jobs played in creating breakthrough innovation at Apple, the next decade would stamp out all uncertainty. In the late 1990s, the music industry was undergoing turbulent change. An algorithm developed by Fraunhofer IIS of Germany had enabled digital audio files to be compressed to approximately one-tenth of their original size. This format was later dubbed MP3. Digital files could now be stored on the hard drive of a computer and shared over the Internet. In the late 1990s several companies introduced portable audio devices to store and play the files, such as Diamond's Rio, Compaq's Personal Jukebox, and Creative's NOMAD jukebox, but none gained much traction. Then in 1999, Shawn Fanning, a student at Northeastern

University, released Napster, a software program that offered a user-friendly way of finding and sharing music online, becoming one of the first widely adopted "peer-to-peer" applications.[44] Napster was free, and by March 2000, five million copies had been downloaded.[45] The great majority of music downloaded through Napster was copyrighted—commercial records and songs. The Record Industry Association of America (RIAA), the trade group that represents the leading music business entities in the United States, became increasingly alarmed and sought a way to stem the flow of pirated music. The RIAA initiated legal action against Napster and its users, and in July 2001 the courts ruled that the Napster service had to be taken offline. However, the genie could not be put back in the bottle. Other MP3 exchange services began sprouting up online, and it was clear that if the record labels wanted to stop the illegal exchange of music, they needed to come up with a better option. Warner Music, BMG, EMI, and RealNetworks teamed up to introduce a subscription service called MusicNet, and Sony Entertainment partnered with Universal to create its own service called Pressplay. However, both were harder to use and offered fewer selections than the illegal exchange services did. The music industry giants needed a better solution, and Jobs was about to offer it to them.

In October 2001, Apple launched the iPod, a portable music player with a sleek shape, an easy-to-use interface, and a hard drive big enough to put "1,000 songs in your pocket."[46] It was a very surprising move for a company whose entire history had been in computers. Analysts and press were openly skeptical; even Apple fans were dubious of the move.[47] However, Jobs had a vision for the Mac as the center of a "digital hub" in the home, and a digital hub had to provide, among other things, music. Jobs didn't like any of the existing portable digital audio players of the time. They either held too few songs or were too heavy or cumbersome to use. The company would have to come up with its own, better design. It took many talented engineers, some external components, and the design talent of Jonathan Ive to come up with what emerged as the iPod. Given the previous lack of success of portable digital audio players and Apple's inexperience in consumer electronics, most people thought the device would fail. They would be proven wrong. Even at $399, a price well above other competing products, the iPod had strong initial sales. The original iPod was compatible only with the Mac, but after a version was released in mid-2002 that was compatible with Windows (a move suggesting that Jobs realized that the iPod could be more successful than Mac computers could ever be), sales took off, reaching over a million iPods sold within a year.

In April 2003 Apple opened its iTunes Music Store. Jobs had struck agreements with the five major record labels (Sony, Universal, BMG, Warner Music Group, and EMI), and he launched iTunes with an initial catalog of 200,000 songs, offered for $.99 each.[48] Although several of the record labels initially balked at selling individual songs or at selling them all for the same price, Jobs countered with "We don't see how you can convince people to stop being thieves, unless you can offer them a carrot—not just a stick. And the carrot is: We're gonna offer you a better experience . . . and it's only gonna cost you a dollar a song."[49] Later, when Jobs was asked why he thought the music industry had been willing to trust Apple, he responded:

> Apple is the most creative technology company out there—just like Pixar is the most technologically adept creative company. . . . Also, almost all recording artists use Macs and they have iPods, and now most of the music industry people have iPods as well. There's a trust in the music community that Apple will do something right—that it won't cut corners—and that it cares about the creative process and about the music. Also, our solution encompasses operating system software, server software, application software, and hardware. Apple is the only company in the world that has all that under one roof. We can invent a complete solution that works—and take responsibility for it.[50]

Apple's cool image, the attractive price point for the songs, and the fact that it could offer music from all five of the major record labels was a recipe for success. iTunes reached 50 million downloads within the first year and quickly became the leading distributor of music online.[51]

In January 2007 Apple made an even more stunning move by announcing the iPhone. To understand how surprising a move this was, it is useful to understand just how brutally competitive the mobile handset industry had become. Although sales of handsets were growing rapidly, the market was also extremely consolidated (Nokia, Motorola, and Samsung collectively controlled about 70 percent of the market), and extreme competition on both price and innovation was the norm. It was almost impossible for smaller companies to compete. This was especially true in the United States, where a large share of mobile phones were sold to a few giant phone service carriers such as AT&T, Verizon, and Sprint, which wielded considerable power to negotiate deep discounts. Furthermore, while on the one hand the emergence of smartphones had prompted consumers to begin to expect much more advanced technologies in their phones, the fact that carriers typically subsidized the purchase price of the phones by building the cost into service contracts meant that most consumers did not have a good sense of the cost and worth of the technology. Most people did not expect to pay more than $200 for a cell phone because most never had—at least not directly. By narrowing the gap in price between basic cell phones and the most sophisticated cell phones, carriers had (probably unwittingly) made it harder for handset manufacturers to charge higher prices for more-sophisticated phones.

Ericsson, once a leading handset maker, gave up the battle in October 2001 and exited the handset business. Palm, the maker of what is considered to be the first successful personal digital assistant, and its offspring Handspring had both evaporated by 2006. Why would Apple want to enter such a competitive, consolidated industry that appeared so unrelated to its core area of expertise?

Ed Coligan, the former CEO of Palm, remarked that it had taken the company a few years of struggle to figure out how to make a decent phone, and "PC guys are not going to just figure this out. They're not going to just walk in."[52] He could not have been more wrong.

In my many years of teaching innovation and counseling entrepreneurs and innovators, I've come to realize that when entrepreneurs and innovators come up with breakthrough ideas, it is often difficult for others (including myself) to understand them. Other people don't see the vision, and they don't feel the thrill felt by the innovator. They often react with deep skepticism. Sometimes the innovator can explain it well enough to bring others on board, but even if she cannot, it doesn't mean the idea isn't a good one. The very things that make an innovator capable of generating and pursuing a breakthrough idea are the reasons that others won't initially understand. Their ability to challenge assumptions and their extreme self-efficacy make them able to conceive of, and commit to, an idea that sounds absurd to others. They are willing to pursue an idea even when everybody else says it's crazy precisely because they don't need the affirmation of others—they believe they are right even if you don't agree. Thus, I now try not to judge the potential of an idea—I'm too often wrong—and instead I advise innovators not to expect everyone to understand. I just try to give them the tools they need to make better decisions based on their own conception of what is possible.

When Apple launched the iPhone in June 2007, the reason for the move became suddenly clear. Not only was the iPhone a thing of beauty, with the clean, smooth lines that Apple had come to be known for, but it also had a remarkable range of functionality accessed through an exquisitely intuitive interface. Many people clearly remember the first time they stroked a finger across the screen of an iPhone and saw the applications scroll by. They didn't slide mechanically; they sailed smoothly, with acceleration and deceleration, like a coaster flicked across a polished table. It was captivating. Furthermore, the interface was so intuitive that toddlers could immediately use it and then expect the television and other electronic devices to work the same way. That interface instantly elevated our expectations about how things should work, which must have put an enormous grin on Steve Jobs's face. Furthermore, there were dozens of applications that became indispensable to people's lives, and the quality of the applications was very carefully controlled so that the user experience would always be seamless. Ryan Block, writing for Engadget at the time, stated, "To date no one's made a phone that does so much with so little. . . . It's totally clear that with the iPhone, Apple raised the bar not only for the cellphone, but for portable media players and multifunction convergence devices in general."[53] The iPhone was, in essence, an evolutionary form of the Mac—a new and beautiful species of the Mac that users would keep with them all day long and that would enhance myriad aspects of their lives. It was a bicycle for the mind that fit in your pocket. It was so in line with Jobs's vision that when we look back now it seems an inevitable move, although it certainly was not obvious to most people in 2006.

Google, which had been designing a phone platform modeled after Windows and Blackberry, quickly pivoted to emulate the iPhone. Its Android devices would look and feel very much like an iPhone but be available from multiple manufacturers and—importantly—have a much wider range of prices. Soon Android and Apple's iOS collectively controlled a commanding share of the smartphone market. This meant that when Apple launched the iPad, which was essentially a tablet version of the iPhone, it was launching a product that could fulfill many people's needs for a personal computer, with an interface that was already well-known and well loved. The iPad's launch must have given Bill Gates a sickening feeling—for the first time since 1983, Microsoft faced a challenger that posed a very real threat of overturning its near monopoly position in personal computer operating systems.[54] By 2011, Apple and Android collectively controlled a larger share of the global computing platform market than Microsoft did. The share of iOS would continue to hover at around 20 percent for many years—bolstered by its devoted following and exceptional hardware but limited by its higher price. Android, which had emulated the style of Apple's iOS but untethered it from expensive hardware, would continue to rise, quickly eclipsing both Microsoft and Apple.

When Steve Jobs and Steve Wozniak had created the Apple I and the Apple II, Wozniak played the role of technical genius, and Jobs played the role of visionary. In the development of the Macintosh, Jef Raskin laid the groundwork for the device, and then Jobs harnessed an entire team of engineers to finish the product. It had taken Edmund Catmull, Alvy Ray Smith, Jon Lasseter, and many other brilliant people at Pixar to make a movie like *Toy Story.* And it took large teams of talented engineers and designers to bring the iPod, iPhone, and iPad to fruition. Is it thus fair to describe Jobs as the breakthrough innovator behind their creation? Without the technological and intellectual resources provided by Woz, Raskin, Ive, Catmull, Smith, Lasseter, and others, many of these products might not have been created. However, Wozniak is quick to admit that without Jobs he would have simply handed out his specifications for the Apple I at the Homebrew Computing Club—Apple would have never been founded, and it is likely that the Apple II would have never been created. Apple's period without Jobs was notably fallow, with only one significant innovation during that time: the Newton, which flopped. When Jobs returned to Apple, the company roared back to life, creating one stunning and unlikely innovation after another. Apple's products under the new reign of Jobs weren't just *good;* they also transformed the way people *lived.* Jobs never strived to simply make a product better—he made products the way he believed *they should be.* He rarely used market research because he felt that most consumers' imaginations were too limited; consumers, when asked what they wanted, would let their ideas be overly constrained by the parameters of products that already existed. Instead, Jobs would think about how the world should work without constraints. His gift of imagination and intuition helped him conceive amazing product ideas; his passion and tenacity brought them to life. As described by Fred Vogelstein in the *New York Times*, "When Jobs ran Apple, the company was an innovation machine, churning out revolutionary products every three to five years," adding, "it hardly needed to be said. When you look back at how the iPhone came to be, it's clear that it had everything to do with the unreasonable demands—and unusual power—of an inimitable man."[55]

Jobs had a vision about what kinds of products he wanted to make and how they would affect the world. He was the creative force that fueled all of these breakthrough innovations that changed our lives. However, he also needed the intellectual and technological resources of others to execute his vision and turn his ideas into reality. It is also true that most of his products were not new-to-the-world ideas: the Altair predated the Apple I, Xerox's GUI was the inspiration for the Mac OS, several portable MP3 devices hit the market before the iPod, and Palm, Handspring, Nokia, and Blackberry all had some version of smartphone before the iPhone was released. Jobs did not invent these product categories. However, what he did was conceptualize products that would revolutionize them. Almost all of Jobs's breakthrough innovations would be in ways that humans interact with technology—ways in which these interactions could be made more intuitive, more beautiful, and decidedly more Zen.

Intellectual and Technological Resources

Steve Jobs's rise to prominence in the computer industry was heavily influenced by where he grew up—Mountain View, the very center of Silicon Valley. Jobs was literally surrounded by engineering expertise; nearly every house in his neighborhood was inhabited by an electronics or computer engineer. In fact, once when a teenage Steve Jobs needed some components he could not afford to buy, he got help from Hewlett (of Hewlett Packard) himself. One of Jobs's most crucial early resources was his friendship with Steve Wozniak, a profoundly gifted engineer who had begun designing computer hardware and software in high school. Although the Altair is widely attributed to be the very first personal computer, Wozniak's Cream Soda Computer was built five years earlier, in 1971, when Wozniak was twenty-one, and it did everything the Altair would later do.[56] Wozniak had also developed (but had not named) the Apple I on his own, before Steve Jobs convinced him that producing the computers could be a business. Jobs was already very interested in electronics and computers when he met Wozniak—it was a key part of their mutual attraction—but without their friendship, it is unlikely that he would have been associated with the rise of the personal computer, and his future would have looked very different.

The most important technological and intellectual resources upon which Jobs would rely were people. We can identify many brilliant engineers and designers who were critical for each of the products associated with Jobs, but he is the link between them. He needed their technical and intellectual skills to enact his vision, and it is clear that he could not have developed most of the innovations for which he is known without them, but it is also clear that those innovations would not have been developed without Jobs's vision and drive.

As we saw with Marie Curie, her life and career were also heavily dependent on unusual access to technological and intellectual resources. Her father was a schoolteacher and a person of extremely wide intellectual interests and expertise. When the Russian authorities removed laboratories from Polish schools, he brought home much of the laboratory equipment and used it to teach his children. Marie was thus steeped in a culture of science and intellectualism from a very early age. Later, she would marry

Pierre Curie, who with his brother had created a state-of-the-art quadrant electrometer. Pierre spent fifteen days working intensely on the electrometer to modify it for Marie so that it would detect very weak currents. To accomplish this, he added another of his discoveries, a piezoelectric quartz that could measure in absolute terms small quantities of electricity and low-intensity currents. He also spent twenty days training Marie to use the complex and finicky equipment to measure the tiny currents generated by Becquerel rays. As noted by one her of biographers, Barbara Goldsmith, "Without Pierre's equipment and instructions, this would have been impossible, a fact which has largely been overlooked."[57]

Elon Musk, Thomas Edison, Albert Einstein, Nikola Tesla, and Benjamin Franklin acquired much of the technological and intellectual resources they needed (at least early in their careers) from books. Each was characterized by multiple sources as a voracious reader. Einstein also drew upon the occasional help of colleagues, and Musk and Edison would go on to realize the importance of leveraging large teams of brilliant people in their innovations, but each began with a larger-than-average appetite for books.

The importance of access to books is epitomized by Franklin. He recognized that books had been an extremely important resource in his acquisition of knowledge, the refinement of his political and philosophical views, and his development of skills of persuasion. He spends many pages of his autobiography talking about the books he read and how they shaped him. Franklin learned to read early, beginning with his father's library of books, most of which were pious tracts about religion. Then, whenever a little money fell into his hands, he would use it to buy more books and, after reading them, would sell them to buy still more books. It was in this manner he read all of the work by John Bunyan (a famous Puritan writer and preacher whose nearly sixty works include *Pilgrim's Progress*) and R. Burton's Historical Collections, comprising some forty titles. It was Franklin's "bookish inclination" that led his father to conclude that he should be apprenticed to a printer.[58] This gave him better access to books, and he soon cultivated relationships with people who visited the printing house and could lend him books. The importance of being able to borrow books must have left a deep impression on the young man; in 1731 he would found the Library Company of Philadelphia, America's first lending library and the predecessor of the free public library.[59]

Interestingly, though access to technological and intellectual resources was important for all of the innovators, most of the innovators I studied had far less formal education than you would expect for the domains in which they worked. As noted, Edison had only a few months of grammar school before being pulled out of school by his mother. Franklin attended two years of grammar school before being indentured to his brother's printing shop. Jobs, Kamen, and Tesla dropped out of college while studying as undergraduates (and technically Kamen never even graduated from high school). Musk excelled at school but dropped out of a doctoral program after two days upon realizing he did not need a PhD. to change the world. Only Einstein and Curie went to graduate school, and of the two, only Curie was noted as a consistently exceptional student.

We should not conclude from this that education and training are unimportant for innovation. If we look more closely at the way that education played a role in the lives of these people, we realize that they were aggressive consumers of education, but they pursued it in their own rhythm and format. Although Jobs dropped out of college, he stayed on campus and sat in on the classes he wanted to attend. Musk rarely attended his college classes but studied on his own and showed up to take the examinations. Franklin and Edison were almost entirely self-taught, and much of Curie's training was also accomplished through her own individually directed study before entering the Sorbonne. Einstein continued to study physics (and made his biggest contributions) while working as a patent clerk. Kamen notes that he relaxes by reading old math and physics textbooks.[60]

IT'S CLEAR THAT ACCESS to technological and intellectual resources was crucially important for the innovators. Common sense might also suggest that the same would be true about access to financial resources. Yet it was surprisingly less important for the innovators studied here. Jobs, to take one example, started Apple with money that he and Wozniak raised by selling Jobs's VW van and Wozniak's HP 65 calculator. Their first order for $50,000 worth of Apple I computers was financed by an agreement to not pay the chip supplier for thirty days. In this way, the computers could be completed and be paid for by the store that had ordered them before Jobs and Wozniak would have to pay the supplier.[61] Later, Jobs would note, "I never worried about money. I grew up in a middle-class family, so I never thought I would starve. And I learned at Atari that I could be an okay engineer, so I always knew I could get by. I was voluntarily poor when I was in college and India, and I lived a pretty simple life even when I was working. So I went from fairly poor, which was wonderful because I didn't have to worry about money, to being incredibly rich, when I also didn't have to worry about money."[62] He would later add, "Innovation has nothing to do with how many R&D dollars you have. When Apple came up with the Mac, IBM was spending at least 100 times more on R&D. It's not about the money. It's about the people you have, how you're led, and how much you get it. . . ."[63]

Curie's story also illustrates how unimportant financial resources were to her innovation. She worked as a governess to put Bronia through school; then Bronia, in turn, helped pay for Marie to move to Paris and attend the Sorbonne. There she scraped by on very little money during her student years, living a spartan existence in a small and cold apartment. Although she received a small scholarship in 1893, she returned it in 1897 as soon as she had her own modest income. Later, she and Pierre would work at fractionating radium in a very modest wooden shack. The pitchblende ore they needed was considered to be a worthless residue after its uranium was removed, and they were able to obtain heaps of it for only the cost of transportation.[64] Even later in life, after having achieved acclaim, Curie was known for her moderate lifestyle. She never patented the radium-isolation process, and she asked that monetary gifts go to the scientific institutions she worked for rather than to herself.[65]

Tesla started his journey to the United States with a small amount of money given to him by his family, but that money (and part of his luggage) were stolen from him on the ship. He arrived in New York with four cents, some poems, and a few belongings. Tesla remained notoriously unconcerned with money for most of his life (and nearly destitute for significant portions of it). He often lived in hotel rooms where he racked up significant debt. Yet with the exception of the tragic debacle at Wardenclyff, he always seemed able to raise enough money for his inventions. The similarly inauspicious arrivals of Franklin in New York and Musk in Canada were noted earlier.

Edison and Einstein developed their first important innovations while earning modest incomes at their regular jobs (Edison as a telegraph operator and Einstein as a patent clerk). Kamen got his start when he was sixteen years old by spending $80 on parts at Radio Shack and then secretly upgrading the lighting system at Hayden Planetarium at New York City's Museum of Natural History. When the surprised chairman of the museum saw the effect of Kamen's work, he agreed to pay him $8,000 under the condition that Kamen do the same for the chairman's other three museums. By the time he started college, he was making $60,000 a year on custom light work[66]—a very good salary for the 1970s and more than his parents were making.

One of the implications of this chapter—and discussed further in the next chapter—is that we can increase breakthrough innovation by finding ways to widen the public's access to technological and intellectual resources. Public libraries were a huge advance in this direction, and digitization of intellectual resources so that they can be more freely distributed and accessed will push that advance further. Finding ways to enable the nonscientist to access scientific resources and expertise—through public laboratories and incubators, for example—could also be extremely beneficial. Breakthrough innovations in science, as we have shown throughout, do not always come from people who pursued the "typical" path of the scientist.

8

"You get creative people, you bet big on them, you give them enormous leeway and support. . . ."

Nurturing the Potential That Lies Within

Our study of the breakthrough innovators—people as different as Benjamin Franklin and Marie Curie—has, I hope, been deeply revealing of the ways they were special in their capabilities, personalities, resilience, and motives. It also reveals that they benefited from situational advantages conferred by time, place, and social networks. These individual factors would be unlikely to work in isolation—for example, being unconventional without having high levels of confidence, effort, and goal directedness might result in rebellious behavior that does not lead to meaningful innovation. Intelligence, self-efficacy, and need for achievement, without unconventionality, might lead to other forms of exceptional performance rather than breakthrough innovation. It is the *convergence* of such traits that increases the likelihood of breakthrough innovation. Furthermore, these traits only *increase* the likelihood of breakthrough innovation; they by no means ensure it. Situational advantages such as resources, timing, and luck also play important roles. Some people with these traits do not become serial breakthrough innovators, and others innovate repeatedly but do so in ways that do not garner widespread recognition.

These are people in a league of their own, and most of us won't play in that league. Their innovative output was to some extent a result of innate traits and situational advantages that are not within our control. Furthermore, these stories reveal the many costs of being a breakthrough innovator. A significant amount of suffering can be a major part of the relentless pursuit of goals, including forgoing personal relationships or relinquishing family ties and obligations. Edison and Franklin abandoned their wives and children for long stretches of time; Curie largely relinquished the raising of her children to her father-in-law. Neither Tesla nor Kamen ever married or had children, and Einstein's familial relationships were, as he noted, rather detached.

The life of the serial breakthrough innovator is not for everyone. Many of the factors that helped them change the world in meaningful ways are inimitable, and many of us would not choose the kind of life they led even if we could. However, understanding *how* these factors helped them to become serial breakthrough innovators is instructive. Often the mechanism linking an innovator's trait to an outcome—for example, separateness leading to the generation of heterodox ideas—is something we can tap even without possessing the trait. Furthermore, the stories of the innovators gives us ideas for how we can increase the likelihood of situational advantage, perhaps by increasing people's access to the resources that help them act on their ideas. Overall, then, understanding what makes breakthrough innovators special simultaneously reveals that there is much we can do to nurture the innovation potential that lies within us all.

Challenging norms and paradigms. A sense of separateness helped the innovators to become original thinkers, freeing them from the constraints of accepted, or acceptable, solutions and theories. For example, Einstein was able to challenge well-accepted principles of Newtonian physics because he stood well outside academic circles and because it was his nature to resist authority. Musk pioneered reusable rockets—something the space industry said was impossible—in part because he was not in the space industry and in part because he wasn't the kind of person who let other people define what was possible for him. Their separation meant that they were less exposed to dominant ideas and norms, and their sense of not belonging meant that even when exposed to dominant ideas and norms, they were often less inclined to adopt them. Being socially detached has its own costs, but the mechanisms by which separateness can prompt innovation provide useful insights about how we can foster it. Leaders of organizations can do much to encourage the kind of creative thinking that leads to fundamentally new kinds of solutions. Giving people flexible roles and autonomy, and demonstrating a tolerance for the unorthodox, will both attract more creative employees and nurture the creative side of existing members. Consider, for example, Al Alcorn's interview of Steve Jobs when he applied at Atari. Alcorn was able to look past Jobs's disheveled appearance and unusual social habits. What he saw was a creative and insightful person, and he found a way to employ him.

To tap the creativity of every member of the organization, it is important to make sure that all employees feel empowered to contribute their ideas—not just those in positions of authority or those in designated creative roles. At Pixar, for example, teams use "dailies," where artists have their ongoing work reviewed by directors and peers. An informal audience of people from all levels in the organization provides direct feedback about both the creative and technical elements of the project. Brad Bird, Oscar-winning director of films such as *The Incredibles* and *Ratatouille,* described the process: "As individual animators, we all have different strengths and weaknesses, but if we can interconnect all our strengths, we are collectively the greatest animator on earth. . . . We're going to look at your scenes in front of everybody. Everyone will get humiliated and encouraged together. If there is a solution, I want everyone to hear the solution, so everyone adds it to their tool kit."[1] At first people were afraid to speak up, but after two months of seeing artists benefit by hearing the blunt suggestions of Bird and others, people began to feel safe enough to contribute their own suggestions.[2]

Pixar is also able to attract and nurture creative people by giving them considerable autonomy. Teams choose their own hours, attire, office arrangements, project management routines, and meeting structure. Teams are also kept small—usually three to seven people, and team leaders are chosen based on their technical expertise and their vision for the project, rather than their seniority. As described by Ed Catmull, president of both Pixar and Walt Disney Animation Studios, "We believe the creative vision propelling each movie comes from one or two people and not from either corporate executives or a development department. Our philosophy is: You get creative people, you bet big on them, you give them enormous leeway and support, and you provide them with an environment in which they can get honest feedback from everyone."[3]

If leaders of organizations want employees to embrace challenging the accepted wisdom, it is also important to abolish practices and norms that require people to come to consensus prior to making decisions or moving forward with a project. Requiring consensus can force people to prematurely converge on ideas; if individuals believe that a consensus must be achieved to move forward, they will be more reluctant to dissent and more ready to pile on to the ideas put forward by others, particularly if they seem uncontroversial (and therefore more likely to achieve consensus). Making consensus the objective runs the risk of making orthodox solutions the objective as well. Consider the development of Apple's first iPod, launched in October 2001. What would have happened if, in the year 2000, Steve Jobs had sought a consensus about where Apple's development efforts should be focused? Would Apple's R&D engineers or product managers have achieved consensus that Apple should enter the consumer portable audio device market—a market littered with failed devices and in which Apple had no experience? Even if all team members have ideas for breakthrough innovations, it is extraordinarily unlikely that they will have the *same* ideas. When you require consensus, you force everyone to focus on the most obvious choices that they think others will agree to, and that is usually an incremental extension of what the organization already does. An organization that seeks more-original ideas should instead make it clear that the objective is breakthrough innovation, not consensus.

It can also be very useful to let teams that disagree about a solution pursue different—even competing—paths. For example, at CERN (the European Organization for Nuclear Research, which operates the Large Hadron Collider), teams of physicists and engineers accelerate and collide particles to simulate the "big bang," in hopes of advancing our understanding of the origins of the universe. However, groups of scientists often disagree about the best solution to particular problems. Management at CERN recognized that a solution that initially appears to be inferior to others could turn out to be actually better if further development is pursued. This means that if solutions have to "compete" to be accepted early in their development, the organization could end up committing major resources to a solution that appears better initially but might not be the best approach in the long run. CERN thus encourages multiple teams to work on their own solutions separately, and only after the teams have had significant time to develop their solution do the teams meet and compare alternatives. In this way CERN helps teams achieve some of the advantages of separateness that the breakthrough innovators reap from their innate sense of detachment. The teams are encouraged to follow their own paths without being constrained by the beliefs of other teams.

Providing time alone. It should also be clear that all children need periods of quiet solitude and should be encouraged to read, write, and experiment with things that reflect their personal interests—it helps them develop their ability to think and create and to define what they believe about how the world works. Elon Musk's escape into science fiction books, and then teaching himself computer programming, helped to craft his independent intellect and ambitious goals. Albert Einstein's meditative musings on the behavior of a compass needle or a beam of light taught him to use thought experiments with which he would later revolutionize physics. Thomas Edison's chemistry experiments in the cellar of his parents' home taught him a patient and persistent method of learning by doing that he would use the rest of his life. Filling up a child's life with team sports, after-school classes, and other extracurricular activities can be extremely valuable for developing social skills or other capabilities, but it should be balanced with the child's need to reflect. Furthermore, a child's nature should inform this balance. If, for example, a child has a naturally introspective or rule-challenging nature, trying to mold her into a charismatic team player through a heavy schedule of participating in team sports or the chorus may not serve her well. It makes much more sense to embrace her unconventionality and help find ways to make it successful for her.

When I give presentations about my research on breakthrough innovators, the people in the audience often find it a relief to see just how many innovators did not do well in school precisely because of their creativity or tendency toward rule challenging. A surprisingly large portion of breakthrough innovators were autodidacts and excelled much more outside the classroom than inside. Although many people will have heard anecdotally that some innovators did not do well in school, the stories here show *why* the innovators such as Edison, Kamen, and Einstein did not flourish in school and *why* they were successful anyway. Some people respond well to structure, but others do much better in a more fluid educational curriculum where they can choose both the direction and pace of their study. I have watched parents become animated and nod eagerly as I described how the very traits that make some people creative also make them struggle with the classroom environment. At the end of my presentations, mothers and fathers have often come up to me to talk about concerns they have had with their children's social development or school performance and about how valuable it was to see that a sense of separateness can have a positive side. They make a breakthrough of their own when beginning to understand the benefits of embracing their child's nature and helping her flourish because of it rather than in spite of it.

Studying these innovators also reveals that when managers want employees to come up with breakthroughs, they should give them some time alone to ponder their craziest of ideas and follow their paths of association into unknown terrain. This type of mental activity will be thwarted in a group brainstorming meeting. Individuals need to be encouraged to come up with ideas freely, without fear of judgment. In both organizations and educational settings, working in teams has become a norm. Teamwork can be very valuable, but to really ensure that individuals bring as much to the team as possible—especially when the objective is a creative solution—individuals need time to work alone before the group effort begins. They should be encouraged to commit their ideas to paper and to flesh each of them out in at least a rudimentary way before they are at risk of being extinguished by social processes. A creative idea can be fragile—easily swept away by the momentum of a group conversation. Almost every team suffers from some degree of groupthink; individuals who are more outspoken or who have forceful personalities can dominate the conversation and the decision making. They can herd a team onto a particular trajectory without even intending to do so. A little isolation and solitude can give other individuals a better chance to develop their creative ideas.

The payoff value of a person working alone on her own projects, tapping into her intrinsic motivation, has been the source of several of Google's most famous products. For example, Google research scientist Krishna Bharat created Google News in the aftermath of the 2001 attack on the World Trade Center to meet his own needs for keeping up with the rapid emergence of news related to the event. The product was so useful that Google launched a beta version for the public in September 2002. Gmail was also an independent project of an engineer at Google. Paul Buchheit, who had previously worked on Google Groups, began working on Gmail in August 2001. Because Google had a large volume of internal e-mail, he wanted to develop a product that would both enable a user to keep her e-mail indefinitely (requiring large storage capabilities) and enable rapid search so that a particular message of interest could be quickly found. The result was Gmail, which was formally launched in 2004.

The benefits of isolation can also apply at the team level. Ideas compete for acceptance in firms, and if exposed to competition too early may be killed off before they have had time to develop. An idea that initially seems a bit better than others can sweep through an organization, killing off competing ones that could ultimately be better with some development. The result can be a "monoculture" where there is too little variety left in an organization to generate new solutions. For example, if one R&D team within a pharmaceutical firm discovers a method of identifying drug targets that seems better than other methods being explored within the firm, other groups may quickly adopt this method, eager to reap similar benefits. If all groups within the firm adopt the same method, however, they are likely to experience too much convergence around the same drug targets and leave other opportunities unexplored. A path that has an initial advantage may thus outcompete other paths that may ultimately have superior benefits. Research spanning fields as diverse as evolutionary biology, small-world networks, "skunk works" in innovation, and organizational learning have all shown that dividing the organization into subgroups and buffering them from one another can help to generate more innovation. For example, it can be advantageous to give R&D teams some physical and cultural distance from the larger organization to prevent the paradigms of the larger organization from quashing the R&D division's heterodox ideas.[4] Jobs knew this intuitively when he set up the Macintosh project in a separate building from the rest of Apple and flew a pirate's flag over its roof.

Separation from the main organization is also often used to keep a new project secret until it's ready for the public. When Lockheed was asked by the US military in 1943 if it could quickly develop a jet fighter to counter the German jet threat, it created a separate organization of a team of aircraft engineers called "Skunk Works." The team was housed in a circus tent next to a manufacturing plant that emitted a pungent smell, leading to the name that the team gave itself. The name came from a running joke in the *Li'l Abner* comic strip about a malodorous place in the forest where a beverage was brewed from skunks, old shoes, and other peculiar ingredients. The project was extremely successful, designing and building the XP-80 Shooting Star jet fighter in just 143 days.[5] Lockheed knew that it had found a winning formula and to this day develops its most revolutionary aircraft in its secretive Palmdale, California, Skunk Works facility, which features a large skunk logo painted on its exterior. Other examples of companies using isolated skunk works to develop breakthrough innovations include Google's Google X, Boeing's Phantom Works, Amazon's Lab126, Ford's Special Vehicle Team, IBM's Thomas J. Watson Research Center, Xerox's PARC, Samsung's Advanced Institute of Technology, and Nike's Innovation Kitchen.[6]

Building self-efficacy. One of the most powerful ways to increase creativity—and other positive outcomes—at both the individual and organizational level is to help people build their sense of self-efficacy. As noted in Chapter 2, creating opportunities for early wins can be extremely valuable for this process. As a young man, when Nikola Tesla proved that his physics professor and the physics texts were wrong, he understood from that moment on that no obstacle could withstand the force of his genius and effort.

To help people to find their own early wins, we can encourage them to take risks by lowering the price of failure and even celebrating bold-but-intelligent failures. A. G. Lafley, who served two stints as the CEO of Procter & Gamble (from 2000 to 2010 and from 2013 to 2015) and was viewed by many as the most successful executive in the company's history, made fearlessness in the face of failure a core strategy of breakthrough innovation at the firm. "We learn," he said, "much more from failure than we do from success."[7] In fact, he celebrates the eleven biggest product failures during his time at the helm in his book, *The Game-Changer.*[8] Similarly, at frog Design, failure is treated as a form of useful progressive experimentation. There is no finger pointing or admonishment; instead, the company uses an end-of-project retrospective framework to rapidly learn from its failures as well as from its successes. Theodore Forbath, Global Vice President of Innovation Strategy at frog Design, notes that "Company leaders can reinforce acceptance of failure by publically celebrating projects that didn't quite meet expected results, but that were successful in providing new learning."[9] Eli Lilly throws parties to celebrate its biggest failures (the ones that did not meet expected results but led to the greatest learning for the organization), and Tata Group gives an annual prize for the best failures in its organization.[10]

Inspiring grand ambitions. The powerful role of idealism highlights the value of cultivating grand goals in the organization that people find personally meaningful. For example, Bristol-Myers

Squibb has a slogan referring to "extending and enhancing human life," and its mission is "To discover, develop and deliver innovative medicines that help patients prevail over serious diseases." Google's well-known mission is "To organize the world's information and make it universally accessible and useful." These lofty goals, if well ingrained throughout the organization, can become an organizing principle that shapes employee behavior even without direct oversight or incentives. When those goals have a social component that employees embrace as being meaningful or intrinsically valuable (such as improving people's quality of life), that intrinsic motivation can increase the amount of effort they invest in their activities. Similarly, nurturing idealism in children increases their likelihood of embracing a work ethic, living a purposeful life, and finding their accomplishments more meaningful and satisfying.

Finding the flow. If managers can tap into people's intrinsic motivators—those rewards that activate their need for achievement or the activities that enable them to experience flow—it should increase innovation and productivity for the organization while simultaneously increasing the satisfaction of the employee. To do so requires both self-awareness on the part of the employee about what she finds intrinsically motivating and enjoyable, and a willingness on the part of the manager to personalize the employment experience. For example, Mihaly Csikszentmihalyi, who has written extensively about flow (described in detail in Chapter 5), gives a detailed example of how one company, Green Cargo, a former division of the Swedish State Railway and Sweden's longest-running rail freight operator, implemented an unusual management system based on flow. First, all supervisors began to receive daily reports from three or four people who worked directly beneath them. The CEO, Lennart Pihl, chose three or four people, each of those chose three or four people, and so forth. Each person was responsible for making sure that those three or four people felt that they were accomplishing something and were enjoying their work. Initially, managers would receive five to ten daily reports from employees at random intervals in response to a timed pager, telling them what the employees were doing at that moment. The employees would also report about the sense of creativity, concentration, and challenge they felt at that moment. If the employees weren't enjoying their work—feeling anxious or bored—the managers needed to ask "What can I do to improve how these people feel?" If certain employees prefer to set their own goals rather than working on a team or prefer to work more with people on a larger team, their jobs are adjusted or their position changed.[11]

After a couple of years the results were showing clearly at Green Cargo: absenteeism and turnover were down, and profitability was up. People came into work in the morning more energized and left in the evening feeling more satisfied that they had done a good job. As Csikszentmihalyi notes,

> The general principle is to find out what your people like to do. Then you give them an opportunity to do that, within the goals of your organization. That's simply allowing their intrinsic motivation to become profitable for the organization. . . . Most people would jump at the opportunity to do what they're really good at, and they would perform better and maybe even make more money, which often brings in more revenue for the company. What's essential is that you get to know your workers. You have to know what they're good at and what they're not good at. Then you have to discover how each person's skills can be connected to the challenges of your company. It may be that you don't need more salespeople. Then people with those skills should be encouraged to find a job elsewhere. . . . We love to do what we're good at. It's the expression of ourselves.[12]

Increasing access to technological and intellectual resources. One of Benjamin Franklin's great insights was that public libraries would give a much wider group of people access to the knowledge obtainable from books, leading him to establish America's first lending library. There was a similar motivation behind Google's ambitious project, started in 2002, of scanning books with the intention of making all of the world's books available online—the ultimate library, accessible from your own home. Books that were still in copyright would be accessible for a charge, earning royalties for their copyright holders, and if those copyright holders could not be found (so-called "orphan books"), royalties would be held for five years in their name. In 2004 Google started scanning; every weekday trucks full of books would pull up to Google scanning centers, where human operators would feed them into machines that could digitize them at a rate of a thousand pages per hour.[13] In 2007 Marissa Mayer, then Vice President of Google Product Search, predicted the entire project would be complete by 2017 (though of course it would need constant updating). One aspect of the project anticipated as the biggest benefit to both consumers and authors—access to the massive repository of out-of-print books that are otherwise invisible and abandoned—turned out to be its Achilles heel. A legal settlement that would have given Google the right to digitize the world's out-of-print books would have also handed it, in essence, a monopoly on out-of-print books. Authors, publishers, and other critics filed objections with the US Department of Justice, which turned down the settlement. By 2017, the company had scanned thirty million volumes—an impressive repository nearly as large as the Library of Congress's thirty-seven million volumes—but only snippets of most could actually be viewed because solutions to the copyright conundrum had yet to be worked out.[14]

In academia a new development is unfolding that is gradually making large numbers of published academic articles available to the public for free. Most academics have two primary jobs. They teach courses for their institutions, and they conduct research that is published in articles and books. At many universities and other research institutions, articles are the primary currency for obtaining tenure, raises, and respect. An academic's "market value" is often very closely linked to the number of articles she has published in journals deemed the most important in the field and to the impact (usually measured in number of citations) of those articles. Some fields also reward academics for publishing books, but usually only if those books also have "scholarly impact." This is what "publish or perish" means. Academics do not typically publish to make money because journals usually do not pay for articles and most academic books generate little income. They publish to achieve impact, which, in turn, earns them tenure, higher pay, and the respect of their peers. They want people to read, talk about, and cite their publications. This means that academics, by and large, want their work widely distributed to both other academics and the public at large. Most top journals share this interest—after all, journals become "top journals" by having a high impact factor (being widely read and cited). Thus, as digital distribution has become widely available and inexpensive, many journals are beginning to offer authors the option to pay a fee to make their work available through an "open access" model. For a fee of a few thousand dollars, the full text of an author's article is made available to any person with a Web browser. This has, unfortunately, raised some ethical questions about the for-profit academic publishers. The top five for-profit academic publishers are responsible for over 50 percent of the academic articles in the natural and medical sciences, and they have very high profit margins—higher than Apple's margins, in fact.[15] Will payments to publishers to have one's scientific work disseminated become the new payola? A sting carried out by the prestigious academic journal *Science* found that more than half of 305 online journals were willing to publish deliberately faked research for a fee, despite the fact that the research contained fatal flaws that should have been obvious to "anyone with more than high-school knowledge of chemistry."[16] That is a disconcerting turn of events, but in the long run, rating systems will presumably evolve that help the consumers of academic articles sort the wheat from the chaff, and we will have open access to high-quality science, an outcome that would make Benjamin Franklin very happy.

So what more can we do? Accelerating the pace at which articles and books are made available online to everyone, free or at low cost, is a start. As illustrated above, we also have to be careful that we do this without undermining the incentives or infrastructure for ensuring the quality of material that is produced or the reader's ability to ascertain that quality. Publishers, editors, and reviewers all serve very valuable functions in helping to screen potential articles and books, selecting those with the most potential and helping to improve them prior to their publication. In our rush to get rid of the barriers to accessing articles and books, we should be careful to avoid doing more harm than good.

There's more we can do, however. Consider Jobs, Curie, and Musk, who were able to tap the expertise of people, not just articles and books. Jobs needed Wozniak and others to help him implement his vision. Curie needed Pierre to show her ways to measure tiny electrical currents. Musk hired the best rocket scientists he could find to help make his dream of reusable rockets a reality. We foster innovation by creating ways for people with ideas to gain access to those with the expertise needed to refine or execute those ideas. We want, in other words, to create ways for people to more easily access the intellectual resources available in other humans. If we can create expertise pools and consortia for sharing intellectual resources and also create incentives to share the physical assets of science such as laboratories and equipment, we might be able to achieve significantly more from our current investment in science, while also opening up science to those without science careers.

The idea of opening up science is especially important to consider. The innovators studied here show that breakthroughs often come not from highly trained specialists in a field, but instead from outsiders who may be trained in other fields or who have relatively little training at all. For example, Kamen never completed an undergraduate degree and had no medical training whatsoever, yet he created the first portable kidney dialysis machine, the first portable drug infusion pump, the iBot mobility wheelchair, and several advanced prosthetic limbs. Musk has only undergraduate degrees in physics and economics, yet he personally designed a prototype for a reusable rocket that is currently revolutionizing the space industry, built an electric car manufacturing company that has been far more successful than anyone ever imagined (and put pressure on other automakers to develop electric vehicles of their own), and is currently building battery systems that are intended to enable people to capture and store solar energy to run their homes.

Outsiders are important to innovation; they often operate in fields where they are highly motivated to solve problems in which they are personally invested. They often look at problems in different ways from those who are well indoctrinated in the field, and they may question (or ignore) assumptions that specialists take for granted. This does not mean that specialized training is unimportant for innovation—specialized scientists account for a very large portion of both incremental and breakthrough innovation—but it means that we do not want to foreclose the opportunities that can arise from enabling nonspecialists to engage in science.

Science has become increasingly professionalized over the last century. Years of training and highly specialized equipment create large barriers between the ordinary citizen and the scientific discovery process.[17] However, a grassroots movement has started to emerge whereby individuals volunteer time, money, and equipment to make the scientific process and resources more accessible to the public. This movement goes by the name of "citizen science" or "community laboratories."[18] Some forms of citizen science engage the public in collecting data in fields such as meteorology, animal populations, and astronomy and then submitting the data to traditional scientists. Other efforts involve creating lab spaces where the public can engage in experimentation, building models, and learning processes typically accessible only to well-established researchers. Examples include BioCurious (in Sunnyvale, California), Genspace (in Brooklyn, New York), and BOSSLAB (in Somerville, Massachusetts). At Genspace, people can sign up to take courses where they learn to genetically modify yeast or grow leather-like textiles out of fungus, or they can pay a monthly fee to have round-the-clock access to Genspace's lab space and equipment to conduct their own experiments.

Unfortunately, these citizen science efforts tend to be underfunded, and many collapse before they become well-known because they fail to raise enough funding to obtain a critical mass of resources necessary to do meaningful work. This is an area where a modicum of government or foundation support could go a long way. Creating grants specifically targeting citizen science initiatives could help these organizations gain the critical mass they need to attract participants and donors.

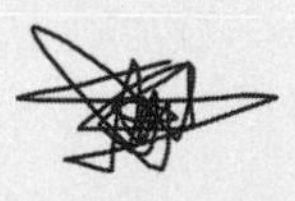

CAREFULLY STUDYING BREAKTHROUGH INNOVATORS reveals the ways in which they were special in their capabilities, their personalities, their resilience, and their motives. It also reveals that they benefited from situational advantages conferred by time, place, and social networks. However, studying breakthrough innovators also gives us insight into how we can nurture heterodox thinking and creativity, and how we can inspire the kind of effort and persistence that is necessary for creative ideas to come to fruition. It also gives us ideas for how we can catalyze situational advantage. Overall, then, understanding what makes breakthrough innovators special simultaneously reveals that there is much we can do to nurture the innovation potential that lies within us all.

Acknowledgments

I would like to thank my editor, John Mahaney, whose suggestions have vastly improved the book. I would also like to thank Joe Porac, Erwin Daneels, Becky Schaumberg, Joe Magee, and the participants at seminars held at New York University, Stanford University, University of Southern California, University of California Irvine, Norwegian School of Economics, Rutgers University, Baruch College, University of Michigan, Karolinska Institute, IESE (Barcelona), SciFoo, Winter Strategy Conference, Carnegie School Organizational Learning Conference, and the Academy of Management Conference for their many helpful comments and feedback. Thanks to my family and friends for their patience and support.

Notes

Introduction

1. In a study I coauthored with William Baumol and Edward Wolff, we searched more than fifty books and numerous online encyclopedias devoted to noted inventors, inventions, and entrepreneurs. However, such lists have significant overlap, and almost all of our entire sample can be found in the fifteen sources we found to be most useful: David Abbot, *The Biographical Dictionary of Scientists: Engineers and Inventors* (New York: Peter Bedrick, 1985); Judy Culligan, *Tycoons and Entrepreneurs* (New York: Macmillan, 1998); Entrepreneurs.about.com; Harold Evans, Gail Buckland, and David Lefer, *They Made America: From the Steam Engine to the Search Engine: Two Centuries of Innovators* (New York: Little, Brown, 2004); Anthony Feldman and Peter Ford, *Scientists and Inventors* (Aldus, 1979); J. Fucini and S. Fucini, *Entrepreneurs: The Men and Women Behind Famous Brand Names and How They Made It* (Boston: G. K. Hall, 1985); Anthony Hallett and Diane Hallett, *Encyclopedia of Entrepreneurs* (New York: Wiley, 1997); Jim Haskins, *African American Entrepreneurs* (New York: Wiley, 1998); George Iles, *Leading American Inventors* (New York: Henry Holt, 1912); www.invent.org; Inventors.about.com; Maury Klein, *The Change Makers: From Carnegie to Gates, How the Great Entrepreneurs Transformed Ideas into Industries* (New York: Henry Holt, 2003); Roger Smith, *Inventions and Inventors* (Salem, 2002); Otha Richard Sullivan, *African American Inventors* (New York: Wiley, 1998); Ethlie Ann Vare and Greg Ptacek, *Patently Female: From AZT to TV Dinners, Stories of Women Inventors and Their Breakthrough Ideas* (New York: Wiley, 2002). Our study ultimately included data on 513 inventors and entrepreneurs.

2. J. Richardson, "How Dean Kamen's Magical Water Machine Could Save the World," *Esquire*, November 24, 2008.

3. Steve Jobs, Stanford University Commencement Address, 2005.

4. Some social scientists reflexively react to outlier case selection as "sampling on the dependent variable," a (poorly named) research design error that introduces theory affirmation bias by selecting cases on the basis of a set of criteria and then using those cases as evidence for the criteria. However, the study here is designed more like backward induction: being a serial breakthrough innovator is, in essence, the independent variable, and we are searching for the traits or circumstances that associate with it. There has been no intentional use of theory about those associations to guide case selection.

5. A. Robinson, *Sudden Genius: The Gradual Path to Creative Breakthroughs* (Oxford, UK: Oxford University Press, 2010).

6. A. Teller, speech at South by Southwest Conference, March 2013.

7. "Edison Sails for Europe on First Trip in 22 Years, to Catch Up with Worries," *Evening World*, August 2.

Chapter 1

1. W. Herrmanns, *Einstein and the Poet: In Search of the Cosmic Man* (Wellesley, MA: Branden, 1983), 14.

2. A. Einstein, *The World as I See It* (1949; repr., New York: Kensington, 2006), 5.

3. P. Frank, *Einstein: His Life and Times*, trans. George Rosen (New York: Da Capo, 1947), 8.

4. S. Baron-Cohen, "The Male Condition," *New York Times*, August 8, 2005; H. Muir, "Einstein and Newton Showed Signs of Autism," *New Scientist*, April 30, 2003; T. Marlin, "Albert Einstein and LD," *Journal of Learning Disabilities*, March 1, 2000; P. Elmer-DeWitt and C. J. Farley, "Diagnosing Bill Gates," *Time*, January 24, 1994; J. Seabrook, "E-mail from Bill," *New Yorker*, January 10, 1994.

5. J. Steinberg, *Einstein: The Life of a Genius* (New York: We Can't Be Beat, 2015).

6. R. W. Clark, *Einstein: The Life and Times* (New York: World Publishing, 1971),14.

7. Ibid., 15.

8. Ibid., 16.

9. *Legendary Scientists: The Life and Legacy of Albert Einstein* (Middletown, DE: Charles River Editors, 2016).

10. P. A. Schilpp, *Albert Einstein: Philosopher-Scientist* (Peru, IL: Open Court, 1949).

11. Denis Brian, *Einstein: A Life* (New York: Wiley, 1996), 4.

12. Ibid., 11.

13. W. Isaacson, *Einstein* (New York: Simon & Schuster, 2007).

14. F. Wishinsky, *Albert Einstein: A Photographic Story of a Life* (London: DK, 2005).

15. B. Hoffman, H. Dukas, and A. Einstein, *Albert Einstein: Creator and Rebel* (New York: Viking, 1972), 32.

16. A. Einstein, letter to Conrad Habicht, 1905.

17. Isaacson, *Einstein*, 115; Erika Fromm, "Lost and Found Half a Century Later: Letters by Freud and Einstein," *American Psychologist* 53 (1998): 1195–1198.

18. A. Einstein, "How I Created the Theory of Relativity" (lecture, Kyoto, Japan, December 14, 1922). See also A. Einstein, *Relativity: The Special and the General Theory* (New York: Henry Holt, 1920).

19. Isaacson, *Einstein*, 133.

20. F. Dyson, "Clockwork Science. A Review of Peter Galison's *Einstein's Clocks, Poincaré's Maps: Empires of Time*," *New York Review of Books*, November 6, 2003.

21. Hoffman, Dukas, and Einstein, *Albert Einstein*.

22. Isaacson, *Einstein*, 15.

23. Isaacson, *Einstein*.

24. Brian, *Einstein: A Life*, 292.

25. Letter by Marie Curie, December 1886, quoted in E. Curie, *Madame Curie: A Biography* (New York: Da Capo, 1937), 72.

26. Marie Curie, quoted in E. Curie, *Madame Curie: A Biography* (New York: Da Capo, 1937), 72.

27. E. Curie, *Madame Curie: A Biography* (New York: Da Capo, 1937), 107.

28. Ibid., 170.

29. B. Goldsmith, *Obsessive Genius* (New York: Norton, 2005).

30. E. Curie, *Madame Curie*, 119.

31. A. Robinson, *Sudden Genius: The Gradual Path to Creative Breakthroughs* (Oxford, UK: Oxford University Press, 2010).

32. See O. P. John and S. Srivastava, "The Big Five Trait Taxonomy: History, Measurement, and Theoretical Perspectives," in *Handbook*

of Personality, ed. L. A. Pervin and O. P. John (New York: Guilford, 1999); D. H. Saklofske et al., "Extraversion Introversion," *Encyclopedia of Human Behavior*, vol. 2 (San Diego: Academic Press, 2012).

33. C. Brennan, *The Bite in the Apple: A Memoir of My Time with Steve Jobs* (New York: St. Martin's, 2013), 30.

34. Public Broadcasting System, *Tesla: Life and Legacy*, www.pbs.org, retrieved May 1, 2017; E. Morris, "Edison Illuminated: The Seventh Volume of Edison's Papers," *New York Times*, March 23, 2012.

35. Mina Miller Edison, "Why Edison Chooses to Be Deaf," *Literary Digest*, August 8, 1925.

36. G. H. Guy, "Tesla, Man and Inventor," *New York Times*, March 31, 1895.

37. A. Van Diggelen, "Elon Musk: His Remarkable Story in His Own Words," *Fresh Dialogs*, January 29, 2013.

38. Einstein, *The World as I See It.*

39. W. Isaacson, *Steve Jobs* (New York: Simon & Schuster, 2011).

40. "iPod Launch," www.youtube.com/watch?v=6SUJNspeux8, October 21, 2001.

41. R. Stross, *The Wizard of Menlo Park* (New York: Random House, 2007).

42. D. K. Simonton, *Origins of Genius* (Oxford: Oxford University Press, 1999).

43. R. L. Brandt, *The Google Guys* (New York: Penguin, 2009), 28.

44. Steve Jobs, "Stanford University Commencement Address," 2005.

45. "Dean Kamen: Part Man, Part Machine," *Telegraph*, October 27, 2008.

46. Ibid.

47. Ibid.

48. A. Vance, *Elon Musk: Tesla, SpaceX, and the Quest for a Fantastic Future* (New York: Harper Collins, 2015), 43.

49. E. Musk, quoted in "Elon Musk Profiled: Bloomberg Risk Takers," www.bloomberg.com, August 3, 2013.

50. F. L. Dyer and T. C. Martin, *Edison: His Life and Inventions* (New York: Harper & Brothers, 1910).

51. C. R. Long and J. R. Averill, "Solitude: An Exploration of Benefits of Being Alone," *Journal for the Theory of Social Behavior* 33, no. 1 (2003): 21–44; T. Amabile, "The Social Psychology of Creativity:

A Componential Conceptualization," *Journal of Personality and Social Psychology* 45, no. 2 (1983): 357–377.

52. Long and Averill, "Solitude."

53. Thoreau entries are from B. Torrey, *The Writings of Henry David Thoreau* (Boston: Houghton Mifflin, 1906).

54. Stross, *Wizard*, 13.

55. M. Diehl and W. Stroebe, "Productivity Loss in Brainstorming Groups: Toward the Solution of a Riddle," *Journal of Personality and Social Psychology* 53 (1987): 497–509.

56. B. Mullen, C. Johnson, and E. Salas, "Productivity Loss in Brainstorming Groups: A Meta-Analytic Integration," *Basic and Applied Social Psychology* 12, no. 1 (1991): 3–23.

57. Letter by Isaac Asimov, *MIT Technology Review*, October 10, 2014.

58. W. Stroebe, B. A. Nijstad, and E. F. Rietzshel, "Productivity Loss in Brainstorming Groups: The Evolution of a Question," in *Advances in Experimental Social Psychology*, ed. M. P. Zanna and J. M. Olson (San Diego, CA: Academic Press, 2010), 2:157-203.

59. Isaacson, *Einstein*.

60. G. Beals, *The Biography of Thomas Edison*, www.thomasedison.com, 1999.

61. W. Isaacson, *Steve Jobs* (New York: Simon & Schuster, 2011), 118.

62. Ibid., 119.

63. J. Richardson, "How Dean Kamen's Magical Water Machine Could Save the World," *Esquire*, November 24, 2008.

64. Ibid.

65. L. Fleming, S. Mingo, and D. Chen, "Collaborative Brokerage, Generative Creativity, and Creative Success," *Administrative Science Quarterly* 52 (2007): 443–475.

66. B. Franklin, *The Autobiography of Benjamin Franklin*, ed. Charles W. Eliot (1791; repr., New York: Tribeca, 2013).

67. Goldsmith, *Obsessive Genius*, 146.

68. Ibid., 173.

69. Ibid., 177–178.

70. Ibid., 178.

71. Al Alcorn, quoted in "Interview with Steve Jobs' 'Only Boss' Alan Alcorn: Exclusive," www.youtube.com/watch?v=odcXGIQuxAg, October 11, 2011.

72. F. Cifaldi, "Steve Jobs, Atari Employee Number 40," *Gamasutra*, October 7, 2011.

73. Isaacson, *Steve Jobs.*

74. J. Cook, "Atari Founder Nolan Bushnell on Managing Steve Jobs and More," www.bizjournals.com, October 20, 2009.

Chapter 2

1. A. Vance, *Elon Musk: Tesla, SpaceX, and the Quest for a Fantastic Future* (New York: HarperCollins, 2015), 24.

2. B. H. Harris, *Technocracy at Work* (New York: State University of New York Press, 1993).

3. M. Melnychuk, "Roots of Adventure," *Windsor Star*, May 13, 2017.

4. J. C. Keating Jr. and S. Haldeman, "Joshua N. Haldeman, DC: The Canadian Years, 1926–1950," *Journal of the Canadian Chiropractic Association* 39, no. 3 (1995): 175.

5. M. Melnychuck, "Elon Musk Inherited a Lifetime of Adventure from His Sask. Family," *Regina Leader Post*, May 12, 2017.

6. Vance, *Elon Musk*, 33.

7. Ibid.

8. S. Pelley, "Fast Cars and Rocket Ships," *CBS News*, March 30, 2014.

9. Vance, *Elon Musk.*

10. M. Chafkin, "Entrepreneur of the Year, 2007: Elon Musk," *INC.*, December 1, 2007.

11. Elon Musk, quoted in "Elon Musk Profiled: Bloomberg Risk Takers," www.bloomberg.com, August 3, 2013.

12. Chafkin, "Entrepreneur of the Year, 2007."

13. "An Evening with Elon Musk," interview with Alison van Diggelen, www.youtube.com/watch?v=zX7I_Rw8QoI, January 24, 2013.

14. S. Outing, "Zip2's Evolving City Site and Portal Strategy," *Editor and Publisher*, August 31, 1998.

15. "Compaq Buys Software Firm Zip2," *Los Angeles Times*, February 2, 1999.

16. A. van Diggelen, "Elon Musk: His Remarkable Story in His Own Words," *Fresh Dialogs*, January 29, 2013.

17. Vance, *Elon Musk.*

18. K. A. Wilson, "The 120-Year History of the Electric Car, in Pictures," *Popular Mechanics*, December 16, 2015.

19. M. V. Copeland, "Tesla's Wild Ride," *Fortune*, July 10, 2008, 82–94.

20. Ibid.

21. A. Williams, "Taking a Tesla for a Status Check in New York," *New York Times*, July 19, 2009, ST7.

22. D. Kreindler, "Tesla Roadster 2.5 S Review: Car Reviews," Autoguide.com, October 12, 2011.

23. J. Cammisa, "2009 Electric Tesla Roadster—Electric Convertible Sport Coupe," *Automobile Magazine*, November 2009.

24. Vance, *Elon Musk*, 211.

25. Pelley, "Fast Cars."

26. Chafkin, "Entrepreneur of the Year, 2007."

27. J. Boudreau, "In a Silicon Valley Milestone, Tesla Motors Begins Delivering Model S Electric Cars," *Oakland Tribune*, June 24, 2012.

28. A. Pasztor, "SpaceX Lofts Commercial Satellite with Reused Rocket in Historic Flight," *Wall Street Journal*, March 30, 2017.

29. C. Hoffman, "Elon Musk, the Rocket Man with a Sweet Ride," *Smithsonian*, December 2012.

30. A. Teller, speech at South by Southwest Conference, March 2013.

31. Chafkin, "Entrepreneur of the Year, 2007."

32. Pelley, "Fast Cars."

33. A. Vance, "Elon Musk, the 21st Century Industrialist," *Bloomberg Business Week*, September 13, 2012.

34. Chafkin, "Entrepreneur of the Year, 2007."

35. A. Bandura, "Self-Efficacy Mechanism in Human Agency," *American Psychologist* 37, no. 2 (1982): 122–147; A. Bandura, *Self-Efficacy: The Exercise of Control* (New York: Freeman, 1997).

36. B. Goldsmith, *Obsessive Genius* (New York: Norton, 2005), 45.

37. E. Curie, *Madame Curie: A Biography* (New York: Da Capo, 1937), 112.

38. Ibid., 116.

39. G. P. Lathrop, "Talks with Edison," *Harper's*, February 1890.

40. A. Bandura, "Self-Efficacy: Toward a Unifying Theory of Behavioral Change," *Psychological Review* 84 (1977): 191–215.

41. Vance, *Elon Musk*, 107.

42. H. Zhao, S. E. Siebert, and G. E. Hills, "The Mediating Role of Self-Efficacy in the Development of Entrepreneurial Intentions," *Journal of Applied Psychology* 90 (2005): 1265–1272; N. Krueger and P. R. Dickson,

"How Believing in Ourselves Increases Risk Taking: Perceived Self-Efficacy and Opportunity Recognition," *Decision Sciences* 25 (1994): 385–400.

43. B. Franklin, *The Autobiography of Benjamin Franklin*, ed. Charles W. Eliot (1791; repr., New York: Tribeca, 2013).

44. W. Isaacson, *Steve Jobs* (New York: Simon & Schuster, 2011), 29.

45. Ibid.

46. Ibid., 30.

47. D. H. Schunk, "Developing Children's Self-Efficacy and Skills: The Roles of Social Comparative Information and Goal Setting," *Contemporary Educational Psychology* 8 (1983): 76–86.

48. See S. Ashford, J. Edmunds, and D. P. French, "What Is the Best Way to Change Self-Efficacy to Promote Lifestyle and Recreational Physical Activity? A Systematic Review with Meta-Analysis," *British Journal of Health Psychology* 15 (2010): 265–288; M. van Dinther, F. Dochy, and M. Segers, "Factors Affecting Students' Self-Efficacy in Higher Education," *Educational Research Review* 6, no. 2 (2010): 95–108.

49. "Bill Bowerman: Nike's Original Innovator," News.Nike.com, September 2, 2015.

50. Ibid.

51. S. S. Al-Zahrani and S. A. Kaplowitz, "Attributional Biases in Individualistic and Collectivistic Cultures: A Comparison of Americans with Saudis," *Social Psychology Quarterly* 56, no. 3 (1993): 223–233; U. Scholz et al., "Is General Self-Efficacy a Universal Construct?" *European Journal of Psychological Assessment* 18, no. 3 (2002): 242–252.

52. G. Joet, E. L. Usher, and P. Bressoux, "Sources of Self-Efficacy: An Investigation of Elementary School Students in France," *Journal of Educational Psychology* 103 (2011): 649–663; S. Ashford, J. Edmunds, and D. P. French, "What Is the Best Way to Change Self-Efficacy?"; A. L. Zeldin and F. Pajares, "Against the Odds: Self-Efficacy Beliefs of Women with Math-related Careers" (paper presented at the meeting of the American Educational Research Association, Chicago, March 1997).

53. F. Pajares, "Current Directions in Self-Efficacy Research," in *Advances in Motivation and Achievement*, ed. M. Maehr and P. R. Pintrich (Greenwich, CT: JAI, 1997), 10:1–49.

54. A. Bandura, *Social Foundations of Thought and Action: A Social Cognitive Theory* (Englewood Cliffs, NJ: Prentice Hall, 1986).

Chapter 3

1. N. Tesla, *My Inventions: The Autobiography of Nikola Tesla* (1919; repr., London: SoHo, 2014), 9.
2. Ibid., 7.
3. Ibid., 283.
4. Ibid., 8.
5. Tesla, *My Inventions.*
6. Ibid., 17.
7. Ibid., 9.
8. M. J. Seifer, *Wizard: The Life and Times of Nikola Tesla* (New York: Citadel, 1998).
9. Tesla, *My Inventions*, 13.
10. Seifer, *Wizard.*
11. "Nikola Tesla and His Wonderful Discoveries," *Scientific American*, May 20, 1893.
12. Tesla, *My Inventions*, 39.
13. Ibid., 13.
14. Seifer, *Wizard.*
15. Tesla, *My Inventions*, 40.
16. Seifer, *Wizard.*
17. Tesla, *My Inventions*, 41.
18. J. J. O'Neill, *Prodigal Genius: The Life of Nikola Tesla* (1944; repr., New York: Cosimo Classics, 2006).
19. Seifer, *Wizard.*
20. Tesla, *My Inventions*, 45.
21. Ibid., 49.
22. O'Neill, *Prodigal Genius*, 56.
23. Seifer, *Wizard*, 26.
24. O'Neill, *Prodigal Genius*, 60.
25. Tesla, *My Inventions*, 54.
26. Tesla, *My Inventions.*
27. Ibid., 7.
28. N. Tesla, "On Electricity," address on the occasion of the commemoration of Niagara Falls Power of Buffalo, January 12, 1897.
29. "Electricity on Animals," *New York Times*, December 13, 1888, 2.
30. O'Neill, *Prodigal Genius*, 83.

31. J. Wetzler, "Electric Lamps Fed from Space," *Harper's*, July 11, 1891, 524.

32. Public Broadcasting System, *Tesla: Life and Legacy*, www.pbs.org, retrieved May 1, 2017.

33. Seifer, *Wizard;* T. C. Martin, "Electrical World Portraits—XII: Nikola Tesla," *Electrical World* 15, no. 7 (1890): 106.

34. F. J. Patten, "Nikola Tesla and His Works," *New Science Review* 1 (1895): 81–87.

35. G. H. Guy, "Tesla, Man and Inventor," *New York Times*, March 31, 1895.

36. W. J. Broad, "Tesla, a Bizarre Genius, Regains Aura of Greatness," *New York Times*, August 28, 1984.

37. USPTO patents 645,576 and 649,621.

38. Public Broadcasting System, *Tesla.*

39. Seifer, *Wizard*, 79.

40. Ibid., 73.

41. Seifer, *Wizard.*

42. "Tesla Opposed to Marriage," *Electrical Journal* 2, no. 3 (1896): 546.

43. E. Jones, *The Life and Work of Sigmund Freud* (New York: Basic Books, 1953).

44. Tesla, *My Inventions.*

45. Ibid.

46. A. Vance, *Elon Musk: Tesla, SpaceX, and the Quest for a Fantastic Future* (New York: Harper Collins, 2015), 237.

47. S. Freud, "The Unconscious," *The Collected Papers of Sigmund Freud* (Oxford, UK: Basic Books, 1959); S. A. Mednick, "The Associative Basis of the Creative Process," *Psychological Review* 69 (1962): 220–232; J. Suler, "Primary Process Thinking and Creativity," *Psychological Bulletin* 80 (1980): 155–165; D. K. Simonton, *Origins of Genius* (Oxford: Oxford University Press, 1999).

48. A. van Diggelen, "Elon Musk: On Critics, Steve Jobs, and Innovation," *Fresh Dialogs*, February 25, 2013.

49. W. Isaacson, *Einstein* (New York: Simon & Schuster, 2007), 14.

50. G. Whitrow, *Einstein: The Man and His Achievement* (London: Dover, 1967), 21.

51. P. Bucky, *The Private Albert Einstein* (Kansas City, MO: Andrews and McMeel, 1992), 148.

52. See, for example, C. Martindale and A. Dailey, "Creativity, Primary Process Cognition, and Personality," *Personality and Individual Differences* 20 (1996): 409–414; Suler, "Primary Process Thinking and Creativity"; C. Wild, "Creativity and Adaptive Regression," *Journal of Personality and Social Psychology* 2, no. 2 (1965): 161–169.

53. C. Martindale, "Biological Bases of Creativity," in *Handbook of Creativity*, ed. R. J. Sternberg (Cambridge, UK: Cambridge University Press, 1999), 137–152; S. J. Lynn and J. W. Rhue, "The Fantasy-Prone Person: Hypnosis, Imagination, and Creativity," *Journal of Personality and Social Psychology* 51, no. 2 (1986): 404–408; L. Hudson, *Human Beings: The Psychology of Human Experience* (New York: Anchor, 1975).

54. M. A. Schilling, "A Small-World Network Model of Cognitive Insight," *Creativity Research Journal* 17, nos. 2–3 (2005): 131–154.

55. M. Benedek and A. C. Neubauer, "Revisiting Mednick's Model on Creativity-Related Differences in Associative Hierarchies. Evidence for a Common Path to Uncommon Thought," *Journal of Creative Behavior* 47 (2013): 273–289.

56. This argument is also invoked in a line of work on "defocused attention." See Martindale, "Biological Bases."

57. N. Cowan, "What Are the Differences Between Long-Term, Short-Term, and Working Memory?" *Progress in Brain Research* 169 (2008): 323–338; R. Engle and M. Kane, "Executive Attention, Working Memory Capacity, and a Two-Factor Theory of Cognitive Control," in *The Psychology of Learning and Motivation*, ed. B. Ross (New York: Elsevier, 2004), 44:145–199.

58. Vance, *Elon Musk*, 32–33.

59. Ibid., 230.

60. A. R. Conway, M. J. Kane, and R. W. Engle, "Working Memory Capacity and Its Relation to General Intelligence," *Trends in Cognitive Sciences* 7, no. 12 (2003): 547–552.

61. E. Jauk et al., "The Relationship Between Intelligence and Creativity: New Support for the Threshold Hypothesis by Means of Empirical Breakpoint Detection," *Intelligence* 41, no. 4 (2013): 212–221; G. Park, D. Lubinski, and C. P. Benbow, "Contrasting Intellectual Patterns

Predict Creativity in the Arts and Sciences. Tracking Intellectually Precocious Youth over 25 Years," *Psychological Science* 18 (2007): 948–952; J. Wai, D. Lubinski, and C. P. Benbow, "Creativity and Occupational Accomplishments Among Intellectually Precocious Youth: An Age 13 to Age 33 Longitudinal Study," *Journal of Educational Psychology* 97 (2007): 484–492.

62. Albert Einstein, quoted by A. Moszkowski, *Conversations with Einstein* (1920; repr., New York: Horizon, 1973).

63. P. A. Schilpp, *Albert Einstein: Philosopher-Scientist* (Peru, IL: Open Court, 1949).

64. V. Kumari et al., "Effects of D-amphetamine and Haloperidol on Latent Inhibition in Healthy Male Volunteers," *Journal of Psychopharmacology* 13 (1999): 398–405.

65. University of Toronto, "Biological Basis for Creativity Linked to Mental Illness," *ScienceDaily*, October 1, 2003.

66. Martindale, "Biological Bases."

67. Tesla, *My Inventions*, 43–44.

68. E. Lhommee et al., "Dopamine and the Biology of Creativity: Lessons from Parkinson's Disease," *Frontiers in Neurology* 5 (2014): 55.

69. E. Strickland, "The Most Dangerous Muse: Parkinson's Disease Gave Her the Gift of Creativity," *Nautilus*, January 15, 2015.

70. Martindale, "Biological Bases"; J. L. Karlsson, "Genetic Association of Giftedness and Creativity with Schizophrenia," *Hereditas* 66, no. 2 (1970): 177–181; I. F. Jarvik and S. B. Chadwick, "Schizophrenia and Survival," in *Psychopathology: Contributions from the Biological, Behavioral, and Social Sciences*, ed. M. Hammer, K. Salzinger, S. Sutton, and J. Zubin (New York: Wiley Interscience, 1973), 57-73; Simonton, *Origins of Genius*.

71. M. Dykes and A. McGhie, "A Comparative Study of Attentional Strategies in Schizophrenics and Highly Creative Normal Subjects," *British Journal of Psychiatry* 128 (1976): 50–56; H. Eysenck, *Genius: The Natural History of Creativity* (Cambridge University Press, 1995).

72. Eysenck, *Genius*.

73. O. Manzano et al., "Thinking Outside a Less Intact Box: Thalamic Dopamine Receptor Densities Are Negatively Related to Psychometric Creativity in Healthy Individuals," *PLoS One* 5, no. 5 (2010): 10670; M. Reuter et al., "Identification of First Candidate Genes for Creativity:

A Pilot Study," *Brain Research*, January 2006: 1069; S. A. Chermahini and B. Hommel, "The (B)link Between Creativity and Dopamine: Spontaneous Eye Blink Rates Predict and Dissociate Divergent and Creative Thinking," *Cognition* 115 (2010): 458–465.

74. O. Arias-Carrion et al., "Dopaminergic Reward System: A Short Integrative Review," *International Archives of Medicine* 3 (2010): 24–30.

75. D. Runes, *The Diary and Sundry Observations of Thomas A. Edison* (New York: Philosophical Library, 2007).

76. R. Mehling, *Hallucinogens* (New York: Infobase, 2003).

77. C. G. DeYoung et al., "Sources of Cognitive Exploration: Genetic Variation in the Prefrontal Dopamine System Predicts Openness/Intellect," *Journal of Research in Personality* 45, no. 4 (2011): 364–371; A. Strobel et al., "Further Evidence for a Modulation of Novelty Seeking by DRD4 Exon III, 5-HTTLPR, and COMT Val/Met Variants," *Molecular Psychiatry* 8 (2003): 371–372.

Chapter 4

1. We are referring here to the common use of the word *idealism*, not the philosophical movement.

2. W. Isaacson, *Benjamin Franklin: An American Life* (New York: Simon & Schuster, 2003).

3. Ibid.

4. B. Franklin, *The Autobiography of Benjamin Franklin*, ed. Charles W. Eliot (1791; repr., New York: Tribeca, 2013).

5. Isaacson, *Benjamin Franklin*, 30.

6. Ibid., 54.

7. Franklin, *Autobiography.*

8. Ibid.

9. Ibid.

10. Ibid.

11. Ibid., 80.

12. Ibid., 101.

13. Isaacson, *Benjamin Franklin.*

14. J. A. L. Lemay, *The Life of Benjamin Franklin*, vol. 3, *Soldier, Scientist and Politician* (Philadelphia: University of Pennsylvania Press, 2008).

15. Isaacson, *Benjamin Franklin.*

16. Ibid., 348.

17. Ibid., 265.

18. A. Druckenbrod, "Scholars Revive a Debate on Whether Ben Franklin Composed a Tongue-in-Cheek String Quartet," *Pittsburgh-Post Gazette*, July 30, 2006.

19. C. Letocha, "The Invention and Early Manufacture of Bifocals," *Survey of Ophthalmology* 35, no. 3 (1990): 226–235.

20. J. Fea, "Religion and Early Politics: Benjamin Franklin and His Religious Beliefs," *Pennsylvania Heritage Magazine* 37, no. 4 (2011).

21. B. Franklin, letter to Thomas Paine, 1785, https://wallbuilders.com/benjamin-franklins-letter-thomas-paine.

22. B. Franklin, letter to Ezra Stiles, March 9, 1790.

23. S. Reiss, "Multifaceted Nature of Intrinsic Motivation: The Theory of 16 Basic Desires," *Review of General Psychology* 8, no. 3 (2004): 179–193.

24. Dean Kamen, quoted in "Dean Kamen: Part Man, Part Machine," *Telegraph*, October 27, 2008.

25. Elon Musk, quoted in M. Chafkin, "Entrepreneur of the Year, 2007: Elon Musk," *Inc.*, December 1, 2007.

26. Elon Musk, quoted in A. Vance, *Elon Musk: Tesla, SpaceX, and the Quest for a Fantastic Future* (New York: Harper Collins, 2015), 260.

27. L. Riddell, "What It Takes to Be the Mother of Tesla's 'Genius Boy,'" *San Francisco Business Times*, July 22, 2011.

28. Elon Musk, quoted in C. Hoffman, "Elon Musk, the Rocket Man with a Sweet Ride," *Smithsonian*, December 2012.

29. A. Smith, "Who Is Elon Musk? Tech Billionaire, SpaceX Cowboy, Tesla Pioneer, and Real Life Iron Man," *Telegraph*, January 4, 2014.

30. *NBC News*, 2000.

31. "Dean Kamen: Part Man, Part Machine," *Telegraph*, October 27, 2008.

32. Dean Kamen, quoted in "Dean Kamen: Part Man, Part Machine."

33. R. Stross, *The Wizard of Menlo Park: How Thomas Alva Edison Invented the Modern World* (New York: Three Rivers, 2007).

34. "Mr. Tesla at Wardenclyffe, L.I.," *Electrical World and Engineer*, September 28, 1901.

35. "When the Man Who Talked to Mars Came to Shoreham," *Port Jefferson Record*, March 25, 1971, 3.

36. M. Seifer, *Wizard: The Life and Times of Nikola Tesla* (New York: Citadel, 1998), 269.

37. E. Curie, *Madame Curie: A Biography* (New York: Doubleday, Doran, 1937), 204.

38. A. Robinson, *Sudden Genius: The Gradual Path to Creative Breakthroughs* (Oxford: Oxford University Press, 2010), 160–161.

39. M. Curie, *Pierre Curie* (New York: Macmillan, 1923).

40. A. Einstein, *The World as I See It* (1949; repr., New York: Kensington, 2006), 4.

41. Steve Jobs, quoted in *The Lost Interview*, Magnolia Pictures, 1990.

42. Steve Jobs, quoted in G. Beahm, *I Steve—Steve Jobs in His Own Words* (Melbourne: Hardie Grant, 2011), 92.

43. Steve Jobs, quoted in B. Burlingham, "The Entrepreneur of the Decade: An Interview with Steve Jobs, Inc.'s Entrepreneur of the Decade," *Inc.*, April 1989.

44. D. Sheff, "Interview: Steve Jobs," *Playboy*, February 1985.

45. Steve Jobs, quoted in David Morrow, "Oral History Interview with Steve Jobs," Smithsonian Institution, April 20, 1995.

46. W. Isaacson, *Steve Jobs* (New York: Simon & Schuster, 2011), 76–77.

47. Quoted in S. Quinn, *Marie Curie: A Life* (New York: De Capo, 1995), 64.

48. Marie Curie, quoted in B. Goldsmith, *Obsessive Genius: The Inner World of Marie Curie* (New York: Atlas Books, 2005), 35.

49. A. Einstein, address given at the Curie memorial celebration, Roerich Museum, New York, November 23, 1934.

50. E. Curie, *Madame Curie*, 266.

51. Ibid., 272.

52. Letter to Hermann Huth, December 27, 1930, 46-756. Einstein Archives, Berlin, Germany, http://alberteinstein.info.

53. R. F. Baumeister, *Evil: Inside Human Violence and Cruelty* (New York: Holt, 1999).

54. See W. Shawcross, *The Quality of Mercy: Cambodia, Holocaust, and Modern Conscience* (New York: Simon & Schuster, 1985), and data provided by Yale University's Cambodian Genocide Program, http://gsp.yale.edu/case-studies/cambodian-genocide-program.

Chapter 5

1. "What Is Life?" *Evening Bee*, November 28, 1891, 7.

2. R. Stross, *The Wizard of Menlo Park* (New York: Three Rivers, 2007), 60.

3. F. L. Dyer and T. C. Martin, *Edison: His Life and Inventions* (New York: Harper & Brothers, 1910), 126.

4. Stross, *Wizard*.

5. "Edison," *Americana*, ed. by F. C. Beach and G. E. Rines (New York: Americana, 1911), 108.

6. T. A. Edison, "Edison and His Mother," *Now: The World's New Thought Journal* 8, no. 2 (1911): 17.

7. Dyer and Martin, *Edison*.

8. Ibid.

9. Edison, "Edison and His Mother," 17.

10. Dyer and Martin, *Edison*.

11. USPTO, patent US90646A.

12. J. E. Relch, "Thomas Edison's First Patent Invention Was an Electronic Voting Machine," *Tech Times*, February 11, 2016.

13. Stross, *Wizard*, 14.

14. Ibid., 16.

15. J. Bofetti, "Heartbreak at Menlo Park: Thomas Edison and Mary Stilwell Edison," National Endowment for the Humanities, Division of Research Programs, https://www.neh.gov/divisions/research/featured-project/heartbreak-menlo-park, March 4, 2014.

16. Stross, *Wizard*, 18.

17. USPTO, patent US174,465.

18. Stross, *Wizard*, 2007.

19. "Prof. Edison's New Telephone," *New York Times*, July 17, 1877.

20. From notes taken by Charles Batchelor at the Menlo Park Laboratory, July 18, 1877.

21. Thomas Edison, quoted in Dyer and Martin, *Edison*, 93.

22. "The Talking Phonograph," *Scientific American*, December 22, 1877, 673–674.

23. Stross, *Wizard*, 45.

24. Ibid., 9.

25. Ibid., 57.

26. Ibid., 66.

27. Dyer and Martin, *Edison*, 125.

28. Ibid., 126.

29. Dyer and Martin, *Edison*, 115.

30. www.uspto.gov.

31. Dyer and Martin, *Edison*.

32. "Mr. Edison's Use of Electricity," *New York Tribune*, September 28, 1878, 4.

33. N. Baldwin, *Edison: Inventing the Century* (New York: Hyperion, 1995).

34. Dyer and Martin, *Edison*.

35. Stross, *Wizard*, 187.

36. Ibid., 191.

37. Dyer and Martin, *Edison*, 504–505.

38. Ibid., 245.

39. Ibid., 273.

40. H. Ford and S. Crowther, *My Life and Work* (Garden City, NY: Doubleday, 1922).

41. "Edison Sails for Europe on First Trip in 22 Years, to Catch Up with Worries," *Evening World*, August 2, 1911.

42. R. Crawford, "Did Thomas Edison Die a Poor Man?" *Modern Mechanix*, January 1932.

43. Dyer and Martin, *Edison*, 345.

44. B. C. Forbes, "Why Do So Many Men Never Amount to Anything?" *American Magazine* 91 (January 1921): 89.

45. Dyer and Martin, *Edison*, 347.

46. N. Tesla, *My Inventions: The Autobiography of Nikola Tesla* (1919; repr., London: SoHo, 2014), 11.

47. M. Seifer, *Wizard: The Life and Times of Nikola Tesla* (New York: Citadel, 1998), 43.

48. Ibid., 67.

49. H. A. Murray, *Explorations in Personality* (Oxford: Oxford University Press, 1938).

50. D. C. McClelland, "Methods of Measuring Human Motivation," in *Motives in Fantasy, Action and Society*, ed. John W. Atkinson (Princeton, NJ: D. Van Nostrand, 1958).

51. O. C. Schultheiss, U. S. Wiemers, and O. T. Wolf, "Implicit Need for Achievement Predicts Attenuated Cortisol Responses to Difficult

Tasks," *Journal of Research in Personality* 48 (February 2014): 84–92; O. C. Schultheiss and J. C. Brunstein, "An Implicit Motive Perspective on Competence," in *Handbook of Competence and Motivation*, ed. A. J. Elliott and C. Dweck (New York: Guilford, 2005), 31-51.

52. S. Jex, *Organizational Psychology: A Scientist-Practitioner Approach* (New York: Wiley, 2002).

53. Stross, *Wizard*, 192.

54. D. C. McClelland et al., *The Achievement Motive* (Oxford: Irvington, 1976); J. W. Atkinson, ed., *Motives in Fantasy, Action, and Society: A Method of Assessment and Study* (Oxford: Van Nostrand, 1958).

55. D. C. McClelland, *The Achieving Society* (Princeton, NJ: Van Nostrand, 1961).

56. J. Rubin, "Review: *The Achieving Society*," *Journal of Economic History* 23 (1963): 118–121.

57. Schultheiss and Brunstein, "An Implicit Motive Perspective."

58. M. Csikszentmihalyi, *Flow* (New York: HarperCollins, 1990), 4.

59. D. Sobel, "Interview: Mihaly Csikszentmihalyi," *Omni*, January 1995, 73–90.

60. Dyer and Martin, *Edison*.

61. A. Vance, "Elon Musk, the 21st Century Industrialist," *Bloomberg Business Week*, September 13, 2012.

62. T. Garland et al., "The Biological Control of Voluntary Exercise, Spontaneous Physical Activity, and Daily Energy Expenditure in Relation to Obesity: Human and Rodent Perspective," *Journal of Experimental Biology* 214 (2011): 206–229; M. Zuckerman, *Behavioral Expressions and Biosocial Bases of Sensation Seeking* (Cambridge, UK: University of Cambridge Publishing, 1994).

63. W. A. Friedman, T. Garland, and M. R. Dohm, "Individual Variation in Locomotor Behavior and Maximal Oxygen Consumption in Mice," *Physiology & Behavior* 52 (1992): 97–104.

64. V. Careau and T. Garland, "Performance, Personality, and Energetics: Correlation, Causation and Mechanism," *Physiological and Biochemical Zoology* 85, no. 6 (2012): 543–571.

Chapter 6

1. S. Quinn, *Marie Curie: A Life* (New York: De Capo, 1995).

2. Ibid.

3. E. Curie, *Marie Curie: A Biography* (New York: Doubleday, Doran, 1937).

4. R. A. Koestler-Grack, *Marie Curie: A Scientist* (New York: Chelsea, 2009).

5. Quinn, *Marie Curie.*

6. Ibid., 41.

7. E. Curie, *Marie Curie*, 49.

8. Marie Curie, quoted in E. Curie, *Marie Curie*, 53.

9. E. Curie, *Marie Curie*, 86.

10. B. Goldsmith, *Obsessive Genius: The Inner World of Marie Curie* (New York: Atlas Books, 2005), 48.

11. Quinn, *Marie Curie*, 89.

12. R. W. Nitske, *The Life of W. C. Röntgen, Discoverer of the X-Ray* (University of Arizona Press, 1971).

13. "Henri Becquerel—Biographical," Nobelprize.org.

14. Goldsmith, *Obsessive Genius.*

15. "The Nobel Prize in Physics 1903," www.nobelprize.org/nobel_prizes/physics/laureates/1903.

16. E. Curie, *Madame Curie.*

17. Goldsmith, *Obsessive Genius.*

18. A. Valiunis, "The Marvelous Marie Curie," *New Atlantis*, fall 2012.

19. www.nobelprize.org/nobel_prizes/chemistry/laureates/1911.

20. A. Davis, "How Marie Curie Helped Save a Million Soldiers During World War I," *The Institute, IEEE*, February 1, 2016.

21. E. Curie, *Madame Curie*, xvi.

22. Letter by Marie Curie, December 10, 1887, quoted in E. Curie, *Marie Curie*, 77.

23. M. A. Schilling, "Technology Shocks, Technological Collaboration, and Innovation Outcomes," *Organization Science* 26 (2015): 668–686.

24. Bono, quoted in W. Isaacson, *Steve Jobs* (New York: Simon & Schuster, 2011), 58.

25. "Rosie the Riveter," History.com, 2010.

26. K. W. Beyer, *Grace Hopper and the Invention of the Information Age* (Cambridge, MA: MIT Press, 2012).

27. Grace Hopper, interview by Angeline Partages for *Oral History of Captain Grace Hopper* (1980), available at the Computer History Museum.

28. Beyer, *Grace Hopper.*

29. A. Hind, "Briefcase 'That Changed the World,'" *BBC Radio*, February 5, 2007.

30. J. Shurkin, *Broken Genius: The Rise and Fall of William Shockley* (New York: Macmillan, 2006).

31. R. S. Kirby, *Engineering in History* (New York: Dover, 1990).

32. A. Atkeson and P. J. Kehoe, "The Transition to a New Economy After the Second Industrial Revolution" (NBER Working Paper 8676, 2001).

Chapter 7

1. C. Brennan, *The Bite in the Apple: A Memoir of My Time with Steve Jobs* (New York: St. Martin's, 2013), 15.

2. Ibid., 7.

3. Ibid., 12.

4. W. Isaacson, *Steve Jobs* (New York: Simon & Schuster, 2016), 16.

5. M. Storper and A. J. Venebles, "Buzz: Face to Face Contact and the Urban Economy," *Journal of Economic Geography* 4 (2004): 351–370.

6. A. Marshall, *Principles of Economics*, 8th ed. (London: McMillan, 1920).

7. Steve Jobs, quoted in *The Lost Interview*, Magnolia Pictures, 1990.

8. W. Isaacson, *Steve Jobs* (New York: Simon & Schuster, 2011), 22.

9. Ibid., 25.

10. Steve Jobs, "Stanford University Commencement Address," 2005.

11. Isaacson, *Steve Jobs*, 41.

12. M. A. Schilling, *Strategic Management of Technological Innovation*, 4th ed. (New York: McGraw-Hill, 2013).

13. Isaacson, *Steve Jobs*, 63.

14. Steve Jobs, quoted in P. Kunkel and R. English, *Apple Design: The Work of the Apple Industrial Design Group* (New York: Watson-Guptill, 1997), 22.

15. Isaacson, *Steve Jobs*, 75.

16. N. Sklarewitz, "From the Very Beginning, Apple Was Born to Grow," *Inc.*, April 1, 1979.

17. R. X. Cringely, *Accidental Empires: How the Boys of Silicon Valley Make Their Millions, Battle Foreign Competition, and Still Can't Get a Date* (New York: Harper Collins, 1996); M. A. Schilling,

Strategic Management of Technological Innovation, 5th ed. (New York: McGraw-Hill, 2015).

18. www.macmothership.com/timeline.html.

19. J. Reimer, "Total Share: 30 Years of Personal Computer Market Share Figures," *ARS Technica*, December 15, 2005.

20. Cringely, *Accidental Empires.*

21. Schilling, *Strategic Management*, 5th edition.

22. Larry Tesler, quoted in R. Cringely, *Triumph of the Nerds*, John Gau Productions, 1996.

23. John Warnock, quoted in Cringely, *Triumph of the Nerds.*

24. Steve Jobs, quoted in Cringely, *Triumph of the Nerds.*

25. A. Hertzfeld, "Pirate Flag," www.folklore.org, August 1983.

26. P. Freiberger and M. Swaine, *Fire in the Valley* (New York: McGraw-Hill, 2000), 357.

27. Isaacson, *Steve Jobs*, 123.

28. C. W. L. Hill, "Apple, 1977–2013," in *Strategic Management: An Integrated Approach*, 11th ed., ed. C. W. L. Hill, G. Jones, and M. A. Schilling (New York: Cengage, 2013).

29. Andy Hertzfeld, "Reality Distortion Field," Folklore.org, retrieved January 20, 2017.

30. A. Vance, *Elon Musk: Tesla, SpaceX, and the Quest for a Fantastic Future* (New York: Harper Collins, 2015).

31. Apple press release, January 24, 1984.

32. "When Steve Met Bill: 'It Was a Kind of Weird Seduction Visit,'" *Fortune*, October 24, 2011.

33. A. Hertzfeld, "A Rich Neighbor Named Xerox," Folklore.org, retrieved January 20, 2017.

34. Steve Jobs, quoted in *Time*, January 14, 2002.

35. Steve Jobs, "Stanford."

36. D. B. Yoffie and M. Slind, *Apple Computer, 2006* (Boston: HBS).

37. "101 Ways to Save Apple," *Wired*, June 1, 1997.

38. "Apple Computer, Inc. Agrees to Acquire NeXT Software Inc," press release, Apple Computer, December 20, 1996.

39. D. E. Dilger, "Apple's 15 Years of NeXT," Appleinsider.com, December 21, 2011.

40. Steve Jobs, speech at the Apple Worldwide Developers Conference, May 13–16, 1997.

41. R. P. Rumelt, *Good Strategy, Bad Strategy: The Difference and Why It Matters* (New York: Crown, 2011).

42. R. Moisescot, Allaboutstevejobs.com, 2010.

43. Hill, "Apple, 1977–2013."

44. Schilling, *Strategic Management*, 5th ed.

45. K. T. Greenfeld, "The Free Juke Box: College Kids Are Using New, Simple Software Like Napster to Help Themselves to Pirated Music," *Time*, March 27, 2000, 82.

46. Steve Jobs, comments on iPod release, October 23, 2001.

47. www.macworld.com/article/1163181/consumer-electronics/the-birth-of-the-ipod.html.

48. M. Amicone, "Apple Took a Big Bite Out of the Market," *Billboard*, April 17, 2004.

49. Steve Jobs, quoted in L. Kahney, *Inside Steve's Brain* (New York: Penguin, 2009), 59.

50. Steve Jobs, quoted in *Bloomberg Business Week*, February 2, 2004.

51. Schilling, *Strategic Management*, 5th ed.; "iTunes Music Store Downloads Top 50 Million Songs," Apple press release, March 14, 2004.

52. R. Ritchie, "History of the iPhone: Apple Reinvents the Phone," www.imore.com, January 9, 2017.

53. Ibid.

54. Schilling, *Strategic Management*, 5th ed.

55. F. Vogelstein, "And Then Steve Said, 'Let There Be an iPhone,'" *New York Times*, October 4, 2013.

56. S. G. Wozniak and G. Smith, *iWoz: Computer Geek to Cult Icon* (New York: Norton, 2006).

57. Goldsmith, *Obsessive Genius*, 71.

58. B. Franklin, *The Autobiography of Benjamin Franklin*, ed. Charles W. Eliot (1791; repr., New York: Tribeca, 2013).

59. www.libraryhistorybuff.org/benfranklin.htm, retrieved January 26, 2017.

60. "Dean Kamen: Part Man, Part Machine," *Telegraph*, October 27, 2008.

61. Wozniak and Smith, *iWoz*.

62. Steve Jobs, quoted in Isaacson, *Steve Jobs*, 105.

63. Steve Jobs, quoted in D. Kirkpatrick, "The Second Coming of Apple Through a Magical Fusion of Man—Steve Jobs—and Company,

Apple Is Becoming Itself Again: The Little Anticompany That Could," *Fortune*, November 9, 1998.

64. Goldsmith, *Obsessive Genius*.

65. E. Curie, *Madame Curie: A Biography* (New York: Doubleday, Doran, 1937).

66. S. Kemper, *Reinventing the Wheel: A Story of Genius, Innovation, and Grand Ambition* (New York: Harper Business, 2005).

Chapter 8

1. H. Rao, R. Sutton, and A. P. Webb, "Innovation Lessons from Pixar: An Interview with Oscar-Winning Director Brad Bird," *McKinsey Quarterly*, April 2008.

2. M. A. Schilling, *Strategic Management of Technological Innovation*, 5th ed. (New York: McGraw-Hill, 2015).

3. E. Catmull, "How Pixar Fosters Collective Creativity," *Harvard Business Review* (September 2008): 65–72.

4. C. Fang, J. Lee, and M. A. Schilling, "Balancing Exploration and Exploitation Through Structural Design: Advantage of the Semi-isolated Subgroup Structure in Organizational Learning," *Organization Science* 21 (2010): 625–642.

5. www.lockheedmartin.com/us/aeronautics/skunkworks/origin.html, retrieved May 11, 2017.

6. M. Nisen, "17 of the Most Mysterious Corporate Labs," *Business Insider*, February 19, 2013.

7. B. Ryder, "Fail Often, Fail Well," *Economist*, April 14, 2011.

8. R. McGrath, "Failing by Design," *Harvard Business Review*, April 2011.

9. T. Forbath, "The Realm of Intelligent Failure," *Rotman Management*, winter 2014.

10. T. Grant, "Failed at Business? Throw a Party," *Global Mail*, May 28, 2013.

11. Mihaly Csikszentmihalyi, interview in *CFA Institute Magazine*, September 2016.

12. Ibid.

13. J. Somers, "Torching the Modern-Day Library of Alexandria," *Atlantic*, April 20, 2017.

14. T. Wu, "Whatever Happened to Google Books?" *New Yorker*, September 11, 2015.

15. S. Buranyi, "Is the Staggeringly Profitable Business of Scientific Publishing Bad for Science?" *Guardian*, June 27, 2017.

16. R. Knox, "Some Online Journals Will Publish Fake Science, for a Fee," www.npr.org, October 3, 2013.

17. L. Z. Scheifele and T. Burkett, "The First Three Years of a Community Lab: Lessons Learned and Ways Forward," *Journal of Microbiology & Biology Education* 17, no. 1 (2016): 81–85.

18. M. Meyer, "Domesticating and Democratizing Science: A Geography of Do-It-Yourself Biology," *Journal of Material Culture* 18, no. 2 (2013): 117–134.

Selected References

Al-Zahrani, S. S., and S. A. Kaplowitz. "Attributional Biases in Individualistic and Collectivistic Cultures: A Comparison of Americans with Saudis." *Social Psychology Quarterly* 56, no. 3 (1993): 223–233.

Amabile, T. "The Social Psychology of Creativity: A Componential Conceptualization." *Journal of Personality and Social Psychology* 45, no. 2 (1983): 357–377.

Arias-Carrion, O., et al. "Dopaminergic Reward System: A Short Integrative Review." *International Archives of Medicine* 3 (2010): 24–30.

Ashford, S., J. Edmunds, and D. P. French. "What Is the Best Way to Change Self-Efficacy to Promote Lifestyle and Recreational Physical Activity? A Systematic Review with Meta-analysis." *British Journal of Health Psychology* 15 (2010): 265–288.

Asimov, Isaac. Letter. *MIT Technology Review,* October 10, 2014.

Atkeson, A., and P. J. Kehoe. "The Transition to a New Economy After the Second Industrial Revolution." NBER Working Paper 8676, 2001.

Atkinson, J. W., ed. *Motives in Fantasy, Action, and Society: A Method of Assessment and Study.* Oxford: Van Nostrand, 1958.

Baldwin, N. *Edison: Inventing the Century.* New York: Hyperion, 1995.

Bandura, A. "Self-Efficacy Mechanism in Human Agency." *American Psychologist* 37, no. 2 (1982): 122–147.

———. *Self-Efficacy: The Exercise of Control.* New York: Freeman, 1997.

———. "Self-Efficacy: Toward a Unifying Theory of Behavioral Change." *Psychological Review* 84 (1977): 191–215.

———. *Social Foundations of Thought and Action: A Social Cognitive Theory.* Englewood Cliffs, NJ: Prentice Hall, 1986.

Baron-Cohen, S. "The Male Condition." *New York Times,* August 8, 2005.

Baumeister, R. F. *Evil: Inside Human Violence and Cruelty.* New York: Holt, 1999.

Beals, G. *The Biography of Thomas Edison.* www.thomasedison.com, 1999.

Benedek, M., and A. C. Neubauer. "Revisiting Mednick's Model on Creativity-Related Differences in Associative Hierarchies. Evidence for a Common Path to Uncommon Thought." *Journal of Creative Behavior* 47 (2013): 273–289.

Beyer, K. W. *Grace Hopper and the Invention of the Information Age.* Cambridge, MA: MIT Press, 2012.

Brandt, R. L. *The Google Guys.* New York: Penguin, 2009.

Brennan, C. *The Bite in the Apple: A Memoir of My Time with Steve Jobs.* New York: St. Martin's, 2013.

Brian, Denis. *Einstein: A Life.* New York: Wiley, 1996.

Bucky, P. *The Private Albert Einstein.* Kansas City, MO: Andrews and McMeel, 1992.

Careau, V., and T. Garland. "Performance, Personality, and Energetics: Correlation, Causation and Mechanism." *Physiological and Biochemical Zoology* 85, no. 6 (2012): 543–571.

Catmull, E. "How Pixar Fosters Collective Creativity." *Harvard Business Review* (September 2008): 65–72.

Chermahini, S. A., and B. Hommel. "The (B)link Between Creativity and Dopamine: Spontaneous Eye Blink Rates Predict and Dissociate Divergent and Creative Thinking." *Cognition* 115 (2010): 458–465.

Clark, R. W. *Einstein: The Life and Times.* New York: World Publishing, 1971.

Conway, A. R., M. J. Kane, and R. W. Engle. "Working Memory Capacity and Its Relation to General Intelligence." *Trends in Cognitive Sciences* 7, no. 12 (2003): 547–552.

Cowan, N. "What Are the Differences Between Long-Term, Short-Term, and Working Memory?" *Progress in Brain Research* 169 (2008): 323–338.

Cringely, R. *Triumph of the Nerds.* John Gau Productions, 1996.

Cringely, R. X. *Accidental Empires: How the Boys of Silicon Valley Make Their Millions, Battle Foreign Competition, and Still Can't Get a Date.* New York: Harper Collins, 1996.

Csikszentmihalyi, Mihaly. *Flow.* New York: HarperCollins, 1990.

———. Interview. *CFA Institute Magazine,* September 2016.

Curie, E. *Madame Curie: A Biography.* New York: Da Capo, 1937.

DeYoung, C. G., et al. "Sources of Cognitive Exploration: Genetic Variation in the Prefrontal Dopamine System Predicts Openness/Intellect." *Journal of Research in Personality* 45, no. 4 (2011): 364–371.

Diehl, M., and W. Stroebe. "Productivity Loss in Brainstorming Groups: Toward the Solution of a Riddle." *Journal of Personality and Social Psychology* 53 (1987): 497–509.

Druckenbrod, A. "Scholars Revive a Debate on Whether Ben Franklin Composed a Tongue-in-Cheek String Quartet." *Pittsburgh-Post Gazette,* July 30, 2006.

Dyer, F. L., and T. C. Martin. *Edison: His Life and Inventions.* New York: Harper & Brothers, 1910.

Dykes, M., and A. McGhie. "A Comparative Study of Attentional Strategies in Schizophrenics and Highly Creative Normal Subjects." *British Journal of Psychiatry* 128 (1976): 50–56.

"Edison." In *Americana,* edited by F. C. Beach and G. E. Rines, 108. New York: Americana, 1911.

Elliott, A. J., and C. Dweck, eds. *Handbook of Competence and Motivation.* New York: Guilford, 2005.

Elmer-DeWitt, P., and C. J. Farley. "Diagnosing Bill Gates." *Time,* January 24, 1994.

Engle, R., and M. Kane. "Executive Attention, Working Memory Capacity, and a Two-Factor Theory of Cognitive Control." In *The Psychology of Learning and Motivation*, edited by B. Ross, 44:145-199. New York: Elsevier, 2004.

"An Evening with Elon Musk." Interview with Alison van Diggelen. www.youtube.com/watch?v=zX7I_Rw8Q0I, January 24, 2013.

Eysenck, H. *Genius: The Natural History of Creativity.* Cambridge University Press, 1995.

Fang, C., J. Lee, and M. A. Schilling. "Balancing Exploration and Exploitation Through Structural Design: Advantage of the Semi-isolated Subgroup Structure in Organizational Learning." *Organization Science* 21 (2010): 625–642.

Fea, J. "Religion and Early Politics: Benjamin Franklin and His Religious Beliefs." *Pennsylvania Heritage* 37, no. 4 (2011).

Fleming, L., S. Mingo, and D. Chen. "Collaborative Brokerage, Generative Creativity, and Creative Success." *Administrative Science Quarterly* 52 (2007): 443–475.

Forbath, T. "The Realm of Intelligent Failure." *Rotman Management* (winter 2014).

Frank, P. *Einstein: His Life and Times.* Translated by George Rosen. New York: Da Capo, 1947.

Freiberger, P., and M. Swaine. *Fire in the Valley.* New York: McGraw-Hill, 2000.

Freud, S. "The Unconscious." *The Collected Papers of Sigmund Freud* (Oxford, UK: Basic Books, 1959).

Friedman, W. A., T. Garland, and M. R. Dohm. "Individual Variation in Locomotor Behavior and Maximal Oxygen Consumption in Mice." *Physiology & Behavior* 52 (1992): 97–104.

Garland, T., et al. "The Biological Control of Voluntary Exercise, Spontaneous Physical Activity, and Daily Energy Expenditure in Relation to Obesity: Human and Rodent Perspective." *Journal of Experimental Biology* 214 (2011): 206–229.

Goldsmith, B. *Obsessive Genius: The Inner World of Marie Curie.* New York: Atlas Books, 2005.

Hammer, M., K. Salzinger, and S. Sutton, eds. *Psychopathology: Contributions from the Biological, Behavioral, and Social Sciences.* New York: Wiley Interscience, 1973.

Harris, B. H. *Technocracy at Work.* New York: State University of New York Press, 1993.

Herrmanns, W. *Einstein and the Poet: In Search of the Cosmic Man.* Wellesley, MA: Branden, 1983.

Hill, C. W. L. "Apple, 1977–2013." In *Strategic Management: An Integrated Approach,* 11th ed., edited by C. W. L. Hill, G. Jones, and M. A. Schilling. New York: Cengage, 2013.

Hill, C. W. L., G. Jones, and M. A. Schilling, eds. *Strategic Management: An Integrated Approach,* 11th ed. New York: Cengage, 2013.

Hoffman, B., H. Dukas, and A. Einstein. *Albert Einstein: Creator and Rebel.* New York: Viking, 1972.

Hudson, L. *Human Beings: The Psychology of Human Experience.* New York: Anchor, 1975.

"Interview with Steve Jobs' 'Only Boss' Alan Alcorn: Exclusive." www.youtube.com/watch?v=odcXGIQuxAg, October 11, 2011.

Isaacson, W. *Benjamin Franklin: An American Life.* New York: Simon & Schuster, 2003.

———. *Einstein.* New York: Simon & Schuster, 2007.

———. *Steve Jobs.* New York: Simon & Schuster, 2011.

Jarvik, I. F., and S. B. Chadwick. "Schizophrenia and Survival." In *Psychopathology: Contributions from the Biological, Behavioral, and*

Social Sciences, edited by M. Hammer, K. Salzinger, and S. Sutton, 57-73. New York: Wiley Interscience.

Jauk E., et al. "The Relationship Between Intelligence and Creativity: New Support for the Threshold Hypothesis by Means of Empirical Breakpoint Detection." *Intelligence* 41, no. 4 (2013): 212–221.

Jex, S. *Organizational Psychology: A Scientist-Practitioner Approach.* New York: Wiley, 2002.

Joet, G., E. L. Usher, and P. Bressoux. "Sources of Self-Efficacy: An Investigation of Elementary School Students in France." *Journal of Educational Psychology* 103 (2011): 649–663.

John, O. P., and S. Srivastava. "The Big Five Trait Taxonomy: History, Measurement, and Theoretical Perspectives." In *Handbook of Personality,* edited by L. A. Pervin and O. P. John. New York: Guilford, 1999.

Jones, E. *The Life and Work of Sigmund Freud.* New York: Basic Books, 1953.

Kahney, L. *Inside Steve's Brain.* New York: Penguin, 2009.

Kemper, S. *Reinventing the Wheel: A Story of Genius, Innovation, and Grand Ambition.* New York: Harper Business, 2005.

Kirby, R. S. *Engineering in History.* New York: Dover, 1990.

Koestler-Grack, R. A. *Marie Curie: A Scientist.* New York: Chelsea, 2009.

Krueger, N., and P. R. Dickson. "How Believing in Ourselves Increases Risk Taking: Perceived Self-Efficacy and Opportunity Recognition." *Decision Sciences* 25 (1994): 385–400.

Kumari, V., et al. "Effects of D-amphetamine and Haloperidol on Latent Inhibition in Healthy Male Volunteers." *Journal of Psychopharmacology* 13 (1999): 398–405.

Kunkel, P., and R. English. *Apple Design: The Work of the Apple Industrial Design Group.* New York: Watson-Guptill, 1997.

Lemay, J. A. L. *The Life of Benjamin Franklin,* vol. 3, *Soldier, Scientist and Politician.* Philadelphia: University of Pennsylvania Press, 2008.

Letocha, C. "The Invention and Early Manufacture of Bifocals." *Survey of Ophthalmology* 35, no. 3 (1990): 226–235.

Lhommee, E., et al. "Dopamine and the Biology of Creativity: Lessons from Parkinson's Disease." *Frontiers in Neurology* 5 (2014): 55.

Long, C. R., and J. R. Averill. "Solitude: An Exploration of Benefits of Being Alone." *Journal for the Theory of Social Behavior* 33, no. 1 (2003): 21–44.

Lynn, S. J., and J. W. Rhue. "The Fantasy-Prone Person: Hypnosis, Imagination, and Creativity." *Journal of Personality and Social Psychology* 51, no. 2 (1986): 404–408.

Maehr, M., and P. R. Pintrich, eds. *Advances in Motivation and Achievement.* Greenwich, CT: JAI, 1997.

Manzano, O., et al. "Thinking Outside a Less Intact Box: Thalamic Dopamine Receptor Densities Are Negatively Related to Psychometric Creativity in Healthy Individuals." *PLoS One* 5, no. 5 (2010): 10670.

Marlin, T. "Albert Einstein and LD." *Journal of Learning Disabilities,* March 1, 2000.

Marshall, A. *Principles of Economics,* 8th ed. London: McMillan, 1920.

Martindale, C. "Biological Bases of Creativity." In *Handbook of Creativity,* edited by R. J. Sternberg, 137-152. Cambridge, UK: Cambridge University Press, 1999.

Martindale, C., and A. Dailey. "Creativity, Primary Process Cognition, and Personality." *Personality and Individual Differences* 20 (1996): 409–414.

McClelland, D. C. *The Achieving Society.* Princeton, NJ: Van Nostrand, 1961.

———. "Methods of Measuring Human Motivation." In *Motives in Fantasy, Action and Society,* edited by John W. Atkinson. Princeton, NJ: D. Van Nostrand, 1958.

McClelland, D. C., et al. *The Achievement Motive.* Oxford: Irvington, 1976.

McGrath, R. "Failing by Design." *Harvard Business Review,* April 2011.

Mednick, S. A. "The Associative Basis of the Creative Process." *Psychological Review* 69 (1962): 220–232.

Mehling, R. *Hallucinogens.* New York: Infobase, 2003.

Meyer, M. "Domesticating and Democratizing Science: A Geography of Do-It-Yourself Biology." *Journal of Material Culture* 18, no. 2 (2013): 117–134.

Muir, H. "Einstein and Newton Showed Signs of Autism." *New Scientist,* April 30, 2003.

Mullen, B., C. Johnson, and E. Salas. "Productivity Loss in Brainstorming Groups: A Meta-Analytic Integration." *Basic and Applied Social Psychology* 12, no. 1 (1991): 3–23.

Murray, H. A. *Explorations in Personality.* Oxford: Oxford University Press, 1938.

Nitske, R. W. *The Life of W. C. Röntgen, Discoverer of the X-Ray.* University of Arizona Press, 1971.

O'Neill, J. J. *Prodigal Genius: The Life of Nikola Tesla.* New York: Cosimo Classics, 2006. First published 1944.

Pajares, F. "Current Directions in Self-Efficacy Research." In *Advances in Motivation and Achievement,* edited by M. Maehr and P. R. Pintrich, 10:1–49. Greenwich, CT: JAI, 1997.

Park, G., D. Lubinski, and C. P. Benbow. "Contrasting Intellectual Patterns Predict Creativity in the Arts and Sciences. Tracking Intellectually Precocious Youth over 25 Years." *Psychological Science* 18 (2007): 948–952.

Pelley, S. "Fast Cars and Rocket Ships." *CBS News,* March 30, 2014.

Pervin, L. A., and O. P. John, eds. *Handbook of Personality.* New York: Guilford, 1999.

Quinn, S. *Marie Curie: A Life.* New York: De Capo, 1995.

Rao, H., R. Sutton, and A. P. Webb. "Innovation Lessons from Pixar: An Interview with Oscar-Winning Director Brad Bird." *McKinsey Quarterly,* April 2008.

Reiss, S. "Multifaceted Nature of Intrinsic Motivation: The Theory of 16 Basic Desires." *Review of General Psychology* 8, no. 3 (2004): 179–193.

Reuter, M., et al. "Identification of First Candidate Genes for Creativity: A Pilot Study." *Brain Research,* January 2006: 1069.

Robinson, A. *Sudden Genius: The Gradual Path to Creative Breakthroughs.* Oxford: Oxford University Press, 2010.

Ross, B., ed. *The Psychology of Learning and Motivation.* New York: Elsevier, 2004.

Rubin, J. "Review: *The Achieving Society.*" *Journal of Economic History* 23 (1963): 118–121.

Rumelt, R. P. *Good Strategy, Bad Strategy: The Difference and Why It Matters.* New York: Crown, 2011.

Runes, D. *The Diary and Sundry Observations of Thomas A. Edison.* New York: Philosophical Library, 2007.

Saklofske, D. H., et al. "Extraversion Introversion." *Encyclopedia of Human Behavior,* vol. 2, 2012.

Scheifele, L. Z., and T. Burkett. "The First Three Years of a Community Lab: Lessons Learned and Ways Forward." *Journal of Microbiology & Biology Education* 17, no. 1 (2016): 81–85.

Schilling, M. A. "A Small-World Network Model of Cognitive Insight." *Creativity Research Journal* 17, nos. 2-3 (2005): 131–154.

———. *Strategic Management of Technological Innovation,* 4th ed. New York: McGraw-Hill, 2013.

———. *Strategic Management of Technological Innovation,* 5th ed. New York: McGraw-Hill, 2015.

———. "Technology Shocks, Technological Collaboration, and Innovation Outcomes." *Organization Science* 26 (2015): 668–686.

Schilpp, P. A. *Albert Einstein: Philosopher-Scientist.* Peru, IL: Open Court, 1949.

Scholz, U., et al. "Is General Self-Efficacy a Universal Construct?" *European Journal of Psychological Assessment* 18, no. 3 (2002): 242–252.

Schultheiss, O. C., and J. C. Brunstein. "An Implicit Motive Perspective on Competence." In *Handbook of Competence and Motivation,* edited by A. J. Elliott and C. Dweck, 31-51. New York: Guilford, 2005.

Schultheiss, O. C., U. S. Wiemers, and O. T. Wolf. "Implicit Need for Achievement Predicts Attenuated Cortisol Responses to Difficult Tasks." *Journal of Research in Personality* 48 (February 2014): 84–92.

Schunk, D. H. "Developing Children's Self-Efficacy and Skills: The Roles of Social Comparative Information and Goal Setting." *Contemporary Educational Psychology* 8 (1983): 76–86.

Seifer, M. J. *Wizard: The Life and Times of Nikola Tesla.* New York: Citadel, 1998.

Shawcross, W. *The Quality of Mercy: Cambodia, Holocaust, and Modern Conscience.* New York: Simon & Schuster, 1985.

Shurkin, J. *Broken Genius: The Rise and Fall of William Shockley.* New York: Macmillan, 2006.

Simonton, D. K. *Origins of Genius.* Oxford: Oxford University Press, 1999.

Steinberg, J. *Einstein: The Life of a Genius.* New York: We Can't Be Beat, 2015.

Sternberg, R. J., ed. *Handbook of Creativity.* Cambridge, UK: Cambridge University Press, 1999.

Storper, M., and A. J. Venebles. "Buzz: Face to Face Contact and the Urban Economy." *Journal of Economic Geography* 4 (2004): 351–370.

Strickland, E. "The Most Dangerous Muse: Parkinson's Disease Gave Her the Gift of Creativity." *Nautilus,* January 15, 2015.

Strobel, A., et al. "Further Evidence for a Modulation of Novelty Seeking by DRD4 Exon III, 5-HTTLPR, and COMT Val/Met Variants." *Molecular Psychiatry* 8 (2003): 371–372.

Stroebe, W., B. A. Nijstad, and E. F. Rietzshel. "Productivity Loss in Brainstorming Groups: The Evolution of a Question." In *Advances in Experimental Social Psychology,* edited by M. P. Zanna and J. M. Olson, 2:157–203. San Diego: Academic Press, 2010.

Stross, R. *The Wizard of Menlo Park: How Thomas Alva Edison Invented the Modern World.* New York: Three Rivers, 2007.

Suler, J. "Primary Process Thinking and Creativity." *Psychological Bulletin* 80 (1980): 155–165.

Teller, A. Speech presented at the South by Southwest Conference, March 2013.

Torrey, B. *The Writings of Henry David Thoreau.* Boston: Houghton Mifflin, 1906.

van Diggelen, A. "Elon Musk: His Remarkable Story in His Own Words." *Fresh Dialogs,* January 29, 2013.

———. "Elon Musk: On Critics, Steve Jobs, and Innovation." *Fresh Dialogs,* February 25, 2013.

van Dinther, M., F. Dochy, and M. Segers. "Factors Affecting Students' Self-Efficacy in Higher Education." *Educational Research Review* 6, no. 2 (2010): 95–108.

Vance, A. *Elon Musk: Tesla, SpaceX, and the Quest for a Fantastic Future.* New York: Harper Collins, 2015.

———. "Elon Musk, the 21st Century Industrialist." *Bloomberg Business Week,* September 13, 2012.

Wai, J., D. Lubinski, and C. P. Benbow. "Creativity and Occupational Accomplishments Among Intellectually Precocious Youth: An Age 13 to Age 33 Longitudinal Study." *Journal of Educational Psychology* 97 (2007): 484–492.

Whitrow, G. *Einstein: The Man and His Achievement.* London: Dover, 1967.

Wild, C. "Creativity and Adaptive Regression." *Journal of Personality and Social Psychology* 2, no. 2 (1965): 161–169.

Wishinsky, F. *Albert Einstein: A Photographic Story of a Life.* London: DK, 2005.

Wozniak, S. G., and G. Smith. *iWoz: Computer Geek to Cult Icon.* New York: Norton, 2006.

Yoffie, D. B., and M. Slind. *Apple Computer, 2006.* Boston: HBS, 2006.

Zanna, M. P., and J. M. Olson, eds. *Advances in Experimental Social Psychology.* San Diego: Academic Press, 2010.

Zeldin, A. L., and F. Pajares. "Against the Odds: Self-Efficacy Beliefs of Women with Math-Related Careers." Paper presented at the meeting of the American Educational Research Association, Chicago, March 1997.

Zhao, H., S. E. Siebert, and G. E. Hills. "The Mediating Role of Self-Efficacy in the Development of Entrepreneurial Intentions." *Journal of Applied Psychology* 90 (2005): 1265–1272.

Zuckerman, M. *Behavioral Expressions and Biosocial Bases of Sensation Seeking.* Cambridge, UK: University of Cambridge Publishing, 1994.

Index

Aarau school, Einstein in, 25–26
academics, and information access, 257–259
access to resources. *See* resources (access to)
accomplishments. *See* achievement
achievement
  in innovators, 16, 179, 180–181
  need for, 178–181
Adler, Alfred, 10
age of Earth debate, 198
Alcorn, Al, 59–60, 247
alone. *See* time alone
Altair computer, 218–219, 239
alternating current (AC) work, 95, 96–97, 98–99, 100–101, 102, 111, 177–178
Amelio, Gil, 150, 229–230
American colonies and unity, 134–137
American Graphophone company, 169
Andreesen, Mark, 68, 83
Android phones, 236–237
animation by computer, 228–229
Apple company
  difficult times, 229–230
  early days, 220–221
  GUI, 224–225
  innovation, 7
  Macintosh, 224–227, 229
  and music, 231–234
  resignation/firing of Jobs, 149–150, 227–228
  return of Jobs, 150, 230–238
Armat, Thomas, 173
art, innovation in, 11, 12
Asimov, Isaac, 47
association paths, 109–111
Atari, S. Jobs at, 59–60, 218
Atkinson, Bill, 224
audio players, 232–233, 249
autism, 22, 23
automobiles. *See* cars
Ayrton, Hertha, 58

Bandura, Albert, 78, 85
Bardeen, John, 208
Baron, Frank, 86
Batchelor, Charles, 97–98, 163, 167
Beach, R. H., 173
Beals, Gerald, 49
Becquerel, Antoine Henri, and "Becquerel rays," 195, 196
Bell, Alexander Graham, 163, 170–171
Bell Telephone Laboratories, radar development, 207–208

Benedek, Mathis, 110
Bharat, Krishna, 252
"Big Five Personality Traits", 113
BIOS code, 221–222
Bird, Brad, 247–248
birth order in family, 9–10
Blastar video game, 67
Block, Ryan, 236
"blue boxes," 81–82, 217
Boguski, Józef, 193
Boltwood, Bertram, 57
Bono, 204–205
books
  access to, 240–241, 257–259
  digitization and copyright, 257
border collies, 184–185
boundary crossing, assumptions in, 5
Bowerman, Bill, 83–84
brain chemistry and creativity, 88, 116–121
brainstorming for ideas, 45–48, 251
Brattain, Walter, 208
breakthrough innovators. *See* innovators
Brennan, Chrisann, 35–36, 213, 214, 217, 224
Bricklin, Daniel, 221
Brin, Sergey, 39, 41–42
Bristol-Myers Squibb, idealism at, 254–255
brokers, in social networks, 54–55
Brown, John Seely, 75
Brunstein, Joachim, 181
Brush, Charles, 169
Buchheit, Paul, 252
Bucky, Thomas, 32
bulb technology, 49, 78, 167–169
Bushnell, Nolan, 60, 218, 220
Byland, Hans, 26

Canada, and Technocracy movement, 64–65
capital, as resource for innovation, 211–212, 242–243
cars
  battery, 173–174
  electric cars, 70–73, 74
Catmull, Edmund, 228–229, 248
celibacy, and inventions, 105
cell phones, 234–237
CERN (European Organization for Nuclear Research), work practices, 249–250, 252
challenges, and flow, 182–183
Chen, David, 54, 55
children, time alone, 250–251
Churchill, Winston, 207, 208
citizen science, 260–261
clustering advantage, 215–217, 238–239
Cocconi, Al, 70–71
coinventors, as social networks, 54, 55
Coleman, Debi, 50, 149
Coligan, Ed, 235
collaboration
  others' help for innovators, 44, 45, 259–260
  social networks in patents, 54, 55
  vs. time alone, 59, 251–253
community laboratories, 260–261

Compaq and early computers, 222
computer animation, 228–229
computers
  access to resources, 237, 238–239
  industry's early days, 218–219, 239
  influence of 60s counterculture, 204–205
  interface/GUI, 222, 223–225, 226
  race for early market, 221–227
  and shocks in technology or economy, 202–203
  situational advantage, 186, 215, 223–224, 237, 238–239, 242
  See also Apple company
confidence. *See* self-efficacy
connections, social, 53–55
consensus *vs.* creativity, 248–250
convergence of time and place. *See* situational advantage
counterculture, influence on innovation, 204–205
Cream Soda Computer, 239
creativity
  association paths, 109–110
  biological processes in, 88, 108–113
  and brain chemistry, 88, 116–121
  vs. consensus, 248–250
  factors and influences, 87–88
  in innovators, 17–18, 247–248
  and intelligence, 87–88, 106–108
  and introversion, 44
  and neuroscience, 88–89
  nurturing at work, 247–248
  and openness to experience, 88, 113–116
  primary process thinking, 108–109
  research on, 4
  separateness and social detachment, 42–45, 47, 59–61, 252–253
  and time alone, 59, 251–253
  and unconventionality, 61
Cringely, Robert, 186
Csikszentmihalyi, Mihaly, 44, 182–183, 255, 256
Curie, Eve (daughter)
  birth, 197
  death of mother, 200
  education of mother, 191, 193
  health of mother, 58
  on mother and father, 34–35, 37, 197
  perseverance of mother, 77, 153
Curie, Irène (daughter), 153, 194, 197, 199–200
Curie, Marie (born Maria Salomea Skłodowska)
  achievements, 32–33
  age of Earth debate, 198–199
  character and traits, 200
  criticism of, 180
  death, 200
  education at university and life in France, 34, 192–194, 196, 201
  education (pre-university), 33, 152, 189–194, 201

Curie, Marie (*continued*)
- family life and childhood with parents, 33, 188–192
- family life with husband and daughters, 34–35, 153, 194–195
- financial resources, 242–243
- health, 58, 190, 191, 197, 200
- historical background and Polish positivism, 151–152, 188–190, 201
- husband's death, 56, 197
- idealism, 146, 151–153
- independent work, 33–34, 51, 193
- intelligence, 189
- marriage and life with Pierre, 34, 194–195
- medical work, 199
- Nobel prizes, 57–58, 196–197, 199
- perseverance, 77–78
- radioactivity work, 195–197, 198–199, 202
- recognition, 198
- scandal about affair, 57–58, 180, 199
- scientific activity and discoveries, 195–200
- self-efficacy, 77–78
- self-learning, 33–34
- self-reinforcing pathways, 51–52
- separateness, 13, 32, 34–35, 37, 51–52, 59, 60–61
- sexism towards, 197–198, 200
- situational advantage for timing, 200–201, 202, 239–240
- social life, 56–58
- women in science, 199, 200
- women in university, 33, 188, 191, 192, 194, 200, 201–202
- work as solace, 34, 197, 199

Curie, Pierre (husband of Marie)
- biographic details, 194
- death, 56, 197
- electrometer and work with Marie, 194, 195, 196–197, 240
- idealism, 146
- marriage and life with Marie, 34, 194–195
- Nobel prize, 196
- separateness, 34

"current wars" (AC *vs.* DC), 98–99, 171

"dailies" at Pixar, 247–248

Dickson, W. K. L., 172

Diehl, Michael, 45–46, 47

diet and idealism, 153–154

disruption in innovation, 6

"divergent thinking," 108–110

Dogood, Silence (B. Franklin), 80–81, 126–127

dopamine and creativity, 116–121

drive
- and hard work, 157–158
- in innovators, 115–116, 177–178
- and need for achievement, 177–178

pleasure of work, 181–185
and working ethos, 176–181
Dudman, Jack, 218
Dyer, Frank Lewis, 168, 175
Dyson, Freeman, 30–31

early wins and self-efficacy, 80–82, 85, 254
Eberhard, Martin, 71–72
echolalia, 22
Edison, Madeleine (daughter), 170
Edison, Nancy (mother), 158, 159
Edison, Samuel (father), 158, 159
Edison, Thomas
achievements, 44
car battery work, 173–174
character and traits, 99, 169–170
childhood, 36, 158–160
drive, 157–158, 161–164, 167–168, 171–176, 179, 183, 184
early successes, 80, 161–162
education and self-education, 36, 42, 98, 108, 158–160
electrical power work and commercialization, 98, 99–100, 169–171
entrepreneurial spirit, 160–163, 166, 171, 174
filaments for light bulbs, 49, 78, 167–169
and flow, 182, 183
health, 158, 166, 170
idealism (lack of), 143–144, 157, 176
intelligence, 108
inventions and scientific activity, 143–144, 159–174
iron ore extraction, 172, 173
kinetoscope, 172–173
and N. Tesla, 97–98, 99–100
need for achievement, 179
nonconformity, 49
patents, 160–161, 168, 179
perseverance, 49, 78
phonograph and telephone work, 163, 164–166, 167, 169–170
power for work, 183, 184, 185
and the public, 166–167
self-efficacy, 78, 80, 175–176
separateness, 14, 36, 44–45
situational advantage, 209
telegraph work, 160, 161, 162, 166
wives and family, 162, 170–171, 172, 179
work as pleasure, 16
Edison General Electric Company, 171
education (formal), and innovators, 17, 211–212, 241, 250–251
See also self-education
"The Education of Women" (Dafoe), 127
effort and persistence in innovators, 18
See also perseverance
Einstein, Albert
achievements, 3
authority disrespect, 3, 24–25, 26–27, 30–31

Einstein, Albert (*continued*)
character and traits, 3, 21, 32
childhood and education, 22–26
on M. Curie, 152–153
diet, 153–154
drive, 115
education at polytechnic, 25, 26–27
first job and early adulthood, 27–28
idealism, 147, 153–154
music and inspiration, 109
nonconformity, 48–49
openness to experience, 114
physics papers and breakthroughs, 28–32
physics self-education, 24, 25, 26
predicted future of, 23–24
as professor of physics, 27, 32
publication of academic papers, 27–29
recognition (lack of), 55, 147
separateness, 13–14, 20, 21–23, 32, 37
social skills, 26
special theory of relativity, 29–31
spirituality and religion, 24–25
wife and children, 27
Einstein, Hans Albert (son), 109
electric cars, development, 70–73, 74
electric commutator and alternating current (AC) work, 95, 96–97, 98–99, 100–101, 102, 111, 177–178
electrometer, 194, 195, 240
endoscopic images, 5–6
energy expenditure, 183–185
England, and American colonies, 135–137
EV1 car, 70–71
extrinsic rewards, 179

failure, and self-efficacy, 84, 254
Fairchild Semiconductor company, 208
faith in own ability. *See* self-efficacy
family, birth order in, 9–10
Fanning, Shawn, 231–232
Favreau, Jon, 75
feasibility and ideas, 47–48
filaments for light bulbs, 49, 78, 167–169
film projectors, 172–173
financial resources, as resource for innovation, 211–212, 242–243
Fleming, Lee, 53–54, 55
flow and pleasure from work, 182–183, 255–256
Forbath, Theodore, 254
Ford, Henry, 174
formal education, as resource for innovators, 17, 211–212, 241, 250–251
France, and American colonies, 136–137
Frank, Phillipp, 22–23
Franklin, Benjamin
beliefs and virtues, 127, 128–131, 134, 137–139, 151
and books, 240–241

character and traits, 124
childhood and family background, 124–125
early successes, 80–81
education and self-education, 125
electrical power work, 132–133
hard work (industriousness), 130–131, 134
idealism, 15–16, 124, 136, 138, 139, 140, 143, 151
intelligence, 107–108
and libraries, 131–132, 241, 256–257
political activity and unity of colonies, 134–137
on population growth, 133–134
and pride, 131
printing work, 125, 128, 130
scientific activity and inventions, 132–134, 137, 139
self-efficacy, 80
slavery and abolition, 137–138
social networks and Junto, 55, 131–132
spirituality and moral philosophy, 124, 125, 128–129, 138–139
writing and oration of, 55–56, 80–81, 125–127, 128–129
Franklin, James (brother), as publisher, 80, 127
Franklin, Josiah (father), 124–125
Franklin, Thomas II (grandfather), 124
Franklin, William (son), 135–136
Frankston, Bob, 221
Freud, Sigmund, 105, 108–109
frog Design, failure at, 254

Gage, Tom, 71
gastrointestinal images, 5–6
Gates, Bill, 23, 226–227, 236–237
General Electric Company, 171
genius, 4, 120
Genspace, 261
germanium diodes, 208
Global Link Information Network (renamed Zip2), 68
GM, electric cars, 70–71
Gmail, creation, 252
Goldsmith, Barbara, 77, 240
Google, 59, 236, 252, 255, 257
Google News, creation, 252
Gracia, Antonio, 73
Gray, Elisha, 163
Green Cargo company, flow at, 255–256
Grossman, Marcel, 27
group
and brainstorming, 45–48, 251
and time alone, 59, 251–253

Habicht, Conrad, 28–29
Haldeman, Joshua (Musk's grandfather), 63–65
Haldeman, Scott (Musk's uncle), 66
Haldeman, Winnifred (Musk's grandmother), 65
hard work
as drive, 157–158
as pleasure, 16
Hayden Planetarium, 243
Henrietta (M. Curie's cousin), 33

hero stories, 83
Hertzfeld, Andy, 50, 225, 226
higher purpose. *See* idealism
Homebrew Computing Club, 219
Hopper, Grace, 206–207
hotel business, innovation and disruption, 6
humanity, self-destruction, 70
Hutchinson, Thomas, 136
hypomania, 119

IBM and early computers, 221–222, 226
iBook and iMac, 231
iBot development, 51, 143
Iddan, Gavriel, 5
idealism
  description and role, 120–121, 139–140, 141, 147, 152, 254–255
  and devotion to cause, 152–153
  and goals, 141–142, 254–255
  in innovators, 15–16, 123, 141, 142–143, 147, 151, 153–154
  as motivator, 15, 139–141
  negative aspects, 144–145, 153–155
  perseverance, 147, 152–153
  and self-denial, 153–154
  source of, 151–152
  and war, 154–155
ideas
  association paths, 109–111
  brainstorming, 45–48, 251
  difficulty of understanding new ideas, 235
  and feasibility, 47–48
  primary process thinking, 108–109
iMac and iBook, 231
information, access to, 257–259
information technology (IT), and shocks in technology or economy, 202–203
innovation
  capital for, 211–212, 242–243
  characteristics and traits for, 1, 3–4, 6–7, 9–10, 13–14, 16–17
  and disruption, 6
  mechanisms in, 16–17
  and outsiders, 5–6, 259–260
  potential for, 6–7, 11, 246–261
  process of, 17–18
  research on, 4, 7
  and shocks in technology and economy, 202–204
  war's impact, 205–208
  See also specific topics
innovators (in general)
  achievements, 16, 179, 180–181
  and books, 240–241
  capital, 212
  commonalities in, 8–11, 13–17
  creativity, 17–18, 247–248
  drive, 115–116, 177–178
  family ties, 246
  formal education, 17, 211–212, 241, 250–251
  idealism in, 15–16, 123, 141, 142–143, 147, 151, 153–154
  information available on, 12–13
  intelligence of, 87, 106–108
  memory of, 89, 112–113

multiple case study, 9
nature *vs.* nurture, 87
one-time *vs.* serial innovators, 7, 10, 11–12
openness to experience, 114–115
others' help, 44, 45, 259–260
parents and working ethos, 176–177, 181
quirks in, 13–14, 16
recognition and praise, 180
research on, 3–4, 7–8, 9–11, 16–17
selection for study, 11–13
self-education, 40–42
self-efficacy, 14, 51, 76, 79
self-reinforcing pathways, 51–52
separateness, 13–14, 21, 23, 35, 247
and situational advantage, 18, 209–210, 211, 240, 246
and sleep, 88–89, 119–120
social networks in patents, 54, 55
study from USPTO, 54
traits and factors (convergence of), 245–246
understanding of new ideas, 235
See also specific innovators

intellectual resources (access to), 212, 238–242, 244, 256–261
intelligence
and creativity, 87–88, 106–108
of innovators, 87, 106–108
and memory, 111–112, 113

interpersonal networks, 53–55
intrinsic motivation, 140
intrinsic rewards, 179
introversion, 35, 44
iPad, 236–237
iPhone, 234–237
iPod, 232–233, 249
IQ of innovators, 106–107
Isaacson, Walter, 48–49
isolation. *See* separateness
iTunes and iTunes Music Store, 233–234
Ive, Jonathan, 231, 233

Jandali, Abdulfattah "John" (Jobs's birth father), 212
Jenkins, C. Francis, 173
jet fighters, development, 253
Jobs, Paul and Clara (Jobs's adoptive parents), 213–214
Jobs, Steve
Apple I and II, 220–221
Apple Lisa project, 224
Atari work, 59–60, 218
and blue boxes, 81–82, 217
character and traits, 8–9, 214, 217, 218, 224–225
childhood and family background, 35–36, 212–214, 216–217
computers development, 81, 147–150, 219–220
demands on employees, 225
early successes, 81–82
education and self-education, 40, 214, 217–218, 242
financial resources, 242

Jobs, Steve (*continued*)
friendship with S. Wozniak, 216–217, 239
and Gates, 226
and Heathkits, 214
idealism, 122, 147–150, 151
and iMac, 231
influence of technological shocks and counterculture, 204–205
intelligence, 214
and interface/GUI of computer, 223–225, 226
Macintosh project, 224–227
music industry and iPod, 232–234
NeXT computers and Pixar, 150, 228–229
nonconformity, 49–50, 59–60
perseverance, 228
research on, 7–8
resignation/firing at Apple, 149–150, 227–228
return to Apple, 150, 230–238
rules disregard, 8, 9
self-efficacy, 81–82
separateness, 35–36, 38
Silicon Valley's influence, 216–217, 238–239
situational advantage for resources, 186, 215, 223–224, 237, 238–239, 242
vision, 148, 237–238, 239
wife and children, 35–36
and Xerox, 222–224
and Zen, 151
Johnson, Craig, 46–47
Johnson, Edward, 167
Joliot-Curie, Irène (daughter of M. Curie), 197
See also Curie, Irène

Kamen, Dean
achievements and innovations, 40, 140–141
character and traits, 8–9
education and self-education, 40–41
financial resources, 243
idealism, 140–141, 143
nonconformity, 50–51
social purpose, 140–141
Kamen, Mitch (brother), 50
Kelvin, Lord, 101–102, 198
kinetoscope, 172–173
Kleiner, Alfred, 29, 32
Kottke, Daniel, 151

L-DOPA, 117, 118
Lafley, A. G., 254
Langevin, Paul, affair with M. Curie, 57, 180, 199
latent inhibition, 116–117
Levchin, Max, 75
libraries, development and access, 131–132, 241, 256–257
Library Company of Philadelphia, 241
lightning and lightning rods, 133
Lippman, Gabriel, 194
Lockheed, 253
long paths of association, 109–111
long-term memory, 111–112

Macintosh/Mac computers, 148–150, 224–227, 229
  See also Apple company
madness and genius, 120
Mallory, Walter S., 78, 173–174
Malthus, Thomas, 133
Manhattan, lighting of, 169
mania, 118–119
maniacal focus, 114
Marconi, Guglielmo, 103–104, 145
Marić, Mileva, 27
Markkula, Mike Jr., 220–221, 224
Mars, travel and colonization, 69–70
Marshall, Alfred, 215–216
Martin, T. C. (Thomas Commerford), 102, 168, 175
mathematics, women's role in WWII, 206–207
Mayer, Marissa, 257
McClelland, David, 178, 180–181
memory
  in innovators, 89, 112–113
  and intelligence, 111–112, 113
Micro Instrumentation and Telemetry System (MITS), 219
Microsoft, 222, 226, 236–237
Miller, Mina (wife of Edison), 170–171, 172, 179
Mingo, Santiago, 54, 55
mobile phones, 234–237
Morgan, J. P., 144–146, 171
mothers of innovators, and working ethos, 176–177
motion picture projectors, 172–173
motivation
  and drive, 178
  and flow, 255–256
  and idealism, 15, 139–141
  research on, 140
MP3 format, 231–232
Mullen, Brian, 46–47
multiple case study of innovators, 9
multiple innovators. *See* innovators
Murray, Henry, 178
Murray, Joseph, 162
music, innovation in, 11
music industry, and S. Jobs/ Apple, 231–234
Musk, Elon
  achievements, 1–2
  association paths and creativity, 110
  business and personal skills, 73–75
  character and traits, 5, 74
  computers and video game creation, 67
  demands on employees, 225
  education and self-education, 41
  electric cars, 70–73, 74
  energy consumption and production, 70
  family background and childhood, 63–67
  financial resources, 212
  and flow, 182–183

Musk, Elon (*continued*)
  idealism and motivation, 122, 141–142
  intelligence, 107
  Internet ventures, 68–69
  memory skills, 67, 112–113
  move to Canada and US, 67, 68
  as outsider, 260
  photographic memory, 112–113
  primary process thinking, 109
  reading and books, 66–67
  rocket science work, 4, 69–70, 74–75, 78–79, 110
  self-efficacy, 14, 66, 69, 70, 73, 74, 75–76, 78–79, 80
  separateness, 14, 37
  space travel work, 4, 69–70, 74–75, 110–111, 141–142
  as student, 67–68
Musk, Errol (father), 63, 67
Musk, Kimbal (brother)
  on Elon, 66, 75, 182–183
  on father, 63
  Internet ventures, 68–69
  move to Canada, 67
Musk, Maye (mother; nee Haldeman)
  on Elon, 66, 142
  family background, 63, 65–66
  move to Canada, 67
  on separateness, 37

Napster, 232
NASA, Mars travel, 69
National Advisory Committee for Aeronautics, 215
Naval Air Station Moffett Field, 215
need for achievement, 177–181
Neubauer, Aljoscha, 110
neuroscience, and creativity, 88–89
New England Courant, B. Franklin in, 80, 126–127
New York Herald, on N. Tesla, 177
New York Times, on N. Tesla, 36
NeXT Computers, 150, 228, 230
Niagara Falls and power, 93, 101–102
Nike shoes, development, 83–84
Nixon, President, 203
"non-exercise activity thermogenesis" ("NEAT"), 183
nonconformity
  and rules, 49–51
  and self-efficacy, 77
  and separateness, 48, 51–52
norepinephrine, 120

"Observations on the Increase of Mankind" (Franklin), 133, 134
O'Dell, John, 74
oil industry, and shocks in technology or economy, 203–204
O'Neill, John, 97, 100
O'Neill, Theo, 74
openness to experience, 88, 113–116
Organization of Petroleum Exporting Countries (OPEC), 203

originality. *See* creativity
Orzeszkowa, Eliza, 151
Osborne, Alex, 45
outsiders, benefits of, 5–6, 259–260

Palo Alto Research Center (PARC), 222–224
parents of innovators, and working ethos, 176–177, 181
Parkinson's disease, 117–118
patents, and interpersonal networks, 54, 55
PayPal, 69
Pelley, Scott, 73
Penn family, 135
Pennsylvania Gazette, 128
perseverance
 and idealism, 147, 152–153
 and self-efficacy, 77–78, 79
personal experience, and self-efficacy, 79–82, 84, 85
personal social networks, and separateness, 53–55
personality traits, 113
Pestalozzi, Johann Heinrich, 25, 26
phonograph, development, 163, 164–166, 167
physical activity, and flow, 183
Pihl, Lennart, 255
PillCam, 5–6
pitchblende ore, 195–196
Pixar, 228, 247–248
Planck, Max, 55
pleasure of work and drive, 181–185
Poincaré, Henri, *vs.* Einstein, 30–31
Poland
 history, 188–190, 201
 positivism and nationalism, 151–152, 191–192, 201
 women in university, 33, 188, 191, 192, 201–202
polonium, 196, 197
potential for innovation, 6–7, 11, 246–261
primary process thinking, 108–109

quadrant electrometer, 194, 195, 240
quirks in innovators, 13–14, 16

radar systems, development, 207–208
radio, development, 103–104
radioactivity work, 195–197, 198–199, 202
radium, 196, 197, 198–199, 202
Raskin, Jef, 224
reality distortion field, 50
recognition and praise for innovation, 180
Record Industry Association of America (RIAA), 232
Regina Leader-Post, 64–65
Reiss, Steven, 140
relativity, special theory, 29–31
"remote associations," 108–110
resources (access to)
 and academics, 257–259
 and books, 240–241, 257–259
 capital for, 211–212, 242–243

resources (access to) (*continued*)
in computer industry, 237, 238–239
education, 211–212, 241, 250–251
example, 200
and innovators, 212
role and importance, 187–188, 211–212, 259–260
technological and intellectual, 212, 238–242, 244, 256–261
reusable rockets, 4, 69–70, 74–75, 78–79, 110
rewards for work, 178–180
Rietzschel, Eric, and coauthors, 47
right place at right time. *See* situational advantage
risk, 79, 178–179
Rive, Peter, and Lyndon, 70
Roberts, Henry Edward "Ed," 218–219
rockets, development, 4, 69–70, 74–75, 78–79, 110
Röntgen, Wilhelm Conrad, 195
Rosenbaum, Ron, 81
Rubin, Julius, 181
rules and nonconformity, 49–51
Rumelt, Richard, 231

Salas, Eduardo, 46–47
Schieble, Joanne (Jobs's birth mother), 212–213
schizophrenia, 118
school. *See* education
Schultheiss, Oliver, 181
science
innovation in, 11–12, 259–260
opening up, 260–261
Scientific American, 165
Scott, Michael, 224
Scully, John, 148, 149, 227, 229, 230
Seifer, Marc, 97, 100, 177–178
self-attribution bias, 84
self-denial, and idealism, 153–154
self-education for innovators, 40–42
self-efficacy
building of, 254
description, 63, 76
and early wins, 80–82, 85, 254
factors in, 79–80
and failure, 84, 254
in innovators, 14, 51, 76, 79
and nonconformity, 77
and perseverance, 77–78, 79
and personal experience, 79–82, 84, 85
process of, 76–77, 78, 79
and risk, 79
source in people, 79–85
and verbal persuasion, 80, 85
and vicarious experience, 79–80, 82–85
self-serving bias, 84
separateness
benefits, 37–39, 42–43, 52, 53–54
causes and explanations, 38–40
costs of, 52–55
and creativity, 42–45, 47, 59–61, 252–253
distress from, 52–53
feelings towards by innovators, 37

in innovators, 13–14, 21, 23, 35, 247
vs. introversion, 35
and nonconformity, 48, 51–52
and personal social networks, 53–55
and secrecy, 253
and self-education, 40–41
self-reinforcement, 39–40, 51–52
and social skills, 39–40, 60–61
as trait, 20, 21
serial innovators. *See* innovators
Serrell, Lemuel, 99
Shaish, Tsipi, 117–118
Shockley, William, 208
shocks in technology or economy, 202–204
Shooting Star jet fighter, 253
Sikorska, Jadwiga, 189, 190
Silicon Valley
emergence, 208, 215
influence on area, 215–217, 238–239
Simonton, Dean, 109
situational advantage
in computer industry, 186, 215, 223–224, 237, 238–239, 242
education and capital in, 211–212
in electricity development, 209
and innovators, 18, 209–210, 211, 240, 246
and resources (*see* resources (access to))
role in innovation, 187–188, 202–203, 209
and timing, 187–188, 200–201, 202, 239–240
transistor development and Silicon Valley, 208–209
and war, 205–207
sixties counterculture, influence, 204–205
Skłodowska, Bronia (M. Curie's sister), 190, 192, 201–202
Skłodowska, Bronisława (M. Curie's mother), 188, 189, 190
Skłodowska, Hela (M. Curie's sister), 189
Skłodowska, Helena (M. Curie's sister), 190
Skłodowska, Maria Salomea. *See* Curie, Marie
Skłodowska, Władysław (M. Curie's father), 188, 189, 190, 191, 192
Skłodowska, Zofia (M. Curie's sister), 189, 190
"Skunk Works" team and facility, 253
slavery and abolition, 137–138
sleep in innovators, 88–89, 119–120
Smiljan (Croatia), 89
Smith, Alvin Ray, 228–229
social detachment. *See* separateness
social movements, influence, 204
social networks, 53–55
social skills, and separateness, 39–40, 60–61
Solar City, 70
solar power, 204

solitude, and creativity, 42–45, 47
space travel innovation, 4, 69–70, 74–75, 110–111, 141–142
SpaceX (Space Exploration), 1–2, 73, 141–142
special theory of relativity, 29–31
Spindler, Mike, 229
Steinmetz, Charles, 104
Stiles, Ezra, 137–138
Stilwell, Mary (wife of Edison), 162, 170
Straubel, J. B., 75
Stroebe, Wolfgang, 45–46, 47
Stross, Randall, 143–144, 157, 166
superordinate goals. *See* idealism
Szczasinska-Dawidow, Jadwiga, 192
Szigeti, Anthony, 96
szlachta class in Poland, 188–189

"The Talking Phonograph" (journal article), 165
Talmud, Max, 24
taxi business, innovation and disruption, 6
teamwork. *See* group
Technocracy movement, 64–65
technological resources (access to), 212, 238–242, 244, 256–261
technology, innovation in, 11–12
telephone, development, 163
Teller, Astro, 75
tenacity. *See* perseverance
Terman, Frederick, 215
Tesla, Dane (brother), 90, 91, 92
Tesla, Djouka (mother), 90, 176–177
Tesla, Milutin (father), 89–90, 93, 94, 95–96
Tesla, Nikola
  achievements, 2–3, 89, 102–103, 178
  association paths and ideas, 110–111
  celibacy, 105
  character and traits, 99–100
  childhood and family background, 89–93
  creativity, 88, 100, 110–111
  drive, 115–116, 176–178
  and Edison, 97–98, 99–100
  education and interests, 93–96, 177
  eidetic and mental images, 91–92, 93–94, 97, 105, 112
  electric commutator and alternating current (AC), 95, 96–97, 98–99, 100–101, 102, 111, 177–178
  electrical power work and commercialization, 97–103, 104–105, 115–116
  faith in own ability, 14
  financial resources, 243
  health, 91, 93, 94, 96, 105–106
  high-frequency phenomena work, 101
  idealism, 144–145
  intelligence and memory, 88–89, 90–91, 93–95, 102
  inventions, 93–94, 96–97, 98–100, 101, 102–105, 144, 177
  manias, 88, 95, 99, 106, 119
  memory skills, 112

move to US, 97–98
and Niagara Falls' power, 93, 101–102
odd behaviors, 88, 92–93
openness to experience, 114
patents, 98–99, 100–101, 103–104, 178
radio work, 103–104
senses and stimuli, 96, 117
separateness, 36
sleep, 88–89
vindication, 180
wireless communications and tower, 104–105, 115, 144–146
working ethos, 176–177
Tesla Models S and X, 74
Tesla Roadster car, 71–73
Tesler, Larry, 223
"Theory of Radioactivity" (M. Curie), 196
Thirteen Virtues of Life (B. Franklin), 128
Thomson, Elihu, 100
Thoreau, Henry David, on solitude, 43
3M company, creativity at, 59
time alone
and brainstorming, 45–48, 251
and creativity, 59, 251–253
vs. group and collaboration, 59, 251–253
importance, 250–252
as self-reinforcing factor, 51–52
Tizard, Henry, 207
transistor, development, 208–209
Tribble, Bud, 50
tzero car, 71
unconventionality, as benefit, 61
Upton, Francis, 157–158
uranium, 195
US Patent and Trademark Office (USPTO), 54, 103–104

Valentine, Don, 220
Vance, Ashley, 113
verbal persuasion, and self-efficacy, 80, 85
vicarious experience, and self-efficacy, 79–80, 82–85
Vietnam War opposition, 204
Villard, Henry, 171
Visicalc, 221
Vitascope, 173
Vogelstein, Fred, 238
voice communication work, 163, 164–166, 167, 169–170
voluntary energy expenditure, 183–185
voluntary fire brigade, creation, 132
vote recorder, 160–161

war, impact on innovation, 205–208
Wardenclyffe Tower, 104–105, 145–146
Warnock, John, 223
Watson, Kevin, 107
Weber, Heinrich, 27
Weber, Max, 180
Wedderburn, Alexander, 16, 136
Westinghouse, George, 100–101, 102
Wetzler, Joseph, 101

Winblad, Ann, 23
Windows system, 226
women
  in university, 33, 188, 191, 192, 194, 200, 201–202
  WWII and innovation, 205–207
working ethos and drive, 176–181
working memory, 111–112, 113
The World as I See It (Einstein), 22
World War I, M. Curie's impact, 199
World War II, impact on innovation, 205–208
Wozniak, Francis, 216
Wozniak, Steve "Woz"
  childhood and father, 216
  computer making and blue boxes with Jobs, 81–82, 148, 217, 218, 219–221, 237, 239
  friendship with Jobs, 216–217, 239
  on Jobs's influence, 237
  skills and traits, 217, 218

X rays, 195, 199
X.com, 69
Xerox and early computers, 222–224, 227
Xerox Palo Alto Research Center (PARC), 222–224

zeal, in innovators, 15
Zip2, 68–69
Zurich Polytechnic, Einstein in, 25, 26–27

Melissa A. Schilling is the John Herzog Family professor of management and organizations at New York University's Stern School of Business and one of the world's leading experts on innovation. Her textbook, *Strategic Management of Technological Innovation* (now in its fifth edition), is the number-one innovation strategy text in the world and is available in seven languages. Professor Schilling is also a coauthor of *Strategic Management: An Integrated Approach,* now in its twelfth edition and one of the leading strategic management textbooks in the world.

© Andrew Steinman

Professor Schilling's doctorate in strategic management is from the University of Washington, where her dissertation research analyzed technology standards battles in high-technology industries. She sought answers to questions such as "How and why are dominant technologies chosen in 'winner-take-all' industries?" and "How do managers make the difficult choice between protecting their technologies with patents or copyrights, versus rapidly disseminating them to build support for their technologies?" This work positioned her on the forefront of research on innovation strategy, with expertise in industries such as smartphones, computers, software, and video games. Dr. Schilling subsequently expanded her research to include other high-technology industries such as biotech, renewable energy, and electric vehicles. Her articles on innovation, creativity, alliances, and modularity have appeared in leading journals such as *Academy of Management Journal, Academy of Management Review, Management Science, Organization Science, Strategic Management Journal, Journal of Economics and Management Strategy, Research Policy,* and *Harvard Business Review.*

B B S

PublicAffairs is a publishing house founded in 1997. It is a tribute to the standards, values, and flair of three persons who have served as mentors to countless reporters, writers, editors, and book people of all kinds, including me.

I. F. STONE, proprietor of *I. F. Stone's Weekly*, combined a commitment to the First Amendment with entrepreneurial zeal and reporting skill and became one of the great independent journalists in American history. At the age of eighty, Izzy published *The Trial of Socrates*, which was a national bestseller. He wrote the book after he taught himself ancient Greek.

BENJAMIN C. BRADLEE was for nearly thirty years the charismatic editorial leader of *The Washington Post*. It was Ben who gave the *Post* the range and courage to pursue such historic issues as Watergate. He supported his reporters with a tenacity that made them fearless and it is no accident that so many became authors of influential, best-selling books.

ROBERT L. BERNSTEIN, the chief executive of Random House for more than a quarter century, guided one of the nation's premier publishing houses. Bob was personally responsible for many books of political dissent and argument that challenged tyranny around the globe. He is also the founder and longtime chair of Human Rights Watch, one of the most respected human rights organizations in the world.

• • •

For fifty years, the banner of Public Affairs Press was carried by its owner Morris B. Schnapper, who published Gandhi, Nasser, Toynbee, Truman, and about 1,500 other authors. In 1983, Schnapper was described by *The Washington Post* as "a redoubtable gadfly." His legacy will endure in the books to come.

Peter Osnos, *Founder*